THE CHASE

HOW *OHIO STATE* CAPTURED
THE FIRST COLLEGE FOOTBALL PLAYOFF

BILL RABINOWITZ

TRIUMPH
B O O K S

This book is available in quantity at special discounts for your group or organization. For further information, contact:

Triumph Books LLC
814 North Franklin Street
Chicago, IL 60610
(312) 337-0747
www.triumphbooks.com

Printed in the United States of America

ISBN: 978-1-62937-177-1
Design and editorial production by Alex Lubertozzi
All photos courtesy of the Columbus Dispatch
Title page photo by Adam Cairns

To Erin,
My wife, the center of my life, my best friend

Urban Meyer went to the 2013 BCS Championship Game full of pride. Against all odds, his first Ohio State team had gone undefeated that 2012 season. ESPN, for whom he had been a color analyst the year before, invited him back as a guest.

As with anything Meyer does, he went to Miami to watch Alabama play Notre Dame not merely as a spectator. He went to observe, to learn. What he saw was sobering. Though the Fighting Irish were the only undefeated team that year other than Ohio State, Alabama was the gold standard in college football. Meyer studied the Crimson Tide beginning with warmups and then throughout their 42–14 rout of the Irish.

Meyer loved his 2012 team. He considered it the foundation of what he wanted to build at Ohio State. But as he watched Alabama, he realized how far his Buckeyes really were from being at that level. *They're so much better than we are right now*, Meyer told himself that night. *We're not even close.*

He needed something bold to convey that to his players. He needed a catchphrase. "'The Chase' started with watching [Alabama] manhandle Notre Dame in the national championship game," he said. "We've got to get there." That night, Meyer sent a text to every player, coach, and staff member: "The Chase is on." Soon after, a huge banner reading "THE CHASE…" was hung above Ohio State's indoor practice field at the Woody Hayes Athletic Center. It stayed for the next two years, a constant reminder of what the Buckeyes were pursuing.

The 2014 Buckeyes would complete their chase, but it would take a season unprecedented in college football history to do so.

CONTENTS

FOREWORD

TEARS STREAMED down my face.

For the entire Ohio State–Oregon national championship game, I was an objective and impartial professional, as my job as college football analyst for ESPN requires.

But before I was a broadcaster, I was a Buckeye. As the confetti fell after Ohio State won the first College Football Playoff championship, the magnitude of the Buckeyes' improbable title hit me. I haven't told a lot of people this, but when the championship was won and we were still on the air, I was overcome with emotion. In an instant, it was as if I'd been transformed back to the 12-year-old kid in Dayton, Ohio, dreaming of such a moment for my beloved Buckeyes. I don't know if it was everything I'd been through on a personal level after moving my family from Columbus to Nashville. But I'd held myself back the entire game and maybe the last three or four years emotionally. Now it all came to the surface with those tears. I was just so proud of what they had accomplished and how they had accomplished it.

It's hard to imagine anyone being a bigger Buckeyes fan than I was as a kid. I grew up at a time when most Ohio State games weren't televised. But WOSU, the public television station, would show the games on Saturday night and Sunday morning with Paul Warfield doing the call. That's how I wanted to experience the game, so I did my best to shield myself from finding out how the Buckeyes did until I could watch the rebroadcast. If I was watching another game and they started to show scores of other games, I'd look away.

I was fortunate to be a good enough quarterback prospect that Ohio State recruited me. When I came to campus for recruiting visits, a graduate assistant named Urban Meyer would often take me from place to place. Even then, you could tell he was destined for success. Just in the way he carried himself, Urban seemed to me to be more like an assistant coach than a GA. I don't know if even Urban knew what was in store for him back then. But his approach, his energy, and the intensity in his eyes made it obvious to me that he'd be a very successful assistant coach and then one day a very successful head coach. We built a relationship then and reconnected in 1995 when I began my broadcasting career and he was an assistant coach at Colorado State. We've stayed close as he moved on to Notre Dame before becoming a head coach at Bowling Green, Utah, Florida, and now Ohio State.

*   *   *   *

WHEN BRAXTON MILLER reinjured his shoulder less than two weeks before the 2014 opener, Ohio State's chances for a championship seemed doomed. Miller was the team's alpha leader, a two-time Big Ten Player of the Year. Who could possibly replace him? J.T. Barrett had never taken a college snap. Cardale Jones hadn't taken a meaningful one, and all anyone knew about him was that silly tweet he'd sent out as a freshman. I know how tough it can be to be thrust into the quarterback job. I went to Art Schlichter's debut in 1978, only to see him throw five interceptions against Penn State. Growing pains are almost an inevitable part of being an inexperienced quarterback. Barrett and the Buckeyes endured them in the loss to Virginia Tech, which proved to be a fork in the road. When the Buckeyes survived overtime at Penn State, you could sense something had changed. I've been at every stadium in the country and Beaver Stadium is as loud and intimidating an atmosphere as I've ever been to, and it's probably the best student section in the country.

Then came the huge win at Michigan State and the win over Michigan, only to lose Barrett in the fourth quarter against That Team Up North. I've been playing or covering college football and probably following it as closely as anybody has for the last 25 years. I know for a fact I've never seen anything remotely close to what we witnessed at the quarterback position at Ohio State, and what it eventually led to—and the pressure that was on Cardale Jones the last three games. But he jumped in against a good Wisconsin team and showed that the moment wasn't too big for him. That's a credit to everything that Urban and offensive coordinator Tom Herman did in practice throughout his career to get Cardale ready for such a moment.

But then Jones had to play against Alabama in the Sugar Bowl when Nick Saban had three weeks to prepare. I worked the earlier semifinal at the Rose Bowl game on New Year's Day between Oregon and Florida State. Immediately after that game, we rushed back to the hotel to watch the Ohio State–Alabama game with about 50 people from ESPN and their families. Taking my family to the Rose Bowl is a family tradition, and my four sons are probably even bigger fans of Ohio State than I am. When the Buckeyes fell behind 21–6, my boys were coming up to me with tears in their eyes. When Evan Spencer completed that magical touchdown pass to Michael Thomas, we were throwing things against the wall. We were going absolutely bonkers. My kids were jumping on the tables. The ESPN executives were just laughing and enjoying how excited everyone was. When Ohio State won that game, it was very, very special to me. It was one of the greatest nights of my life as a Buckeyes fan.

Then Ohio State dominated Oregon to win the national title. For the third game in a row, Cardale was in complete control. I was mesmerized by the way he played and represented himself and carried himself. It's easy with hindsight to say, "Well, I knew those quarterbacks could do it." I have news for you. That's probably the first time in college football history that that has happened and maybe the last time that a team can win the championship with its third quarterback.

That's a big reason I had those tears running down my face after the Oregon game. I was just so proud of what they had accomplished and the way they had accomplished it. It was a storybook ending with Cardale Jones and the way he played in those three games. But it was more about the way the team represented itself. It was the epitome of no *I* in team. They didn't care who got the credit. They played with a chip on their shoulder, yet they didn't talk a lot of trash. It was exactly the way I would want Ohio State to carry itself. It's very easy for an Ohio State fan to say, "That's my Buckeyes, I knew they could do it." But with all the hurdles and distractions and things they had to overcome, what they achieved last year just...doesn't...happen.

Urban Meyer had won championships before. He won them at Florida. He's now won them at Ohio State. He'll probably win more at Ohio State. But he'll never have another year like 2014. I don't know if anybody will have a year like 2014.

In *The Chase*, Bill Rabinowitz doesn't just recap what happened. He tells the behind-the-scenes story that really sheds light on a magical season. I followed the Buckeyes as closely as anybody, and what I love in this book is the insight behind the story, the way Bill explains the *how* and the *why* as well as the *what*. A team doesn't overcome all the adversity that Ohio State faced just by accident. It's the product of training, sacrifice, and character, as *The Chase* documents. This book brought back so many memories. For an Ohio State fan, to be able to chronicle that and relive it is something to cherish for years to come.

—Kirk Herbstreit

PROLOGUE

BRAXTON MILLER dropped back to pass, and for a moment, it looked like Ohio State's 2013 season might end in triumph after all. Wide receiver Corey "Philly" Brown made his cut on a crossing pattern and got behind the Clemson secondary. A touchdown and a come-from-behind Orange Bowl victory was within Ohio State's grasp.

But Miller, the two-time Big Ten Player of the Year, underthrew Brown. Clemson linebacker Stephone Anthony made a leaping interception. In that instant, the Buckeyes' chances of tempering the disappointment of a Big Ten Championship Game loss to Michigan State with a bowl victory ended with a 40–35 loss.

To Urban Meyer, the 24-game winning streak at the beginning of his Ohio State tenure suddenly felt like a distant memory. All he could think about was that his team was now on a two-game losing streak. He soon would be forced to contemplate the tough decisions he'd need to make to get his team back on track.

Defensive coordinator Luke Fickell didn't see the interception. He was by the bench, preparing his players for a Clemson possession if Ohio State scored. He was too much in the moment to give any thought about the changes that lay ahead for him, his defense, and even his family.

Chris Ash was watching on TV from Fayetteville, Arkansas. Content to be the defensive coordinator at Arkansas, he had no idea that he'd soon be hired to fix Ohio State's leaky pass defense.

Larry Johnson was watching from State College, Pennsylvania. His future was suddenly unclear after 18 years as a Penn State assistant coach following the departure to the NFL of head coach Bill O'Brien. But he had no idea he'd soon join Ash in Columbus.

Offensive line coach Ed Warinner was on the sideline. In minutes, his thoughts would turn to the soon-pressing question of how he could possibly replace four senior starters who'd been the foundation of the Buckeyes' offensive success.

Tight end Jeff Heuerman was on the field for the interception. The thought quickly hit him—hard—that he and his fellow seniors-to-be would enter their final season without having won a championship—that is, if he even chose to return to Ohio State.

J.T. Barrett stood on the sideline wearing a headset. He hadn't played a snap as a freshman redshirting from a knee injury and was determined to contribute in 2014, though he dared not expect more than to be the holder on field goals.

Cardale Jones didn't even wait for the game to end before walking to the locker room. It had been another season of waiting, and his prospects of ever seeing significant playing time at Ohio State looked dim. Still, he resolved to himself that he'd work hard enough to put himself in position to be the backup in 2014.

Wide receiver Evan Spencer was in the locker room, hazy from medication given to him after he broke his fibula earlier in the game. The son of a Buckeyes star, Spencer would begin his final season determined to secure his own legacy.

Wide receiver Michael Thomas, who redshirted as a sophomore after not being able to crack the lineup early in the year, asked himself, *Could I have made a difference?*, and vowed that in 2014 he would.

Darron Lee stood on the sideline, another redshirting freshman who saw an opening for playing time and was determined to seize it. In a few hours, he'd have a conversation with another freshman redshirt that would resonate throughout 2014.

Linebacker Curtis Grant walked off the field after a third straight disappointing season. The solution, he thought, would be to transfer, and he had every intention of doing so.

Shelley Meyer, who'd experienced the thrilling highs and agonizing lows of her husband's coaching career, sat in the stands. As disappointed as she was, she was confident that her husband would not fall into the despair that such losses used to bring. And that confidence surprised her.

Cornerback Doran Grant, victimized like so many other Buckeyes defensive backs the last three games of the season, stood at the 50-yard line when Anthony intercepted the pass. In his mind, Grant was already plotting how to be the leader the secondary needed.

Defensive tackle Michael Bennett had been considering turning pro after his junior season. But the disappointing ending to the season ended those thoughts. He knew he couldn't end his college career this way. He was already prepared to get back to work.

As for Braxton Miller, all he knew was that his shoulder hurt like hell.

1

BACK FROM THE BRINK

THOSE WHO KNEW Urban Meyer best weren't worried, though history told them they should have been. But the Meyer after the 2013 season was a different coach than he had been at the end of his six years at Florida. He was just as passionate, just as intense, just as demanding. But he had perspective and self-awareness. He had stared into the abyss. It scared him to his core.

Even though his Florida teams won national championships in 2006—crushing Jim Tressel's favored Buckeyes 41–14—and 2008, the thrill of victory dissipated for Meyer after a stunning coaching ascent that began at Bowling Green and then Utah. After losses, Meyer would stay up until the wee hours of the morning diagramming punt plays, desperate to find solutions that might not exist. He ate poorly and lost weight, about 30 pounds one year. He needed sleeping pills and a beer to fall asleep. When his older daughter, Nicki, came home from Georgia Tech for winter break in 2009 after not seeing him for months, she was shocked by how gaunt he was. The low point came that year after Florida lost in the Southeastern Conference title game to Nick Saban's Alabama Crimson Tide. Late that night, Meyer was stricken by chest pains. Shelley called 911. It turned out that the pain was caused by esophageal spasms and could be treated. But Meyer knew he couldn't go on long like this. He announced his resignation, only to rescind it days later. He coached the Gators in 2010, but after a disappointing season, he resigned again, this time for good. Losing and the pressure—imposed internally and externally—to avoid defeats had driven him to the brink.

"It was going to be a bad ending," Meyer said of the path he was on.

After Ohio State's 12–0 season in 2012, Meyer's wife, Shelley, admitted that a part of her wouldn't have minded a loss that year. With no postseason possibility, there were no lasting consequences from a defeat. Even though she was confident that her husband had learned from his past, a loss in a season like that would have served as a test.

"I thought it was more of a [for-]fun season," she said. "Let's just go see how we can do. Then we went 12–0, and you go, 'Why did we have to go 12–0 the first season?' How do you follow that up? Then the pressure's on because the next season you are playing for the Big Ten championship, hopefully."

When Ohio State did lose to Michigan State in the 2013 Big Ten title game and then to Clemson, the reckoning was at hand. But Shelley, head strength coach and longtime Meyer right-hand man Mickey Marotti, and others closest to Meyer had come to believe he could handle it.

"Urban was of course very disappointed, but he didn't react as devastatingly as he did at Florida when we'd lose a game," Shelley said. "At Florida, if we lost a game, he really shut down. He didn't do that after the Michigan State game. I was totally fine with how he felt about losing that game, which was very disappointed, but [only concerned with], 'What could we have done better?'"

That was how Marotti viewed it as well.

"I didn't worry about that one bit," Marotti said. "He was great. He approached it great. It was, 'Here are the problems. What's the solution?' Then we went to work."

*   *   *   *

IT HAD TAKEN a long time to reach that point of serenity. Urban Meyer was born in 1964 in Toledo to Urban "Bud" Meyer and his wife, Gisela. The family then moved to Ashtabula in the far northeastern corner of Ohio. Bud, a chemical engineer, was a loving father to Urban and his sisters, Gigi and Erika, but also demanding—particularly of his son. On Friday nights after Urban's high school football games for Saint John, Bud would make his son analyze game film with him, questioning him about plays he messed up. One time in high school, Meyer brought home a C from school. His father read him the riot act.

"I grew up in a very driven household," Urban said. "Any lack of effort was unacceptable."

Baseball was his best sport. The Atlanta Braves drafted Meyer as a shortstop in the 13th round of the 1982 draft. But his pro career washed out in two seasons after an elbow injury. He enrolled at the University of Cincinnati and became a walk-on defensive back and special-teamer on the Bearcats football team. Meyer had an undistinguished playing career, but it wasn't because of lack of effort.

"Urban was gifted in terms of being motivated, and not as gifted athletically," said Dan Sellers, a UC teammate. "He was always the first guy in drills. He was the kind of guy who'd run through a brick wall for a coach. I had a lot of respect for him."

His football career may have been forgettable, but he left UC with a degree that would prove invaluable. Meyer switched from major to major until settling on psychology. He was particularly fascinated by theories about what motivated people.

Meyer left Cincinnati with more than a degree. He also found his future wife. The first time Meyer saw Shelley Mather, she was holding a *Playboy* magazine with the centerfold open. It was at a Greek Derby Day mixer, and her sorority was in a competition to get a Sigma Chi to smile or laugh without touching him.

"That was so unlike me," she said. "I was this farm girl. I was so conservative. But I had to help my sorority win the competition. Comparing me to the centerfold of *Playboy* magazine was very funny, so I just flipped over this centerfold. I had to stop him because he was going to fly right by me. I said, 'Does this look like me?'"

Meyer did crack a big smile but didn't stop long enough to introduce himself. A day or two later at another Derby Day event, Meyer did notice Shelley and struck up a conversation with her, though he didn't connect her with the *Playboy* stunt.

"He didn't even remember that it was me who did that," she said with a laugh.

Soon enough, though, he was smitten.

"I do know that very early on I knew she was the one," Meyer said. "She was tough. I loved her toughness. She was beautiful. She was real smart."

Meyer was hired as a graduate assistant at Ohio State under Earle Bruce. Shelley, who became a psychiatric nurse, followed him to Columbus, though they didn't see each other that much because of their busy work schedules. To make ends meet, Meyer took an additional job on the graveyard shift for Consolidated Freightways, operating a forklift and loading trucks. They were married in 1989 and would eventually have three children, Nicki, Gigi, and Nate. Meyer climbed the coaching ladder as a college assistant, starting at Illinois State and then Colorado State, where he again coached under Bruce, and then Notre Dame under Lou Holtz. In 2001 he was offered the Bowling Green head coaching job.

Meyer contemplated turning down the Falcons job. Bowling Green was a downtrodden program. Holtz set him straight. Of course, it's a bad job, he told Meyer. If it were a better job, Bowling Green would have offered it to someone more proven. Meyer had become enamored with the spread offense as an assistant coach and set about implementing it at Bowling Green. The basic concept behind the spread is to force a defense to have to defend the entire width as well as length of the field to create mismatches. It was wildly successful. Meyer spent two years at Bowling Green before Utah hired him. In his second season in 2004, Utah went undefeated. Florida then hired him, and he reached the pinnacle twice before it all crashed down. Even his seemingly unshakable self-confidence was rattled.

"To be a successful coach—we've got to be honest here—you've got to be a little cocky," Shelley said. "I always thought Urban was a little cocky, even the moment I met him. Cocky in a very, very confident way, not a jerk, not narcissistic. But you have to be confident, and that comes off as being a little cocky sometimes.

"He lost that. When things went bad at Florida, he lost that part of him and that was what really scared and upset me. If you lose that, it's hard to get it back."

When Meyer stepped down for the second time at Florida, he did not foresee returning to coaching anytime soon. "I planned on at least five years [off]," he said. But after only a couple of months, the itch to coach returned, and he told Shelley, "I can't take this anymore." Her reaction? "She looked at me and said, 'You're out of your mind.'"

Because of her training as a psychiatric nurse, Shelley understood that he needed time to decompress and sort through the withdrawal from coaching. She cautioned patience, as hard as it was for him. ESPN hired Meyer as an analyst, and part of his duties involved traveling to programs and meeting with coaches and players to see what made them successful. One of the trips was to Stanford University in Palo Alto, California, to talk with Cardinal quarterback Andrew Luck.

It would be a trip that would change his life, though not because of Luck. Before leaving for California, Meyer had lunch with ESPN football analyst Todd Blackledge, a friend. Blackledge gave Meyer a book, *Lead...for God's Sake!* by an obscure author named Todd Gongwer. Meyer is given books all the time. Most collect dust.

He stuck Gongwer's book in his briefcase and didn't give it much thought. On the flight to California, looking for a way to pass the time, he pulled it out. Gongwer's book is a parable about a high school basketball coach who loses his way. Expected to compete for a state championship, the team gets off to a slow start. The coach pushes harder and harder, figuring that only that can produce results. It proves counterproductive. His team flounders and his life begins to spiral out of control. Counsel from the school's mysteriously wise custodian gradually helps the coach realize that the relationship with his players, not the single-minded pursuit of victories, is the essence of successful coaching.

Gongwer did not set out to write such a book. He spent his early adulthood in rural Indiana as a business executive and assistant basketball coach at Bethel College, an NAIA school. He did not think of himself as an author. "I'd experienced a number of disappointments in my life—business failures and not achieving what I'd wanted to in any of those spheres in my life," he said.

In 2002, at age 32, he was living in Cincinnati when he hit rock bottom, questioning his life's purpose. One day, he got on his knees and cried in his bedroom. Gongwer's two-and-a-half-year-old son saw him, put his hand on his dad's shoulder, and said, "It's okay, Daddy. It's okay."

At that moment, he had an epiphany.

"I've told that story hundreds and hundreds of times, and still I usually get choked up telling it," Gongwer said. "I remember how powerful that was to me. It was like God sent him into the room and said, 'You want an answer? Open your eyes. You're so caught up in pursuing all these other things and you're letting all these other things destroy your health, your relationship with your wife, and your relationship with others closest to you.'"

Gongwer had always been interested in leadership philosophy, and over time came to believe that he should write a book on the subject. For two weeks, he sat down to write a fairly standard leadership book. It went nowhere. Gongwer then decided to write it as a fictional short story.

"It just poured out," he said. "By the time I got two-thirds through the book—I didn't have plot or characters; I did not know where it was going—I was telling my wife, 'This story is unbelievable. Something is going to happen with it.' It was weird."

Gongwer believes that God had used him as a vessel to tell the story. Though the story has a strong faith component to it, he is wary of describing it as a Christian book because of the way he believes that term has been twisted. Living in tiny Wakarusa, Indiana, and knowing publishers' rejection rate of first-time authors, Gongwer decided to self-publish in 2010. Slowly, the book began to find an audience, particularly among coaches. One of the early readers was Jim Tressel, who made the book mandatory reading for his Ohio State assistants.

"My recommendation would be that every coach at every level read this book," Tressel said. "I have given dozens of them to coaches all over the country."

Gongwer watched Meyer's 2009 resignation press conference from his parents' house. He told his dad and brothers then that he wished he could get Meyer a copy of his book. Unbeknownst to Gongwer, Blackledge eventually would. When Meyer finally pulled it out on the flight to Stanford and began reading, it hit him like a thunderbolt. He felt as if Gongwer had written the book for him, which Gongwer said is a common response. At dinner that night with Stanford coach David Shaw, Meyer found himself wanting to cut it short so he could get back to his hotel room and finish the book. After dozing briefly—Meyer doesn't sleep much anyway—he got up at 4:00 AM and finished the book while walking across the Stanford campus, his cell phone light illuminating the book.

"It kind of rebooted everything," Meyer said. "The story of that high school coach is kind of a similar thing that a lot of guys go through."

When he got back to his hotel room, Meyer saw Gongwer's email on the book jacket and fired off an email. He wrote that he considered the book essential reading for any coach and offered to help promote it. When Meyer's email popped into his account, Gongwer at first thought some friends had pranked him until he read the message.

"I about fell out of my chair," he said.

When they spoke on the phone right after Gongwer read the email, he realized what an impact the book had on Meyer. "This was a guy who was scared for his health, knew what he was doing to his relationships around him, both his family and the people he was working with," Gongwer said.

To Meyer, one scene in the book particularly resonated. "When the coach kicks the Gatorade and then the star player goes in and punches the wall and breaks his hand…" he said, "it was a spiritual rebirth for me right there. I felt God was talking to me, saying, 'You've got to reorganize.'

"I forgot the 'why.' I got caught up in how many games we won and [forgot] the real reason—and that was the players. There was no money. I never dreamed of having [a $4.5 million salary, his base compensation in 2014]. I got in because I love players. Getting involved with them has always been my passion."

Meyer and Gongwer, along with Blackledge, met in Chicago when Meyer was there for ESPN. Gongwer later flew to Meyer's home in Florida to shoot a promotional interview for the book. Meyer wrote the foreword when a publisher agreed to distribute the book. They still stay in contact. Gongwer said he's careful not to infringe on Meyer's time, but will send Meyer a text if he sees something potentially problematic.

"He'll very graciously say, 'Stay on me,'" Gongwer said.

Said Meyer, "He's my unpaid sports psychologist."

Shelley Meyer said that the book's impact made it easier for her and her children to endorse the idea of Meyer returning to coaching. "I could sense some peace in him after reading the book," she said. "He was in the middle of this mess. He just had a lot of questions about his life. That book really helped him get started settling down and [focused on] where he wanted to go."

When Ohio State athletic director Gene Smith called in late November 2011 to discuss the Buckeyes' opening, Meyer knew he was ready. He missed the competition, but he understood that winning, however important, did not supersede everything else. His family, however, still had reservations about his ability to coach while retaining balance in his life. One day while in class at Georgia Tech, Nicki Meyer wrote a list of rules in her pink notebook that her father would have to agree to before she would give her blessing. Rule No. 1: My family will always come first. Meyer treated Nicki's rules, which became known as the Pink Contract, seriously. He signed it, and it would be prominently displayed in his office as a constant reminder of the coach and man he wanted and needed to be.

2

TURNING THE PAGE

THE MOOD AFTER the Orange Bowl was somber, not just because of the loss but because of the departures to come. The 2013 Buckeyes had rolled through the regular season undefeated. They had to rally to beat Northwestern and Iowa and had a narrow escape against archrival Michigan when Tyvis Powell intercepted a two-point conversion attempt in the final minute in a 42–41 victory. Otherwise, the Buckeyes were seldom challenged. Ohio State outscored opponents by almost 23 points per game. The Buckeyes had a powerful ground game with running back Carlos Hyde and wondrously elusive quarterback Braxton Miller behind an offensive line featuring four multi-year starters. Three of them—Jack Mewhort, Corey Linsley, and Andrew Norwell—would start in the NFL as rookies. The defense featured linebacker Ryan Shazier and cornerback Bradley Roby, who'd be first-round picks, and a stout defensive line. But the secondary never recovered from the loss to injury of its leader, safety Christian Bryant, early in the season. The pass defense was exposed in the Michigan game and then bludgeoned in the postseason. Ohio State finished 110th nationally in yards allowed through the air in 2013.

Still, if the second-ranked Buckeyes had beaten No. 10 Michigan State in the Big Ten Championship Game, they would have played Florida State for the national championship in the final year of the Bowl Championship Series system. It was not to be. Two silly defensive pass-interference penalties on the Spartans' first possession set the tone. Ohio State rallied with 24 straight points after falling behind 17–0, but Michigan State scored the final 17 points to stun the Buckeyes 34–24. The 40–35 loss to No. 12 Clemson in the Orange Bowl denied the Buckeyes a major consolation prize.

In the Sun Life Stadium locker room, the seniors said their goodbyes. Several spoke to the team. Philly Brown delivered the most powerful farewell speech. Once on the outs with the coaching staff, Brown had grown into a respected leader. Brown was on the cusp of his dream of making it to the NFL, which he would do with the Carolina Panthers. But that wasn't on his mind.

"He was crushed after the game," Ohio State wide receivers coach Zach Smith said. "I mean, tears. He spoke to the guys coming back and told them, 'I would give anything right now—*anything*—to have one more year of college. Don't ever forget this feeling right here. All off-season, keep this feeling. Remember this game and the last game, because it's not supposed to happen like this, and it's not going to happen like this for you next year.'"

There was no chance that Ohio State's players would forget the feeling. Head strength coach Mickey Marotti, whose official title is assistant athletic director for football sports performance, is Meyer's longtime confidant. When the team's off-season conditioning program convened later in January, he had the team's video director, David Trichel, produce a "lowlights" tape of mistakes and missed opportunities in the Michigan State and Clemson games. The video showed Spartans players clutching roses for earning their trip to Pasadena. It showed Clemson tossing oranges in victory. Worse, the video was in slow motion, as if to twist the knife.

"It was awful," Marotti said. "There were tears. Coach Meyer couldn't even watch it. He wouldn't come in. He couldn't watch it.

"I wanted them to remember because if you don't remember the past, you're condemned to repeat it. We said we will do everything in our power to make sure you remember how it felt. It caught their attention."

Every Wednesday at 5:30 AM for four weeks, a new video was shown for their viewing displeasure. Cornerback Doran Grant had to endure a clip of Clemson star wide receiver Sammy Watkins catching a touchdown pass on him. "It was really hard to watch because the whole team is watching you miss that opportunity," Grant said.

Like Meyer, tight end Jeff Heuerman felt sick watching the videos. In perhaps the pivotal play of the Michigan State loss, he missed a block on linebacker Denicos Allen on a fourth-down play that resulted in Miller being stuffed. Michigan State scored on its ensuing possession to seal the victory. Heuerman and Miller, who were moved to the front of the team meeting room as seniors-to-be, cringed as the video played.

"I remember just looking at each other like, *You've got to be shitting me*," Heuerman said. "It was real tough."

It was particularly tough for Heuerman because he knew he didn't need to be in that room reliving the mistake. After the Orange Bowl, he contemplated entering the NFL Draft. But the memory of the missed block on Allen contributed to his decision to stay. He just wouldn't have felt right leaving for the pros when he'd played at Ohio State for three years without helping to deliver a championship.

"That play beat me up," Heuerman said. "I was down for a while after that play. Even the first week of bowl practice, I was down about it. I felt it was my fault."

Encouragement by Meyer, offensive coordinator Tom Herman, and tight ends coach Tim Hinton helped boost his spirits. "I remember Coach Herman pulled me aside in the locker room [after the Michigan State game], and he told me if he had it to do over again he'd do the same again, that if he had one guy to make a block or make a play, it'd be me."

After four weeks of showing different lowlights videos, Marotti's final one was filled with highlights so at least they remembered that the 2013 season wasn't a complete disaster.

* * * *

THE BUCKEYES TEAM that needed to be molded for 2014 was a far better one, in body and mind, than the one Meyer inherited two years earlier. In 2011 the Buckeyes finished 6–7. They hadn't lost that many games in a season since the 19th century. It was a season in which Ohio State was just trying to keep its head above water. Head coach Jim Tressel had been forced to resign in May because of NCAA violations stemming from the tattoo-and-memorabilia scandal, and Luke Fickell served as the head coach. Hired at the end of November, Meyer stayed in the background for his first month, assembling a staff and getting organized. Meyer had his first meeting with the team the morning after the Buckeyes' Gator Bowl loss to Florida. Several players were absent or tardy for that meeting and another one a couple days later. It was obvious how deep the problems were. At Meyer's direction, Marotti moved up the start of the off-season conditioning program. The workouts were brutal. Players were forced to do grueling workouts in the bitter January cold. They could not wear Ohio State gear. Some players were reduced to wearing socks on their heads to try to stay warm. They were kicked out of their own locker room. In sum, they were beaten down so they could be built back up.

Players in January 2014 weren't exiled outside. That wasn't necessary. But in Marotti's first meeting of the off-season, he spelled out his goals. "I'll give it to you verbatim," he said, "It was to reemphasize the foundation of our total program. To develop toughness, accountability, and leadership. To develop relentless attitude, effort, strain. To improve as a player. Our mantra was, 'Our best players have to be our best workers.' That hadn't been the case around here, for whatever reason."

Marotti had that mantra on a sign above his office in the weight room, except he crossed out "workers" and replaced it with "grinders."

* * * *

MEYER'S COACHING STAFF had remained completely intact after Ohio State's undefeated 2012 season. That wouldn't be the case after 2013. Co–defensive coordinator/safeties coach Everett Withers, the only assistant without Ohio ties, left to become head coach at James Madison in Virginia. Meyer had much regard for Withers as a person, coach, and recruiter. Withers had been instrumental in the signings of five-star prospects Vonn Bell in 2013 and Raekwon McMillan the next year. But Meyer believed that the professional chemistry between Withers and Fickell, whom he'd retained as defensive coordinator after much consternation, was merely good, not great. Withers had been a defensive coordinator for 11 years, and Meyer sensed that he wasn't comfortable in a No. 2 role. So when the James Madison job opened, he jumped at it, even though it represented a pay cut.

Meyer talked to as many as 10 candidates for Withers' replacement, but the one he wanted was Arkansas defensive coordinator Chris Ash. In 2012, while at Wisconsin, Ash devised a game plan that flummoxed Ohio State. The Buckeyes' offense sputtered before finally awakening in overtime for the victory. When Wisconsin head coach Bret Bielema unexpectedly left for Arkansas, Ash went along. Ash and Tom Herman are close friends, and Herman asked him if he was interested in the Ohio State job. Ash was, but with trepidation. He was a coordinator in the Southeastern Conference, whose teams had won seven straight national titles before Florida State ended the streak. On paper, a co-coordinator job was a demotion. Ash was happy in Fayetteville and comfortable with Bielema. His fiancée and son were settled there. Herman was the only one on Ohio State's staff that he knew. But he wanted to be a head coach someday. He knew how many of Meyer's assistants had become head coaches after having success with him.

"Anytime you're in a situation like that, it's a little scary," Ash said. "But I've gotten where I'm at in this profession because I'm willing to take risks, and I'm not afraid of challenges. I knew this was a risk and a challenge, but I knew if we pulled it off, the goals I have long-term I'd be able to pull off."

To Meyer, the Ash hiring was critical. Meyer wasn't happy with the pass-defense philosophy, which was too often passive. He wanted to hire someone to implement an aggressive approach that would challenge every pass. The model, as much as any team, was Michigan State's. Most defenses, including Ohio State's until then, are constructed with a front-to-back philosophy: The first priority is to stop the run to force a team to have to rely on the pass. With Ash, the Buckeyes' first priority would be to stop the pass, so a back-to-front mentality had to be ingrained.

"I knew I could fix it as long as Coach Meyer let me do the things I knew I could do and as long as the other guys on the staff were willing to work together to make it happen," Ash said. "There was no doubt or lack of confidence in the ability to fix it. This is Ohio State. You have good players. What I needed to do was get players to buy into me and what I was selling. I needed to get the other coaches on staff to buy into me."

But there was still an issue that needed to be resolved. Fickell remained the defensive coordinator, though he wasn't necessarily the people's choice given the defensive struggles. Meyer heard the chatter, and he acknowledged that the thought of letting Fickell go crossed his mind. Meyer had been impressed with the selflessness and loyalty that Fickell showed after he transitioned from head coach back to assistant after the 2011 season. Meyer believed Fickell was an excellent man and coach. But results matter.

"I had to make a decision about if I [should] retain Coach Fickell," Meyer said. "There were a lot of people in my ear about whether to keep him or not. That was pretty intense, the month of January. I never got as close as some people thought about making a change, but I knew we needed a home-run hire on the back end [of the defense]."

During all this, Fickell did what he always did, starting from the time he was a three-time state championship wrestler at Columbus DeSales High School and a Buckeyes nose guard in the 1990s. He put his head down and worked. His job status was beyond his control. Why worry about it? When Meyer was hired, Fickell told him that he should do what he felt was best for the program and not feel any obligation to keep him. The same applied now. Fickell drove to Indianapolis for a coaches convention and met with Ash there. For more than two hours, they talked about football philosophy and how they would mesh.

"I said that I have no ego," Fickell recalled. "I explained to him who I was and that the most important thing to me was being successful."

Working with Ash wasn't the only change Fickell faced. As head coach in 2011, he hired his former Ohio State roommate and teammate Mike Vrabel as an assistant to round out his staff. After a distinguished NFL career in which he won three Super Bowls, Vrabel quickly became a rising star as a defensive line coach. But after the Orange Bowl, Vrabel stunned everyone at Ohio State by leaving for a job with the Houston Texans after former Penn State coach Bill O'Brien took the head coaching job there.

That wouldn't be the only way O'Brien's move affected the Buckeyes. Larry Johnson had been the esteemed defensive line coach at Penn State for 18 years. Six of his players had become first-round NFL picks, including the 2000 No. 1 overall pick Courtney Brown by the Cleveland Browns. Johnson was a top-flight recruiter. His recruiting territory overlapped with Fickell's in the mid-Atlantic region, though they'd never met.

"I called him, 'The Ghost,'" Fickell said. "I recruited against him, but I never saw him and he always beat me, so I called him 'The Ghost.'"

Fickell could recall getting only one player—Conner Crowell—whom Johnson coveted. Johnson had applied for the head coaching job at Penn State after O'Brien left. When Vanderbilt's James Franklin was hired instead, Johnson decided he didn't want to go through another coaching transition. He'd done that two years earlier after Joe Paterno was fired following the Jerry Sandusky sexual-molestation scandal. Johnson's presence helped with the transition under O'Brien. He took inspiration with how Penn State players endured despite crippling NCAA sanctions.

"It's probably the toughest thing I've ever done in coaching, but also probably the proudest thing I've ever seen," Johnson said. "Because I saw a bunch of seniors who refused to die, refused to quit. Every day you went to practice, you picked your head up and kept going on. But when you walked out of the building, there were a lot of tears. You really had to stay strong for the players because you knew they'd bought into it."

The decision to leave Penn State was a hard one. He said he wasn't bitter about not getting the head job. But he prayed about it and concluded it was time to move on. He figured he'd take time off, at least for a year or two, and then see about getting back into coaching. Meyer knew about Johnson's reputation. He'd considered contacting him in 2012 before deciding to retain Vrabel. So Meyer figured he'd pursue Johnson this time.

"My daughter, Teresa, is probably my biggest fan," Johnson said. "She said, 'Dad, it's time for other players and other kids to get a chance to know who you are.' I thought about that and said, 'You might be right, Teresa.'"

Johnson met with Meyer at the same Indianapolis coaches convention and quickly agreed to take the job. On January 12, off to Columbus he went. One of the first things that required was a wardrobe makeover. Penn State's dominant color is blue. About all Johnson had in his closet were blue suits and blue ties. That wouldn't go over well at the Woody Hayes center. Anything blue—even pens—is banned from the facility because Michigan's colors are maize and blue. Johnson had to make repeated trips to Men's Wearhouse for his wardrobe makeover.

"Every week I would go do that so I wouldn't be wearing the same suit or pair of pants," he said.

How much did Johnson spend there? "I'm pretty embarrassed to tell you," he said.

Changing a wardrobe is easy. Changing a defense is not. Fickell's first meeting with the defensive coaches set the tone. "The minute we walked into the room, [Fickell] said, 'This is *our* defense,'" Johnson said. "'This is not Chris Ash's defense, Larry Johnson's defense, my defense, or [cornerbacks coach] Kerry Coombs'. It's our defense. Let's do this together.' That meant he had to be willing to change and give in to things that he's done in the past. He was very unselfish in the sense he was all about team. The only thing he cared about was, How can we be better? The terminology we changed a little bit, and he said, 'Okay, I'm cool. It's good.' When we walked out of the room, we were unified. The credit goes to Luke."

Both Ash and Johnson gave up a lot to come to Columbus for a shot at a championship. They could only go on faith that their bold move would work out. What Meyer thought was that he'd accomplished what he hoped—make two home-run hires. Only time would tell.

* * * *

FOR THE STARTERS who would be seniors, particularly on that maligned defense, there was resolve that 2014 would be different than the end of 2013. At the first meeting of the off-season, Fickell told players he wouldn't tolerate any more negativity, any more blaming others.

"We are a defensive unit, and we are all together," Michael Bennett remembered Fickell saying. "We loved it. That's what we'd been waiting for. He said it's on the leadership and so it starts with the coaches and it trickles down to the seniors and then it trickles down to the rest of the team."

Bennett had once been one of those skeptical players. The son of two West Point graduates who had raised him to think for himself, Bennett had done just that his first three years at Ohio State. Especially in 2012, he was resistant to the tough-love approach instilled by Meyer.

"I refused to be broken," he said.

As the only senior starter on the defensive line, Bennett knew the time had come to be the leader he knew he could be. He vowed to be more positive, less questioning. He was never a heavy drinker, but he pretty much stopped partying entirely to serve as an example to younger players.

"I wanted them to look at me and see that I was making the sacrifices necessary for what we want to accomplish," Bennett said. "That's not always easy in college, so I wanted the guys to understand that it's worth it."

For Doran Grant, that process had already started. Roby didn't play in the Orange Bowl because of a bone bruise. Knowing that he'd be playing with all underclassmen in 2014, Grant assumed a leadership role in bowl practices. "That's when I started to get those guys going, hug them up and [let them] know I'm the guy they can trust to be the leader and take them to the next level the next year," he said.

But the other Buckeye senior-to-be named Grant had a completely different attitude in early January 2014. Linebacker Curtis Grant, who is Doran's second cousin [Doran is also a second cousin to wide receiver Devin Smith], might have been the poster boy for the Buckeyes' defensive underachievement. He had been a five-star recruit out of Virginia, rated the second-best player in the country by one recruiting service. He said he planned to sign with Florida until Meyer left. Grant's lofty rating only served to magnify what a disappointment he had been in his first three years as a Buckeye. As a sophomore in 2012, coaches had so little faith in him that they shifted a fullback, Zach Boren, to linebacker in midseason out of desperation. During his junior season, Grant's father died unexpectedly, and he took the loss hard.

"I didn't want to play football anymore," Grant said. "I felt I couldn't do anything right. He's the one who got me started playing football, so it was like, 'What do I do now?'"

His play reflected his indifference. He was better than he had been as a complete non-factor as a sophomore, but only marginally. "I was so angry at Curtis Grant at the Orange Bowl," Meyer said. "He wasn't on any special teams. He wasn't serious, wasn't preparing to go win and beat Clemson, and that's why we lost. His unit was an embarrassment—the linebacker corps. We had one great player [Shazier] and a bunch of guys who weren't very good and weren't trying."

When Withers got the job at James Madison, Grant all but booked a one-way ticket back to his native state. "I was very close," Grant said. "I was getting ready to call Coach Withers. I had called my mom. I was mad because Coach Fickell and I had a very tough conversation. I told my mom, 'I'm out of here.' The only reason I stayed at Ohio State was that my mom asked me to stay and not quit. I was like, 'Okay, Mom.'"

Neither he nor Fickell would divulge the precise details of their talk, but it's safe to assume that Fickell told him that he was unhappy with the way he was handling his business off the field and dissatisfied with his play on it. Grant had every reason to believe that he would see little playing time. The Buckeyes had signed five-star freshman Raekwon McMillan, the crown jewel of their 2014 recruiting class. McMillan was the future, and if Ohio State had its druthers, the present as well.

Grant's mom, Gloria, called Fickell shortly after her son's talk with him. Curtis knew that he could be hotheaded and make rash decisions. She beseeched him to take the long view and stick it out at Ohio State.

"It took me about two weeks to make up my mind," Grant said. "I kept telling the guys I'm about to leave. But I couldn't leave my boys. We've got such a tight brotherhood. I made Raekwon a promise that I was going to take care of them and Josh [Perry] and the guys. I wanted to be a man of my word."

The turning point came one day during weightlifting drills. Grant could see that Marotti and his staff were heaping pressure on Perry because coaches believed that the junior-to-be, ready or not, would have to be the unit's leader. Perry is an uncommonly mature guy and a diligent worker, but he was still finding his way. Grant could see that Perry was buckling under the pressure. "There was a lot on my shoulders, and it happened so quickly that it was hard for me to deal with," Perry said.

At first, Grant admitted, he was so disenchanted that he didn't care that Perry was struggling. He felt unwanted. Why worry about anyone else? "My dad had died, and I just didn't really care about anything," he said.

Until he'd gotten to Ohio State and his career spiral began, he'd always prided himself on being a helpful leader. Now he saw himself at a final crossroads as a Buckeye. He could wallow in self-pity, or he could pledge to rise above it. He decided he couldn't live with himself if he didn't give it a shot. "If we were going to win something and all my other buddies were doing well," he said, "why am I going to be the only slacker in the group? That's not cool."

But would his pledge stick? There was no way to know.

While Grant had his crisis of doubt, Eli Apple was simply trying to finish simple runs. He had been a blue-chip recruit when he enrolled at Ohio State at age 17, but the cornerback never got on the field as a true freshman, taking an unplanned redshirt. Even worse, the New Jersey native was the only one in his recruiting class who hadn't shed the black stripe on his helmet. Freshmen have to earn the removal of the stripe by doing something in practice that causes coaches to accept them as full-fledged members of the team. For Apple, it was a daily, painful reminder of where he stood.

Now, for reasons he couldn't identify, his body was betraying him in basic off-season conditioning drills. His endurance was gone. He had lost weight. Apple had started noticing the problem late in the 2013 season, and it got progressively worse.

"When we'd have to do long-distance running, I would pass out, literally," he said.

He started beating himself up about it, wondering whether he was simply mentally weak. Coaches and teammates tried a tough-love approach. Ohio State's entire program is based on constant competition. If one member of a team in a drill isn't pulling his weight, they all pay the price. The low point came when Chris Carter, a 340-pound defensive tackle, beat him in a sprint. To fellow cornerback Doran Grant, that was the final straw. As much as Grant wanted to be a positive leader for his fellow defensive backs, he couldn't stomach that.

"I specifically remember [safety] Cam Burrows yelling at him," Grant said. "'Man, I'm not running anymore because of you!' and just pushed him to the ground. I kind of mushed him in the face because we were like, 'Man, what's wrong?' It's tough-guy time in the winter, and we were trying to get everybody going."

Apple was expected to compete for the starting cornerback job opposite Grant that Roby played in 2013. Apple was definitely not looking like he would be that guy. Worse, his football manhood was being questioned. As the criticism mounted, Apple began to doubt himself. Many cornerbacks carry themselves with an air of bravado. It's a position that requires unshakable confidence and a short memory. Few players are exposed on bad plays the way beaten cornerbacks are. But Apple's personality is more laid-back.

"Eli is the kind of person who on his best day and worst day looks the same," said his mother, Annie.

Now teammates and coaches mistook his placidity for indifference. Apple decided to suffer in silence. He didn't go to teammates and volunteer that his energy was sapped. He didn't admit how scared he was. He said nothing. He just tried to get through each day. Finally, Kerry Coombs had seen enough. He took Apple aside and told him that it was time for him to see doctors to see if something was physically wrong with him. It proved to be a turning point for Apple and the Buckeyes.

3

A CLASS FOR THE AGES

WHEN URBAN MEYER took the Ohio State job at the end of 2011, he had to scramble to salvage the 2012 recruiting class. Meyer and most of his staff simply didn't have the time to develop the relationships that are so vital in enticing prospects. Some recruits were wary of joining the Buckeyes because of the bowl ban imposed by the NCAA for the 2012 season. A few backed away. Even so, the Buckeyes closed strong and finished with a top-five class that included Noah Spence, Adolphus Washington, Joshua Perry, and Michael Thomas. But that would prove to be a mere prelude to a 2013 recruiting class that seems destined to be regarded as legendary. Seven became starters as sophomores or redshirt freshmen in 2014, including Joey Bosa, J.T. Barrett, Ezekiel Elliott, and Darron Lee.

It did not happen by accident. Recruiting permeates every decision Ohio State makes as a football program. Meyer pushed for more night games—and got them—because of the prime-time exposure it provides and because more prospects can attend those games. It can be difficult for a high school player to make it to Columbus for a noon Buckeyes game after playing in his own game on Friday night. Even the football facility at the Woody Hayes Athletic Center is designed to appeal to recruits. The Buckeyes redesigned their locker room in 2014, with a new water wall as the centerpiece. When Meyer walks through the facility, he said, he constantly thinks, "How does that look to an 18-year-old?" Videos of Buckeyes stars and big games, particularly against Michigan, blare from TVs built into the wall. It's part office, part Ohio State museum.

"Everything is recruiting," Meyer said. "If someone says, 'I want to do this,' my first question is, 'How does that help recruiting?'"

When Meyer arrived, he wasn't deterred by a sort of gentlemen's agreement among conference coaches that once a prospect committed to a school, he was off limits to others. Wisconsin's Bret Bielema was irked when the Buckeyes pried away a Cleveland prospect, offensive lineman Kyle Dodson, who'd committed to the Badgers.

"We're very aggressive," Meyer said. "I think it's well-documented when we first got here that some people were upset with how aggressive we were. 'If a guy was committed somewhere else, what are we doing calling that kid?' I made the comment that if our guy doesn't call, that's a real big problem."

If a player reaffirms that he's solidly committed to another school, Ohio State will back off. But Meyer wants that call made. "I think times have changed a little bit," Luke Fickell said. "If you're not talking to a kid every two days, he's pushing, pushing, pushing. 'Hey, we've got to get him on the phone.'"

Wide receivers coach Zach Smith, the grandson of former Buckeyes coach and Meyer mentor Earle Bruce, said Meyer demands that recruiting is every assistant coach's top priority, followed by player development and then X's and O's. Some head coaches let their assistants handle most of the recruiting duties. That makes sense to some degree because NCAA rules limit when head coaches can visit recruits. But Meyer is deeply involved in the process and, like his predecessor, has a gift for closing the deal.

"When Jim Tressel was here, he was the best recruiter on our staff," Fickell said. "Urban Meyer is the best recruiter on our staff. There are a lot of [head coaches] who don't want to put the time and effort into it. He does put the time and effort into it. Then there are guys who put the time and effort into it, but just don't have the charisma and personality to be a great recruiter. Well, he does. He has that charisma. He has that personality. It comes naturally to him."

As a player, Smith passed up other offers to walk-on at Bowling Green just to learn from Meyer. He said that Meyer is "by far" the best recruiter he has ever been around. "He was a psych major for a reason," Smith said. "I remember as a player at Bowling Green—people used to laugh about it—you'd go into a one-on-one meeting with Coach Meyer and you'd walk out saying, 'I just committed. I didn't want to commit. What just happened?'"

Meyer said he believes he's effective because he has a good product to sell—Ohio State, athletically and academically—and because he's honest. He doesn't promise playing time. He does promise the opportunity to earn it. "I don't think I BS people," he said. "Sometimes that turns people off, and we don't get them. Honesty is a big key to who we are."

Take the case of Jalin Marshall, who was a star option quarterback at Middletown High School. At 5'10", he understood that he'd probably play another position in college. "There were a lot of teams that told me I could start at quarterback for their team," Marshall said. "I felt I wasn't ready to do that and that was a lie. I thought they would move me. Coach Meyer just told me straight up what he wanted to do. I felt there was more honesty in the relationship."

*　*　*　*

MEYER IS THE ONE who typically seals the deal with recruits, but a prospect's first interaction with Ohio State is typically with a guy who wasn't a football player and whose original plan was to become a doctor. Director of player personnel Mark Pantoni grew up in Sarasota, Florida, and got his undergraduate and master's degrees at the University of Florida. But as medical school approached, and knowing how long he'd have to train to be a doctor, he realized he wasn't sure that was the path he wanted. Pantoni began volunteering in the Gators' track-and-field program. He had developed a fan's passion for football recruiting and began helping out in the football office. Whatever mundane job he was assigned, he did eagerly. Eventually, he was given the job of taking recruits around campus. He did so well at that and other tasks that coaches took notice. Meyer, who won a national championship in his second season at Florida in 2006, wasn't necessarily one of them.

Asked when Meyer finally noticed him, Pantoni half-joked, "Probably after a year."

But Pantoni's tireless work ethic did eventually catch Meyer's attention, and he got a job as a recruiting program director. When Meyer took the Ohio State job, Pantoni came along. Now Meyer regards him as one of the most vital people on his staff, along with director of football operations Brian Voltolini, player development coordinator Ryan Stamper, video director Dave Trichel, personal administrative assistant Amy Halpin, and advisor Hiram de Fries. To followers on Twitter, Pantoni has become well-known for tweeting "BOOOOOMMM!!!!" when a prospect commits and using the word "swaggernaut," which he said he took from former *American Idol* judge Randy Jackson. But funny tweets are a miniscule fraction of his work day. Day after day, he watches video of prospects and develops relationships with players the Buckeyes want to pursue. Pantoni will use any resource available to spot prospects. He looks at recruiting services. He learns about players from Ohio State coaches who've heard about players through their grapevines. If a player is deemed to be worth watching, Pantoni or one of his three interns will watch entire game video of that kid, not just highlights. Pantoni estimates that 95 percent of colleges look only at highlight tapes.

"I don't know if it's laziness or what the excuse is," Pantoni said. "I think that's to our advantage. We want to be able to distinguish the bad from the good. A highlight tape is all good. By watching the whole games, it paints the true story of a kid."

That, obviously, takes much more time. An average workday in the office for him and his three interns starts at 7:00 AM and lasts until 10:00 PM several days of the week. He hopes to look at 20 prospects—typically two games per player—in a day. By NCAA rules, a person with Pantoni's job title is not permitted to evaluate film, only to screen and edit it. Only coaches can. But once a coach gives him the go-ahead, Pantoni tries to engage a prospect on social media. The key, Pantoni said, is to have a light touch. Pantoni's opening line to a player might be something like, "Hey, I just got some popcorn and gummy bears and watched your tape and you're an impressive player." Of the thousands of potential recruits that come onto Ohio State's radar in a year, Pantoni will initiate contact with about 200. From there, he'll eventually develop a close relationship with about 30 that the Buckeyes are particularly serious about signing. By the time a player visits Ohio State's campus, he often thinks of Pantoni as almost a long-distance big brother, even if they've never met in person. Director of high school operations Greg Gillum is in charge of logistics once a recruit arrives for his campus visit. "He's great at relating to kids and their families and knows everything about this place," Meyer said. "If he gives a tour of the Woody Hayes facility, I'll go on it because he knows so much."

While the goal is to get a kid to sign on the dotted line on signing day, Pantoni said he never talks recruiting with a prospect. "We talk about anything but," he said. "Think about it. They're getting hit by 20-something schools every day about recruiting, recruiting, recruiting. Even our coaches are hitting them about recruiting. You have to be different. You have to be funny and talk their language and be able to relate to them. So I'm sending them silly videos of guys being dunked on or talking about shoes or LeBron [James] or anything that might get their attention.

"At first it might be difficult to even get them to respond. You have to stand out. You have to get them to like you. Then really that relationship starts to build because they're like, 'This guy cares about me other than recruiting. He doesn't talk recruiting with me. He wants to get to know me on a personal level,' and we joke back and forth."

The job can be all-consuming and yet it must be done with one arm essentially tied behind his back. In addition to the NCAA rule prohibiting him from evaluating video, he is not allowed to initiate any conversations with a prospect. Pantoni is permitted to message a prospect and ask him to call, but he can't dial the phone first. He isn't allowed to call a player's high school coach. He's not even allowed to go to a high school game, whether or not there's a player Ohio State is recruiting.

On Saturdays of home games, Pantoni's work day is even longer than usual. He'll start at 7:00 AM and often isn't done until 1:00 AM. Pantoni is married, and his wife, Kristin, was due to deliver twins the following spring (which she did in June 2015, a girl and a boy). Pantoni said that Kristin is used to his work hours and is supportive and understanding, but even she has her limits. The fact that he must always be reactive and can't initiate communication with recruits can be an issue.

"There are times when the phone goes off or a top recruit DMs me and I need to DM him back," Pantoni said. "Sometimes she'll get frustrated. 'When does this end? Does it ever end?'"

Even on vacation, he'll tend to succumb to his competitive side and reach for his cell. Kristin will then remind him where they are. If that doesn't work, she has been known to confiscate his phone. When does she return it?

"When she sees I start turning white and get the shakes," he said with a laugh.

* * * *

OHIO STATE'S recruit evaluation process is finely tuned. Each position has prototypes. The Buckeyes crave speedy players. But so does every program. They prefer players with multi-sport backgrounds and put a premium on those who have won championships. Ohio State has a particular interest in how a prospect plays in pressure situations. Ohio State delves into a prospect's academic performance and his family life. The Buckeyes will try to find out about his girlfriend if he has one. When a coach visits a high school, he'll talk to the cafeteria worker, secretary, janitor, and anyone else who can answer how a kid truly behaves and treats people.

"You've got to listen," Pantoni said. "That's what Coach Meyer always says. Ask questions. Listen. Gather information."

A kid might be a five-star talent, but if he's judged to be a jerk, Ohio State will move on. "We won't recruit them," Pantoni said. "There's a zero percent chance of having success if you have those on your team. We'd rather have a three-star [player]—not as talented—but he's going to work harder, [have] no ego, [and be a good] locker room guy. That's how we want to build. Ideally, do you want to have an elite player? Yes, you do. But you have to make sure they fit the culture here, and it's a unique culture."

It might help that Pantoni claims not to know whether a player is rated by recruiting services as a five-star or three-star player. He doesn't want to be biased when he looks at video. The same applies to overall team recruiting rankings.

"If you were to ever ask me where we're ranked in recruiting, I literally have no idea, and I don't care," Pantoni said. "Coach Meyer always asks where we rank, and I'll say, 'I don't know.'"

But recruiting is as much art as science. It's about gut feel and projection. Sometimes, it comes down to how hard an assistant coach is willing to push for a player. No two recruitments are the same, and each one has its own element of drama, some more than others.

Take Ezekiel Elliott's. Elliott was a star running back at the John Burroughs School, a prestigious private college preparatory school in St. Louis. He committed to Ohio State on April 1, 2012, and faxed in his letter of intent on National Signing Day. "I knew once I stepped on campus that it was a special place," he said. "You could just feel the energy."

But in between his commitment and signing day, there was plenty of drama. Elliott's father, Stacy, was a football player at Missouri, where he met his wife, Dawn, who was a heptathlete on the Tigers' track team. Stacy's playing background and his occupation as a gang specialist made him wiser than most parents about the sales pitches from recruiters. "I could be a salesman if I wanted to," he said. "To persuade young people from killing each other, you've got to be pretty good."

Stacy now is close to Meyer and even serves as an unofficial liaison between the program and parents. Meyer said that he expects to remain close with Stacy and Dawn for the next 30 years. But the relationship between Meyer and the Elliotts became contentious during recruiting. After Ezekiel committed, Stacy got wind that the Buckeyes were also pursuing another blue-chip running back, Derrick Green. Stacy wasn't happy and told Meyer as much. "I told him, 'I don't like this relationship. It's like we're courting to get married, and you can see other women, but I can't see other men,'" Stacy said.

For his part, Meyer didn't appreciate a father trying to dictate to him who he could and couldn't pursue. The best players, he believes, don't care who else a coach is recruiting because they have faith that they'll win any competition. Stacy had questions about his son's role in the offense, to the point where he picked up a marker and diagrammed plays on the board during one visit to find out how Ezekiel would fit in the Buckeyes' offense. "[Meyer] would say, 'Stace, you just have to trust me,'" he said. "It was never about trusting Coach Meyer. It was about the best situation for my son."

At one point, Meyer was so frustrated by what he considered Stacy's excessive involvement that he considered pulling Ezekiel's scholarship offer. "I found out...that it was very wholesome and pure because Stacy loved his kid so much and wanted the best for him," Meyer said.

The truth is, the Buckeyes didn't actively recruit Green, who would sign with Michigan. Elliott did his own sleuthing on social media and concluded that Meyer hadn't been talking with Green. Ohio State even called Green and told him not to attend the Friday Night Lights recruiting showcase that year. But Elliott's recruitment did go down to the wire. The weekend before signing day, Elliott took an official visit to Missouri. When Ezekiel went to a Missouri basketball game, fans serenaded him with a chant of "M-I-Z! E-Z-E!" Ezekiel said that he visited Missouri just to make sure that he'd made the right decision to go to Ohio State, that he really wasn't wavering.

The Buckeyes weren't so sure.

"I thought, *Oh, my God, we might lose him,*" Pantoni said.

Though Elliott's parents by then were firmly back in Ohio State's camp, the visit tugged at their emotions. At the last minute, other schools including Alabama, Texas, and Florida State tried to make a late push. On signing day, Stacy or Dawn told Ohio State that Ezekiel would sign with the Buckeyes. But the Burroughs School wouldn't allow a signing ceremony until after school was out to prevent disruption to the academic day. Finally, the fax arrived. Elliott was a Buckeye.

Elliott was part of a 2013 class ranked No. 2 nationally, barely behind Alabama. But recruiting rankings guarantee nothing. "I think we knew we had the ability," Elliott said. "But when we got on campus, what were we going to do? Were we going to live up to the hype, or be just another class?"

They would answer that soon enough.

In just their second year on campus—and many of them redshirt freshmen—seven members of Ohio State's 2013 recruiting class would be starters. Elliott would blossom in the second half of 2014 and put together a three-game stretch in the postseason unprecedented in Ohio State history. Defensive end Joey Bosa would be a unanimous All-America selection. Five-star safety Vonn Bell, whose surprise announcement on signing day that he'd become a Buckeye capped the 2013 recruiting class, would lead the team with six interceptions. Linebacker Darron Lee, a high school quarterback, would become the biggest surprise on a defense that finally proved worthy of recapturing the Silver Bullets reputation it had long sought. Marshall would become a dazzling playmaker, saving the Buckeyes against Indiana and making key plays in other games down the stretch. Cornerback Eli Apple would help solidify the Buckeyes' secondary. Left guard Billy Price, signed as a defensive lineman, would mature into the final effective piece on an offensive line that shattered expectations.

And then there was the quarterback from that 2013 recruiting class. J.T. Barrett wouldn't play in the postseason, but he would lead the Buckeyes to it, against all odds.

4

PIECES ALIGNING

IN THE LOCKER ROOM after the Orange Bowl loss, Braxton Miller spoke of how badly his right shoulder throbbed. He had absorbed a couple of big hits against Clemson, one early in the game and then another late that left him wincing. But the injury did not at first seem to be of major concern. As the calendar turned from January to February, though, the pain in his shoulder hadn't subsided much.

"For a few weeks I had been under the assumption that it was a rehab-able injury and wasn't that big a deal," offensive coordinator Tom Herman said. "When the progress became so slow, I was like, 'Okay, guys, it's been six weeks, and the kid is not even picking up the ball. Something's not right here.'"

Urban Meyer said he wasn't worried until doctors said surgery was needed. "Anytime you do surgery, you get a little concerned," he said. "But I thought he'd be fine."

Doctors operated in late February at the Ohio State University Medical Center. Ohio State released a brief statement saying that Miller had had a "minor outpatient" procedure. It wasn't minor. Miller had a partially torn labrum that included a few chipped pieces of bone. The doctors' prognosis was that it would be July before Miller was likely to be 100 percent healed.

Miller wasn't the only one coming off surgery when spring practice began. Days earlier, Meyer had a procedure to relieve pressure from an arachnoid cyst near his brain. Headaches caused by the cyst had been an issue for Meyer earlier in his coaching career before he learned to manage his temper. Meyer was on the field for the first day of practice. Miller would be a spectator throughout spring ball, though coaches did their best to keep him engaged, in part by having him wear a video camera on his cap during practice.

With Miller out, Cardale Jones and J.T. Barrett shared snaps. Neither had proven much at that point in their careers. Jones was blessed with a great arm and size, and questions about everything else, starting with his maturity. Sitting in class as a freshman, he sent a tweet he would long regret. "Why should we have to go to class if we came here to play FOOTBALL," he tweeted. "We ain't come to play SCHOOL classes are POINTLESS."

Jones was suspended for one game—he was redshirting any-way—but the tweet became the extent of his public image. He was a third-stringer in 2013 behind Miller and Kenny Guiton and saw mop-up action in three games. His stats for the season: 1-of-2 pass-ing for three yards. A skimpy résumé to be sure, but more than the blank slate that Barrett's was. Barrett tore the ACL in his right knee in the fifth game of his senior season at Rider High School in Wichita Falls, Texas. He enrolled at Ohio State the following Jan-uary and spent his first year on campus rehabbing and then serving as the quarterback for the scout team. He had a reputation for poise and maturity, but his physical gifts were reputed to be merely above-average.

Still, quarterback wasn't considered that big of an issue. Miller was expected back in time for the regular season, and the Buck-eyes had plenty of other pressing problems. On defense, they had to find successors to Ryan Shazier at outside linebacker and Brad-ley Roby at cornerback, and fill both safety spots. They also had a hole at defensive end, though they expected that to be temporary. Before the Orange Bowl, Noah Spence was ruled to be in vio-lation of the Big Ten's substance-abuse policy. After he success-fully appealed, claiming that someone had slipped ecstasy into his drink, what would have been a one-year suspension was reduced to three games.

On offense, Ohio State had to replace top wide receiver Philly Brown and their beast of a running back, Carlos Hyde. After redshirting his first season on campus, hybrid back Jalin Marshall looked poised to make his mark. But in the third practice of the spring, he tore the meniscus in his left knee.

Around the same time, Jeff Heuerman suffered an injury that could have ended his career. Heuerman, who already had a broken nose from a tug-of-war mishap during off-season conditioning, caught a pass on an out route near the end of a no-pads practice. As he was running, someone stepped on his foot.

"I was like, 'Dang, that hurt,'" Heuerman said.

He tried to go for another play or two. In the training room after practice, team doctor Chris Kaeding examined Heuerman's foot. Heuerman could tell from Kaeding's face that the injury was serious. Tests showed that Heuerman had suffered a Lisfranc injury—a fracture of the bones or tear in the surrounding ligaments in the midfoot.

"There are guys who've never really come back from it," Heuerman said.

A decade ago, he said, treatment involved putting a cast on the foot for up to two months. Sometimes, the foot would heal properly. Sometimes, it wouldn't. Now the preferred treatment is surgery in which a sort of tightrope is placed around the ligament to strengthen it. The recovery time, though, is five to six months. After a discussion with Meyer and Heuerman's dad, Heuerman had the operation the next day at the Cleveland Clinic. He would be on crutches with a non-weightbearing cast for eight weeks and in a walking boot for another two months. This was not how Heuerman envisioned the start of his senior season.

With capable junior Nick Vannett as Heuerman's replacement, the Buckeyes weren't panicked over the tight end position. The offensive line, however, was a major concern. The Buckeyes had to replace four multi-year starters from a unit that had dominated in 2012 and 2013. The only holdover was junior Taylor Decker. He understood the huge responsibility he faced in helping get his linemates up to speed. Decker grew up in the Dayton suburb of Vandalia as a huge Ohio State fan. "My whole bedroom was Ohio State," Decker said. "Ohio State blanket, posters. I wanted to be a Buckeye."

But Ohio State's staff under Tressel didn't offer him a scholarship. Decker committed to Notre Dame. Fighting Irish offensive line coach Ed Warinner and tight ends coach Tim Hinton, who was the point man for Decker's recruitment, then left South Bend to join Meyer's staff. Warinner said he promised Notre Dame coach Brian Kelly when he left that he wouldn't call any Fighting Irish commitments to try to lure them to Ohio State, and Decker first thought he'd stick with his commitment. But as time passed and he realized that Warinner and Hinton—his two biggest ties to Notre Dame—were now in Columbus, he thought about seeing if Ohio State might have interest. So Decker talked it over with his family and high school coach Greg Bush, who called Ohio State. "I stayed out of it," Warinner said. "But I told Coach Meyer that there was no doubt he'd be a top NFL player one day."

Meyer offered a scholarship, and Decker accepted. As a freshman, Decker impressed his linemates early with his football intelligence, and he battled with converted tight end Reid Fragel for the right tackle spot. Fragel, a senior, barely won the job. Decker took over the next year. The four seniors didn't make life easy for him. The offensive line had been a revelation in 2012 and they weren't about to let Decker be the weak link in 2013 without doing everything in their power to change it. By the end of the year, Decker played on a par with them. Then, after the Orange Bowl, they were gone.

"Jack Mewhort came up to me," Decker recalled, "and said, 'This is your unit now. You're the leader.'" It was a daunting task. Even Decker faced a major challenge, switching from right tackle to left tackle. The second starter figured to be Pat Elflein. He had filled in admirably after right guard Marcus Hall was ejected from the Michigan game and suspended for the Big Ten title game. Hall had flipped off the crowd in Ann Arbor with both hands following an on-field fight between the archrivals. Well, if you're going to be ejected, you might as well go down with fingers a-blazin'.

Beyond Decker and Elflein, there were only question marks. The Buckeyes signed Chad Lindsay, a part-time starter for Alabama in 2013 who transferred and was immediately eligible as a graduate transfer. He was the smart-money choice to start at center. One alternative was Jacoby Boren, the last of three brothers to play for the Buckeyes. But at only 6'1" and 285 pounds, Boren looked like he was too small for the job. Antonio Underwood got the first starter's reps at left guard, though he hadn't proven much to that point. Three other line candidates were converted defensive linemen—senior Joel Hale, redshirt freshman Billy Price, and fifth-year senior Darryl Baldwin. Hale started at defensive tackle in 2013, though his playing time diminished after Adolphus Washington was moved inside from end after the emergence of Joey Bosa. Price was the team's strongest guy in the weight room, but understandably raw as an offensive lineman. Baldwin was given the nominal edge at right tackle, but it was more by default than merit.

While there was borderline panic about the line by outsiders, inside the room was steely determination, led by Warinner. For him, coaching at Ohio State was the culmination of a dream. He grew up as the son of educators in the village of Strasburg, south of Canton. His dad, Paul, played for Paul "Bear" Bryant at Kentucky before becoming a teacher and coach and eventually a superintendent. His mom, Gale, was a teacher and then a librarian. In high school, Warinner was a four-sport athlete. At Mount Union College, he played football and baseball and was a student assistant with the basketball team. Warinner started as a premed major, with hopes of becoming a pediatrician. But his labs schedule conflicted with practices and he switched majors, expecting to follow in his dad's career path. Warinner became a graduate assistant at Michigan State, where he met his wife, Mary Beth. He then coached at Army for 13 seasons and for three at Air Force. In 2007 he became the offensive coordinator at Kansas, where he'd previously served as offensive line coach. The Jayhawks have traditionally had a dismal program. Head coach Mark Mangino and Warinner knew they had to be creative to compete with Big 12 powers such as Oklahoma, Texas, and Nebraska.

"We changed the culture," Warinner said. "We went to no-huddle in 2007 and went to high tempo and a quick passing game, spread offense, audibling from the sideline. That was where we broke new ground."

The quarterback would approach the line after being given a play call. Then he'd look at the sideline and get instructions based on a defensive alignment whether to run that play or change it. Eventually, the Jayhawks devised a sign-language system in which every word Warinner wanted to communicate to his quarterback would be signaled in from the sideline.

"Where to throw it, who to throw it to, what to do, how to do it," Warinner said. "That was unheard of then. We were one step ahead of everybody then. So we rolled through college football."

Kansas—Kansas!—won its first 11 games of the 2007 season, reaching No. 2 in the rankings, before losing to No. 3 Missouri in the final regular-season game. The Jayhawks then beat No. 5 Virginia Tech in the Orange Bowl. Kansas averaged 42.8 points per game, second-most in the country.

"I was a little bit surprised," Warinner said. "I knew it all made sense to me because it was something I worked on in my mind for 20-some years. But to actually have the players and personnel [execute it].… It just all came together. Once we got rolling, it was pretty good. It was real good."

He went to Notre Dame in 2010. While Warinner was getting ready to board the team bus the morning after the Fighting Irish lost the 2011 Citrus Bowl, Meyer called to ask him about the Ohio State offensive line job. The chance to come back to Ohio for the first time since college was too enticing to turn down. Until the Buckeyes' opener in 2012, his players didn't quite know what to make of Warinner. He was so intense and demanding in practice that they worried he would be a frothing mess during games. Instead, he shocked them by how calm he was. The hard work, they realized, had already been done. Games were the time to show it. Ohio State's line became the sturdy foundation of the offense's success in 2012 and 2013. Now, with an almost entirely new cast, the pressure was on Warinner again.

"The perception in the room was that [outsiders] were looking for a reason for us not to be good, and we're not going to give them one," he said. "It gave us a chip on our shoulders and motivation to grind," Warinner said. It was as if Warinner and his players exiled themselves to a secret retreat. His mindset? "Don't talk to anybody," he said. "Tell your wife and kids to avoid listening to all the noise. Don't go out to dinner. Don't be seen in public. Just stay away from everybody and grind."

Above the area of the practice field where the offensive line worked was that "THE CHASE..." banner. It was a constant reminder of their challenge. "We looked at it every day running out there for practice," Baldwin said. "Anytime something would happen or we'd get down, we just had to remember what we were doing it for. It's so much bigger than anything we could have done individually. Coach Meyer would remind us, 'Remember what we're chasing.' After practice, the same thing. There was such an emphasis on it, there was no way we could forget it."

But Warinner was playing with a half deck in the spring. Chase Farris, expected to compete for one of the spots, was out after knee surgery. Lindsay never became healthy enough to assert himself. He eventually had to quit without playing a down because of repeated neck and shoulder stingers. Hale also would be bothered by a back injury that would keep him out of the mix for most of 2014.

"It was kind of tough to say [what we had]," Decker said. "But everybody was a good athlete. All were strong. All could run. It was a matter of whether we could execute it on the field. That's where Coach Warinner had to coach us up." Decker described Warinner as the hardest worker on the coaching staff. "He works that way because he cares so much about us," he said. "He spends so much time with us that we're like his sons. He sees us more than he sees his own son. In spite of that, he demands perfection of us. He's tough on us, and it's not always what you want to hear. His biggest thing is effort. If you play hard as an offensive line, you can do a lot of things wrong. But you'll still be all right just because of your effort and toughness."

But as spring practice ended, more questions than answers remained.

"I think I'd named two starters—Decker and Elflein," Meyer said. "I was panicky. Coach Warinner wasn't, because he knew more than I knew. He's with them every day."

*   *   *   *

ON DEFENSE, the Buckeyes were enthusiastic about the aggressive new pass defense that Chris Ash was installing. "Once I met with Coach Ash and he explained the defense in the off-season going into spring ball," Doran Grant said, "I was like, 'I'm liking this, because we can challenge.' It was a big adjustment. The safeties played tighter. The corners played press every snap. It was a zone-match defense. For corners, it was basically man-to-man every play. It gave us the opportunity to challenge everything."

But the transition to that defense took a blow on the first day of practice. Sophomore safety Vonn Bell, who had an interception making his starting debut in the Orange Bowl loss, injured his knee when his cleat got caught in the turf while breaking up a pass. He had torn the medial collateral ligament in his knee and would be out the rest of the spring. The news was better elsewhere in the secondary. Cornerback Eli Apple was back on the field. Tests had revealed an iron deficiency as the cause of his lack of endurance and energy during off-season conditioning.

"You've got guys getting on you, saying this and that about you, and you start to believe it and doubt yourself," Apple said. "It was definitely a relief to find out it was something beyond my control." Medication began to ease the symptoms, though he said he never felt 100 percent during the 2014 season. But at least he could now compete for the job with Gareon Conley, the other top contender for the spot opposite Doran Grant. On student-appreciation day, when Meyer invites students to attend practice at the Woody, Apple finally shed the black stripe on his helmet. He'd had that stripe for so long that he almost forgot he was regarded as a second-class citizen until one of the freshmen pointed it out. "That's when it kind of put a fire in me like, *Okay, it's time for me to get this off*," Apple said.

He felt great in warmups, and it carried over to practice. He repeatedly locked up receivers in practice. Afterward, the helmet stripe was removed. More than a year after he arrived on campus, Apple was a full-fledged Buckeye at last.

Apple wouldn't win the job in the spring. He and Conley would battle deep into training camp. But another player did come out of nowhere to seize a job. Darron Lee was not one of the marquee linebackers in Ohio State's 2013 recruiting class. Mike Mitchell from Texas and Trey Johnson from Georgia were the ones projected to become starters. Neither panned out. Mitchell would transfer after his freshman season in part to be closer to his father, who had serious health issues. Johnson's career ended prematurely because of arthritis in his knees.

The Buckeyes weren't sure what they had in Lee when they signed him. In fact, it took a long time for the Buckeyes to even want to sign him. Lee was primarily a quarterback at New Albany High School near Columbus. His college position wasn't clear. He attended Ohio State camps several times in hopes of earning an offer. Luke Fickell was in his corner. Meyer wasn't. At one OSU camp, Lee showed up wearing tie-dyed socks. "They were my lucky socks, man," Lee explained. If Fickell had known Lee was going to wear them, he said he'd have discouraged him. "A New Albany quarterback wearing tie-dyed socks," Meyer said. "That's not what I'm looking for."

But Lee did show impressive quickness the final time he attended camp, and Meyer liked how persistent Lee was in returning to camp after camp in hopes of finally earning an offer. Fickell pleaded with Meyer to extend an offer, which he did. At his first weigh-in as a Buckeye, Lee nudged the scale at 197 pounds. Lee was tried at safety and wide receiver, but Mickey Marotti believed his frame would support enough weight to become a linebacker. Lee's first year was a washout. He played five plays on special teams before a groin injury caused him to take a redshirt. He bided his time and gradually gained weight—and more—under Marotti's strict tutelage.

"He wasn't the toughest cookie in the cookie jar," Marotti said. "He was athletic. He was one of those guys I took under my wing and beat the living shit out of, physically and mentally. I was in his grill all the time, just coaching him as hard as you could possibly coach him. I didn't let him sneeze the wrong way."

It is a tenet of the Ohio State program under Meyer that if you push players to the brink, it strengthens their resolve. They've endured and invested so much that walking away ceases to become a palatable option. By the Orange Bowl, it was apparent that Ryan Shazier would head to the NFL, opening a linebacker spot. Confident by nature, Lee was determined to take advantage of it.

At 3:40 AM the night of the Clemson loss, he knocked on the hotel room door of Billy Price, who was still awake. For more than an hour, they talked outside on the balcony. "I said, 'I didn't want to feel this anymore. I don't want to lose anymore,'" Lee recalled.

The two made a vow that they would do everything in their power to make a difference in 2014, and that started with earning a starting spot. "We had that conversation and we never had to remind each other," Lee said. "He knew and I knew."

While Price struggled to adapt to his new position, Lee quickly became the talk of spring practice. "Darron Lee was just all over the field, hitting things left and right, chasing down stuff," Curtis Grant said. "I was like, 'Where did this kid come from?' I always told him that he was cocky. I like that about him, the way he plays his game."

One play in particular stood out to Lee. In the Wednesday practice before the spring game, Dontre Wilson got the ball on a reverse and had a clear path to the end zone. Wilson is one of the fastest players on the team. A linebacker shouldn't catch him.

"He probably had at least 15 yards on me," Lee said. But Lee caught him and, in his words, "destroyed" Wilson. "I put my foot in the ground and I hawked him down at the 1," he said. "He woke up real woozy after that."

Ohio State had found its strongside linebacker.

*   *   *   *

AS FOR THE quarterback battle for what looked to be the backup job, Jones was ahead. Barrett was disappointed with his play. Though he hadn't taken a snap in 18 months, Barrett was frustrated that he had let bad plays linger in his mind. "Three plays would go by and I'd still be thinking about what I messed up," he said.

But it's not as if he expected to be the starter when the season began. At a family reunion back in Wichita Falls, relatives asked him how much he expected to play in 2014. He told them he'd be happy if he could contribute on the field by earning the job as the holder for field goals.

In the forgettable spring game, Barrett barely completed half of his passes—17-of-33—for 151 yards. Jones wasn't any better. He was 14-for-31 for 126 yards.

Barrett was still considered starter material down the road. Jones? Not necessarily.

Until the end of spring practice when he broached the subject with offensive coordinator Tom Herman, Meyer had been skeptical about Jones' potential as a starter. "I remember for the first time asking Tom, 'Do you think he can play at Ohio State?'" Meyer said. "Until then, I didn't think he could. But you saw glimpses in the spring that he was a very talented guy. Up until then, I hadn't seen it."

But for both Jones and Barrett, it seemed an academic question. In everyone's mind, the Ohio State quarterback in 2014 would be Braxton Miller.

5

BROTHERHOOD OF TRUST

EVEN NOW, Urban Meyer isn't quite sure why he approached Tim Kight that night in 2013. Divine intervention perhaps, he now thinks.

Kight was at the Meyers' house for a fundraiser for Athletes in Action, a Christian athletic fellowship organization. It was a large gathering. Meyer finds those uncomfortable. He made an escape from a room and spotted Kight, who was holding a soda in one hand and hors d'oeuvres in the other. Meyer stopped to ask him if they'd ever met.

"People who know me know there's no chance I would ever do that," Meyer said. "But I went right up to him. Something said to me, 'Hey, you know that guy.'"

Meyer and Kight hadn't met, but soon it felt as if they had. Meyer asked Kight what he did for a living. Kight replied that he was a leadership development consultant. Since his college days as a psychology major, Meyer has been fascinated by the topic of motivation. He and Kight became immersed in conversation.

"We sat there, and I couldn't get enough," Meyer said.

Kight told Meyer about his company, Focus 3, and explained what he calls the "performance pathway." At its heart is a maxim: leaders build culture, culture shapes behavior, and behavior produces results.

"That's the physics of performance," Kight explained. "It's non-negotiable. That's always at work in every team, whether you know it or not. The coaches who don't know that's happening are missing a big piece, and those who do know what's happening have a competitive advantage, because they can intentionally build leadership, culture, behavior."

The next morning, Meyer called him. It was the beginning of a relationship that Meyer believes was instrumental to the Buckeyes' 2014 success. Their first meeting came too far along in the 2013 off-season to implement Kight's full system for that season. Meyer in fact had already been actively trying to enhance his team's leadership. The undefeated 2012 team was blessed by senior leaders who, after early resistance, bought into his coaching. Meyer said he will be eternally grateful to those seniors, especially players like John Simon, Zach Boren, Etienne Sabino, and Garrett Goebel. Because of Ohio State's NCAA sanctions, they could have transferred and played elsewhere right away. None did, even though they knew Ohio State would not have a postseason. "I didn't recruit them," Meyer said. "I didn't know them. To me, they set the foundation."

Meyer could see early in 2013 off-season conditioning that, without those departed players, the foundation was a bit soft. The offensive linemen did their part, as did a few others, but overall, there was a void. Mat drills are perhaps the quintessential Ohio State drill under Mickey Marotti. It's as basic as it gets. One player tries to reach one end of a wrestling mat while another does everything in his power to stop him.

"Our mat drills bordered on pathetic," Meyer said. "The worst I've ever seen. We had these great players run out the door [after 2012], and all of a sudden you've got these kids [remaining]. Our best players weren't bad guys. They turned out to be really good guys."

But they weren't setting the right tone. If players were supposed to start workouts at 6:00 AM, too many would walk in at 5:59, Meyer said. Class attendance became a minor issue. Off-season conditioning is designed to test minds as well as bodies, and the Buckeyes weren't acing the test.

"When it got hard, pains in the ass surface," Meyer said. "And they were surfacing." He said that he and Marotti panicked. Every year, Meyer had formed what he calls a leadership group of players. They met with him weekly to keep the team on course. Meyer usually didn't settle on the players for the leadership group until after spring practice. In 2013 he decided the issue was too dire to wait. "We started this in February, it was so bad," Meyer said.

Meyer picked 19 players for the group. He believed the sessions went well. "But it was kind of grab-bag," Meyer said. "I wouldn't think about what we would teach until that day."

He was a little over a month into the program when he met Kight. Almost immediately, some of Kight's ideas were implemented. Players began wearing rubber wristbands reading E+R=O—Event plus Response equals Outcome. That's at the core of Kight's philosophy. Things—or events—happen, good and bad. People have no control over that. But they do control how they respond to those events, and that determines the ultimate outcome. A proper response is considered "above the line." One that's not is "below the line."

As the 2013 season unfolded, the leadership issues became exposed. Christian Bryant's injury in the Big Ten opener against Wisconsin was particularly devastating. The safety was the defense's vocal leader. "I think we didn't have complete leadership," defensive tackle Michael Bennett said. "We had guys who were really good leaders. But we weren't all together. We were still blaming each other and pointing fingers and kind of still more individuals than a team."

After the two losses at the end of the 2013 season, Meyer knew how tempting it might be to deflect responsibility, to do what he calls "BCD"—blame, complain, and defend. He was determined not to let that happen. He wanted to get under the hood and get to the core of whatever deficiencies existed. The easy solution might have been to fire coaches, but that's never been Meyer's way. Nor is it to blame players. "It takes time, effort, and guts to find out what the problem is," Meyer said. "Sometimes it's not pleasant. It's not pleasant at all. We went on a mission to find out what the problem was, and I think we did. It went to the trust element that I felt."

Kight would be part of the solution to fixing it. If Todd Gongwer's book re-sparked the "why" in what drove Meyer as a coach, Kight would formalize the "how" his leadership beliefs would be implemented. Meyer has long had tenets for the culture he wants. The most frequently invoked are "4 to 6" and "A to B." The average length of a play is four to six seconds. Meyer demands that players give maximum effort from snap to whistle, and "4 to 6" is code for that. The "A to B" is also as basic as it sounds. Players should go from Point A to Point B as fast as possible. Those are Meyer's commands for on-field performance. What Kight helped him do was instill his overall philosophy into his assistant coaches and players.

"It was a systematic approach to teach what we were already doing," Meyer said. "Our whole program is about how you respond. But his terminology and way of doing it were exactly what we needed."

All good coaches consider themselves educators, and most put leadership among the most important qualities a team needs. But Meyer believes that leadership has too often become just a buzzword. "*Leadership* in athletics is the most overused and misunderstood word," he said. "Leadership—and I'm not proud to say this—for me and most is a quote, a video, and you move on. How you run an offense is not a quote and a video, either. That's why there are so many bad offenses. You have to have a plan to teach it. Our leadership training in the past was Coach Mick and me. Obviously, it wasn't all bad, but it wasn't a game-changer."

The Buckeyes firmly believe that the program Kight taught in 2014 was. Starting in the spring, Kight held formal classroom seminars with the Buckeyes coaching staff. The aim was to strengthen what Meyer calls the power of the unit. There are nine positional units on a football team—defensive linemen, quarterbacks, wide receivers, etc. Each would be held accountable for its performance.

The Buckeyes lost to Michigan State, Meyer believes, because not all nine units were up to standard.

"The goal is not to win a national championship," Meyer said. "It's to have all nine units be strong, which is playing at maximum capacity."

The starting point for maximizing performance in each unit would be to build trust. "It's just a little theory I have that before you can get great results, you need teamwork," Meyer said. "Before you can ask people to give you teamwork, you need commitment. Before you get commitment, they have to trust you. If they don't trust you, they have no trust. The trust can't be on a team level. It's impossible. It's too many people. It's got to be on a unit level."

The workshops that Meyer asked Kight to teach were called the "Brotherhood of Trust." Each week, coaches sat with notebooks just as they would in a typical school. Meyer was there, too, glasses perched on his nose, Kight said, pencil in hand, as eager or moreso than anyone to learn.

Kight has run plenty of seminars for corporations and teams. He said he has never seen the follow-through that he got with Ohio State. The sessions were originally scheduled for 45–60 minutes apiece, but they typically stretched to 90 minutes because the coaches were so engaged. "Everyone really intends to do it," Kight said of other clients. "But after the workshop is over, you really don't hear from the leaders anymore. There's no follow-up. They don't work hard at application. Employees will often tell us, 'Your training was the most profound experience we've ever had. We absolutely loved it. But since you guys left, no one hardly talks about it anymore.' But at Ohio State it was very different. From Day 1, Urban and the coaching staff, particularly Urban, constantly used the tools. He talked about it. He applied it. He discussed it formally and informally."

It helped that Kight is a former athlete, which helped him click with coaches and players. He won the 1971 scholastic national championship in the 330-yard intermediate hurdles while at

Worthington High School near Columbus. Kight ran track at UCLA after transferring from Ohio State. He became a pastor and did consulting work for businesses before deciding to switch to that full-time, with an emphasis on motivation. "I've always been intrigued by peak performance," he said. "I've always wanted to know what makes the best tick."

The more he worked with Meyer, Kight became transfixed by the rare combination he saw in him—remarkable intelligence coupled with the intellectual curiosity and openness to new ideas. "He's curious and hungry," Kight said. "If there's something that's true, there's something new, there's something that's different, something that's better or something that's helpful, he has no problem whatsoever saying, 'I'm not good enough at that.' None whatsoever. If he sees something that he needs to be better at and he knows he's not good enough, he gets a resource to help him. There is zero ego in that guy at that point."

With his confident and no-nonsense demeanor, Meyer can give off the air of someone who knows the answers. Meyer is so hyper-focused on tasks at hand that occasionally he'll walk by someone in a hallway without even acknowledging the person. He said he is aware of that and is trying to better about it. But tight ends coach Tim Hinton, who was a graduate assistant with Meyer at Ohio State in the mid-1980s, said that Meyer is the best listener he knows. "He is the most intense, continuous listener of anybody I've been around," Hinton said. "That's a skill, and that's not an easy skill. It's off the charts, in my opinion."

When Meyer hears something that he believes is helpful, he's willing to try it. One night while at home after spring practice ended, Chris Ash watched an instructional video by Seattle Seahawks coach Pete Carroll advocating rugby-style tackling. Because rugby players don't wear helmets, they try to tackle low, leading with their shoulders. By not using their heads to hit, they were less prone to concussions, a major issue in football.

Ash did substantial research and became convinced that Ohio State should coach that style of tackling. He knew that persuading his fellow Buckeyes coaches, particularly Meyer, would be a challenge. These weren't rookie coaches. They'd coached tackling a certain way their entire careers. But after he pitched his case, Meyer agreed to change. The result, Ash believes, is that Ohio State players had fewer injuries while tackling and missed fewer tackles, which had been a problem with recent Buckeyes teams.

"People think he's so arrogant," Shelley Meyer said, "and arrogance can mean that you think you know everything or are the best at everything. He knows he doesn't know everything. I think he's okay with that now. Maybe that's part of what's changed in him now. He knows he's got people to go to, to help him figure things out so he can get the answer. He is way more humble than he was at Florida. That's part of his perspective."

Kight said Meyer continually peppers him with "how" questions. How do we do this? How can we be better at that? Meyer says that's because he knows the danger of thinking he knows it all. "I'm a great thief," he said. "I'll go to incredible depths to find out what makes an organization tick, a coach tick, or a player tick and [finding out] 'How did that happen?'"

Meyer counts Nike CEO Phil Knight, NFL commissioner Roger Goodell, New England Patriots coach Bill Belichick and Philadelphia Eagles coach Chip Kelly among his close friends. But in conversation, he usually moves past small talk quickly. He is constantly seeking knowledge. "My closest friends are guys who share a common outlook," Meyer said. "It's very rarely, 'Hello, how are you doing?' It's, 'What've you got?'"

Meyer continually picked Kight's brain, and his enthusiasm for Kight's teachings permeated the staff. The newest assistant coaches—Larry Johnson and Chris Ash—were among the most excited.

"I thought it was the best thing that ever happened not only for the alignment of the coaching staff but as far as transferring the information to the players," Johnson said. "I think we all had a sense of purpose. Coach Meyer drove this thing: 'This is who we are. This is what we're going to do better than anyone in the country, and it's going to start with leadership.' You'd think, *Man, this is boring*. But every day you got something new about how to connect with players and what's important to players." Johnson said that without that connection, tapping into a player's full potential is almost impossible. On some days, that meant putting aside, say, the schematic plan for installing a blitz. Instead, he'd talk to them about his background and experiences so that they could see he'd been through some of the same issues they faced.

Meyer mandated that his position coaches do three things with their players before the season: invite them to dinner at the coach's house, do a community-service project together, and set aside a day for a fun activity. Hinton, for example, took his players out on a ski boat.

During the season, the talk in meeting rooms doesn't always involve X's and O's. "What we do here as well as anybody in the country is we have a lot of campfire chats in our room," Hinton said. "We spend an awful lot of time talking non-football issues with our players. Coach Meyer does not want you to start a meeting with just football. Start with academics, start it with a social issue of the day. Laugh a little bit, cry a little bit. There are times we'll talk about real issues, and we've had guys stand up in front of their room and have tears in their eyes and cry in front of their buddies because they'll be talking about something that means something to them. When you get a relationship that gets to that point where they're not afraid to bleed on each other, there's a bond there."

That was particularly beneficial for the new coaches. Ash said that he also spent more time than ever talking about leadership with his players than he did X's and O's. Every meeting would begin with a nugget of leadership. "A lot of people talk about leadership training and character building and chemistry on the team,"

Ash said. "The reality is, not a lot of people invest the way they need to make that happen. It doesn't happen overnight. It takes time and effort, and [Meyer] put in the time and effort with Tim Kight to make us as coaches learn it and go teach our players."

Day after day, the E+R=O was drilled into their heads. Adversity was going to happen. How would they respond? "It was communicated non-stop," Ash said. "It was beat into their brains. It wasn't motivation. It was manipulation. We brainwashed them to buy into it."

Kight had a strong feeling that the coaching staff had embraced his teaching one day in spring practice. He said that Ash came off the field and told Fickell, "Man, I coached below the line today. I've got to change that." Ash felt he'd been too angry and edgy. He'd yelled too much at his players. That Ash felt comfortable enough to confide that in Fickell was particularly significant, Kight believed. Usually, a new coach is reluctant to show weakness, particularly in talking with a guy from whom outsiders believe you've usurped some responsibility.

"There was zero of that," Kight said. "None. Luke didn't use that against Chris. Chris didn't try to hide that from Luke. You had high character by Luke, high courage by Chris, a willingness to use the tools he's being taught, not hesitating, being open and authentic and making changes."

Too often, a team can be undermined by turf wars among coaches. That hadn't been an issue in Meyer's first two years at Ohio State, but the potential is always there. Coaches are ambitious people, competitive by nature, eager for advancement and justifiably insecure in an occupation not known for job security. To get them working seamlessly is a huge challenge even in the best of circumstances. But Meyer mandated it, Kight facilitated it, and the coaches embraced it.

What mattered, though, was not so much that the coaches got it, but whether they could transfer the overall message to their players.

Coaches were given leeway to how they delivered the message. A soft-spoken coach like Larry Johnson wouldn't say it the same way as cornerbacks coach Kerry Coombs, whose passion oozes from his pores.

"I don't want them to be robots," Meyer said. "I don't want them to be Tim Kight or me."

Senior offensive tackle Darryl Baldwin said the message got through. He said the E+R=O mentality helped players get through the grind of practice without going on autopilot. One day, the offensive linemen even wrote "ATL" for "Above the Line," and taped it on their helmets.

"I think it played a huge role in everything," Baldwin said of the leadership training. "It made you evaluate yourself and see how you were doing and how you could improve and how you're helping the team. You really have to look yourself in the mirror every night and say, 'Am I doing everything I can for this team? It brought leaders out in everyone. It made everyone accountable for their unit. They didn't want to let the team down. That's where the whole 'brotherhood' came into play."

In those smaller, positional units, trust was gradually built back up. The goal was to instill qualities that would not only help the Buckeyes on the field but in their lives beyond football. That kind of talk is commonplace everywhere. Meyer was determined to make it more than talk.

Its roots began a week after Meyer's Florida team dominated Oklahoma in the BCS title game to win the 2008 national championship. Basking in the glow of a second title, Gators coaches were meeting, and one of the assistants, Chuck Heater, commented about the players' post-football futures. Coaches were being paid handsomely. So were athletic directors. Programs were in the midst of a facilities arms' race. The system was awash in money, and the players, even if they graduated, faced uncertain futures. Times had changed, Meyer knew, since he graduated in the 1980s when a college degree almost ensured a decent job. That wasn't the case anymore. But he believed that football players had experiences that would serve employers well.

"You don't want to stereotype negatively or positively," Meyer said. "But they are used to performing in front of millions of people, understand the essence of teamwork, discipline, hard work, and commitment. How many people want to hire those people? Everybody."

But the demands of playing big-time football preclude some of the options a non-athlete would have. They can't get a job during the school year, for example. A question nagged at Meyer. "When the cheering stops," he said, "how are they going to be ready?"

In his last couple years at Florida, he began a program to prepare his players for life after football. At Ohio State, it has become a bona fide program called Real Life Wednesdays, with player development coordinator Ryan Stamper as the point man. Players are taught the basics of personal finance—how to balance a checkbook, how to understand credit scores, and "Who's this FICA guy?" as Meyer put it, to teach them about payroll taxes. Prominent business leaders— including Limited Brands head Les Wexner, JPMorgan Chase CEO Jamie Dimon, and Cleveland Cavaliers owner Dan Gilbert—spoke to the players. The highlight was a job fair in which players, dressed in business attire, met representatives from almost 100 companies. Cornerback Doran Grant said that he had about six emails the next day, with one requesting an interview. Ezekiel Elliott received three internship offers for the summer as a result, his father said. The program is taken so seriously that juniors are not allowed to participate in preseason camp unless they have finished a résumé certified by the program's academic advisors.

"I haven't heard of a school yet that's done half the stuff we've done," said Curtis Grant, who said he had filled two large folders with information from business contacts. "I'm very appreciative because at the end of the day, that's what matters."

6

BRAXTON DOWN

BRAXTON MILLER was going to be a different quarterback in 2014. That, he knew. In his first three years at Ohio State, Miller had been a run-first, pass-second quarterback. Part of that was because Miller was simply a spectacular runner. Raw speed combined with incredible elusiveness made him a threat to turn even a broken play into a touchdown. Entering 2014, he had run for 3,054 yards and 32 touchdowns. He averaged 5.5 yards per carry, and that's misleading because in college football, unlike the NFL, sacks count against a quarterback's rushing totals. Particularly in his first two years, Ohio State had to rely on Miller's legs because, even though he had a strong arm, he lacked the supporting cast around him to be much of a pocket passer. But as his senior year approached, he wanted that to change.

"I've got a lot of talent around me," Miller said in July 2014. "Why not show that talent off? It'll be fun to watch those guys run for the ball, attack the ball, and make plays for me. If I need to use my feet while scrambling, I'll do it. But other than that, I'd rather sit in the pocket and let it rip."

Miller had changed in other ways. Reserved by nature, he had gradually become a team leader. One day, Miller was driving on campus when he noticed a freshman who'd been having a difficult adjustment to college. Miller pulled over and encouraged the player to keep his chin up. Urban Meyer's eyes lit up as he relayed that story.

"That's huge," he said.

Early in his Ohio State career, Miller had gotten by more on talent than preparation. Meyer arranged a meeting for him with former NFL general manager Bill Polian, so that Polian could tell Miller what he would need to do to succeed as a pro. He also had him meet with Chip Kelly, the Eagles' coach. Miller had always put in his time in the film room, but the best quarterbacks practically live there. Miller was now doing that.

Miller had become a father in July 2012 when his son, Landon, was born. But he hadn't told anyone on the team other than his roommate, backup quarterback Kenny Guiton, for months afterward about it. "Because I didn't trust them," Miller said. "I'm sure they never had a quarterback as high-profile that had a child. I thought he was just going to judge me, like, 'I don't know what type of kid he is.' That's why I really didn't tell anybody."

When he finally told Meyer, the coach was supportive and told him he'd help him any way he could. When Meyer came to Ohio State, he and Miller bonded quickly. Miller's father, Kevin, remembered being surprised shortly after Meyer's hiring to see coach and player chest-bump when they greeted each other. That early superficial bond had now deepened. Meyer's affection for Miller had grown in their years together. Meyer believed Miller had a future as an NFL quarterback if he continued to grow in the mental side of the game. "If he makes the same progress that he made from Year 1 to Year 2 to Year 3 and makes the same jump, [it's a] no-brainer," he said. "If he doesn't, 50-50."

It was clear which possibility seemed more likely to Meyer. "He's matured," he said. "He's a sponge now. That means he can't get enough."

Miller had thought about turning pro after his junior year. The shoulder injury changed that. But his goal for the 2015 draft was clear. "First round for sure," he said. "I see myself as one of the top guys coming out."

But first there was unfinished business. He wanted to earn his degree, which he was due to complete in December. He was a leading Heisman Trophy candidate, but that was secondary in his mind to winning that elusive Big Ten championship and maybe something beyond. As for his shoulder, Miller seemed unconcerned. Rehab from the February surgery appeared to be going well. He had been tossing a football for a while with no ill effects. Coaches were going to limit Miller's throws to prevent him from overdoing it, but they fully expected him to start the season opener against Navy on August 30.

*   *   *   *

ELSEWHERE, though, questions abounded. When Ohio State's preseason camp began on August 4, about half of the 22 starting positions were undetermined. On defense, the line was set, with an asterisk. Noah Spence's substance-abuse suspension would keep him out for the first two games. Steve Miller and Rashad Frazier were the top contenders to fill in. When Spence returned, the Buckeyes believed, they might have the best defensive line in the country.

Darron Lee's breakthrough in the spring made the Buckeyes feel better about that unit. Joshua Perry was solid at the other linebacker spot. Senior Curtis Grant and freshman Raekwon McMillan were to battle in one of the more intriguing duels of camp. The secondary was more unsettled. Eli Apple had gotten treatment for his iron deficiency and was feeling much improved. He and Gareon Conley competed for the cornerback spot opposite senior Doran Grant. At safety, Tyvis Powell, Vonn Bell, and Cam Burrows were battling for the two spots.

On offense, sophomore Ezekiel Elliott was considered the front-runner to replace Carlos Hyde at running back. "As soon as Carlos graduated, I told Urban Meyer that this kid is going to be as good if not better than Carlos," running backs coach Stan Drayton said.

But Elliott was not a shoo-in. Senior Rod Smith finally seemed to have gotten his act together on and off the field. Talent had never been an issue for Smith. Now it looked like he might be one of those guys for whom it finally clicked as a senior. Freshman Curtis Samuel had dazzled during the spring and was now looking like a viable candidate as well. Recruited more as a hybrid back, Samuel had shown surprising toughness to go with his speed during spring practice.

Wide receivers coach Zach Smith said in the spring that his spots were up for grabs, even though three-year starter Devin Smith was back and fellow senior Evan Spencer was fully recovered from his broken leg suffered in the Orange Bowl. Devin had long proven himself as a deep-ball playmaker, but not a complete receiver. Michael Thomas, whose poor practice play in 2013 resulted in an unexpected redshirt year as a sophomore, had reemerged in the spring. Then there was junior-college transfer Corey Smith, who was regarded as the most physically gifted receiver on the team. "We had two guys who were starving, and we had two guys who were good kids, who worked hard and were going to be seniors," Coach Smith said.

At the hybrid position, sophomore Dontre Wilson and redshirt freshman Jalin Marshall were loaded with potential, but each had much to prove. Originally committed to Oregon, Wilson was a prized late addition to the 2013 recruiting class. He's blessed with rare speed but proved one-dimensional as a freshman. Marshall's first season never got off the ground. He got a concussion early in training camp and by his own admission was immature in his work habits. His attempts to make a lasting impression in spring practice in 2014 ended with the meniscus tear, though it was healed by the summer.

From the start of camp, Zach Smith was encouraged by what his players were doing. In 2011, Buckeyes receivers were a disaster. No one caught more than 14 passes, an embarrassment for a program like Ohio State's. They improved each of the next two years, but still weren't up to lofty Buckeye standards. Now Smith believed they would be in 2014. "They had a great camp," he said. "They were understanding concepts, understanding the purpose of our concepts, and how to attack defenses, which is next-level stuff at my position. They really ate it up."

Except for one particular day. That happened to be when ESPN broadcaster Joey Galloway, one of the best receivers in Ohio State history, showed up. Smith said the receivers had their worst day in a full year. "It was awful," Smith said. "They got covered. They were getting held by DBs. Just getting abused. The grind of two-a-days had gotten to them. They had a bad day, which happens. But it figures that it's the day Joey Galloway is there."

Disappointed by what he's seen—former Buckeyes take particular pride in their position group—Galloway texted Smith after practice and asked to speak to the receivers the next day. "He started off by saying, 'You all are the nicest group of receivers I've ever been around,'" Smith recalled. It was not a compliment. Galloway said he watched them pat defensive backs on the butt after they threw receivers to the ground. He told them that if a cornerback held him during practice or game, he'd issue a warning—don't do it again or prepare to pay the price. He told the receivers that they lacked swagger and confidence. Then he offered $1 to the first receiver who started a fight with a defensive back the next day.

"He was joking about the fighting, but it was sending a message that you have to be so confident to play this game at a high level that you will not let anybody touch you," said Smith, who added his own dollar to the challenge. The next day, Smith said, the receivers had the best practice of camp. The dollar bills remain on Smith's office wall. To be in compliance with NCAA rules, even $2 rewards to players are forbidden. Maybe when they graduate…

*   *   *   *

TRAINING CAMP is a grind for everybody, and sometimes under-the-radar players can do things to single themselves out. One Buckeye did by something he didn't do. Nik Sarac was a walk-on from Cleveland who'd made his mark on special teams. Meyer believed Sarac, a premed major, had earned a scholarship. But when Meyer offered it to him, Sarac turned it down, saying that his family could afford the cost of college and asked Meyer to award the scholarship to someone else in need. That decision forever earned him Meyer's respect.

Then there was another walk-on, a newcomer who was a backup heavyweight on the wrestling team. Kosta Karageorge was hard to miss. He was a defensive tackle whose rawness as a football player was exceeded only by the size of his personality. Karageorge was a familiar presence on campus, riding his motorcycle with his unruly hair and beard and a heavily tattooed body. Though playing time seemed like a longshot, Karageorge embraced every aspect of football. "I've never seen a guy so excited to go out to practice," left tackle Taylor Decker said. "He would always run out on the field and yell that he couldn't wait to hit somebody. He loved that physicality."

He had the same aggressiveness in the weight room. "I remember the very first day in the weight room," defensive tackle Adolphus Washington said. "All he wanted to do was lift heavy weights. He didn't want to do a warmup. He just wanted to put five plates on there and lift it. We used to think it was hilarious."

Karageorge also made his mark at meal time. In 2014 the NCAA lifted its rule restricting the amount of food a team can serve its players. Nobody took advantage of the buffet more than Karageorge. "Oh, he loved it," defensive tackle Michael Bennett said. "He'd always sit down with the widest smile on his face. He loved all the steak. He ate as much as he could."

But Karageorge provided more than comic relief. Every day after practice, he'd work with graduate assistant Vince Oghobaase on his technique. "It was a joy to see him—and the players—when he won his first one-on-one," defensive line coach Larry Johnson said. "Everybody cheered and jumped up and down because it was all coming together for him. Our players loved him."

* * * *

IT'S RARE THAT a team emerges unscathed from injury during camp. The most notable early one was a broken left wrist suffered by Ezekiel Elliott when he was hit after catching a pass in a seven-on-seven drill. "I didn't realize it was broken at first," Elliott said. "I finished practice, and afterward, I couldn't move my hand. I thought something had to be up."

X-rays revealed the fracture, and he had surgery two days later in which a pin was inserted to stabilize the area. He missed about 10 days of practice before returning with a cast. "At that point, I was scared," Elliott said. "It was my job to lose. Not being able to play in camp was kind of scary. I was afraid of what the outcome would be. We had a lot of great backs in the room."

As for Braxton Miller, his return was coming along slower than expected. Even with limits on the number of throws, Miller's shoulder was sore. "We didn't anticipate the roller coaster," offensive coordinator Tom Herman said. "We knew we were going to have him on a pitch count, but we thought we'd have him every day or more frequently than whatever it was the first 15 days of training camp. But it was just soreness. The way it was described to me was that it was the muscles around the shoulder, not the actual injury or the labrum itself."

With Miller mostly sidelined, Cardale Jones and J.T. Barrett continued their duel to be the No. 2 quarterback. Jones entered camp ahead of Barrett, but that changed as camp progressed. Ohio State charts almost every conceivable metric—completion percentage, sacks, interceptions, touchdowns, etc. Coaches believed the offense ran slightly smoother and more consistently with Barrett.

"He was more efficient," Meyer said after the season. "You started to witness the leadership skills that are so important at that position. His grasp of the offense was outstanding." On August 16, Meyer told the media that Barrett had edged past Jones. It was considered minor news then. Two days later, it wouldn't be.

The pass was a routine one, just a seven-yard swing pass. But as soon as Miller threw it, he crumpled to the ground at the Ackerman Road practice field, screaming in agony. Everyone understood instantly what had happened. Miller had reinjured his surgically repaired shoulder. Practice, normally full of chatter, fell silent. Miller was taken to a tent and examined by medical personnel. Tests confirmed that his labrum had torn again. "The amount of hours that kid put in, to see him roll on the ground like that, it was one of the worst things I've ever seen," Meyer said. "The whole team was shocked for I'd like to say a week, because it happened right in front of everybody."

He called Shelley walking off the practice field. At first, she thought it was a joke.

"I couldn't believe it," Shelley said. "We didn't know how bad it was, but he said, 'I think it's bad.' I just thought, *Well, there goes our season.* That's exactly what I thought. We were going to have this great season. He'd probably win the Heisman, probably go to the national championship. I just thought there's no way now."

Meyer returned to his home in the suburb of Dublin that night instead of staying at the team hotel. Shelley said she was pleasantly surprised by how calm he was. He didn't sleep well but wasn't the wreck he would have been at Florida. "It wasn't like, 'Woe is me. We're going to lose every game,'" she said. "He was just thinking, *How do I fix this?* That's the way he always is. He says, 'Don't talk to me about the problem. Figure out a solution.'"

Meyer smiled when told after the season that Shelley described him that night as calm. "I hid it very well," he said. "I couldn't sleep. My heart bled."

He knew how much work Miller had put in to become a complete quarterback. He'd put in so much time in rehab, so many hours in the film room. "And in three seconds it's gone," Meyer said. "I know Braxton and his family very well, and it was devastating. That was number one. Number two was, where do we go? We have a really bad offensive line. We have a group of receivers that's very inexperienced. Your best tailback is gone, and he was a great player. The pass defense last year was pathetic. You've got problems."

But Meyer was better equipped to cope with them. The changes in him, starting with reading Todd Gongwer's book and the leadership seminars with Tim Kight, had taken root. "What I learned on the journey is you can't control what you can't control," he said. "E+R=O."

Meyer would ask questions to find out what went wrong. He challenged Mickey Marotti, asking if the rehab was handled properly. Did Miller do his part? Did Ohio State? Did the surgeon? "Not many people are comfortable talking about that," Meyer said. "I don't care. Obviously, it failed. It's not as easy as, 'Why did a play fail?' It's usually because someone made a mistake. I was looking for an answer and never really got one, which is not uncommon."

Even a definitive answer wouldn't have changed anything. Regardless of why, Ohio State's season had been turned upside down in a matter of seconds.

That night, Evan Spencer texted Barrett to tell him that his teammates had faith in him. But it wasn't Barrett's job just yet. The next day, Tom Herman had to compartmentalize his thoughts—sympathy for Miller balanced by the pressing reality that he had to get a quarterback ready. He told Barrett to continue to do what he'd done to overtake Jones. Herman told Jones the competition wasn't over yet. "I said, 'Go beat him out. You've got 10 days here. Go beat him out. You guys were right neck and neck as of yesterday. Go take the job from him.'"

That came close to happening.

"Oh yeah, very close," Meyer said. "The leadership and the take-charge approach by J.T. is what put him on top. He was less prone to mistakes. Cardale would do great things and then throw the ball to the other guy."

Other position battles remained unsettled. Despite concerns about his size, Jacoby Boren had won the center job. Darryl Baldwin had solidified his spot at right tackle, but the guard spot opposite Pat Elflein hadn't been adequately filled. The receivers would share snaps, which would continue during the season. Elliott, despite his broken wrist, would be the No. 1 running back. On defense, Curtis Grant, for now, had held off Raekwon McMillan at middle linebacker, though both would play. At cornerback, Eli Apple had overtaken Gareon Conley, in part because Conley was dealing with a back injury. At safety, Tyvis Powell and Cam Burrows got the nod. Burrows edged out Bell partly because Bell was coming back from his knee injury and coaches weren't thrilled with his practice habits.

But with so many new faces, and the devastating loss of Miller, Meyer ended training camp believing the ceiling was pretty low for the 2014 Ohio State Buckeyes. He figured that with an inexperienced quarterback and an unproven line, Ohio State would have to be conservative on offense and hope to win with defense and special teams. He was already looking ahead to 2015. The Buckeyes were ranked No. 5 in the preseason Associated Press media poll, but that voting was done before Miller's injury.

"I'm embarrassed to say this—I'm not proud of it—but I was kind of saying, 'Okay, let's have a good year here developing these young players so we can have a good season the next year,'" Meyer said. "I just didn't see the makings of a championship team. I thought we were looking at a 9–4 or 8–5 team."

7

BARRETT'S DEBUT

DON'T BE LIKE Braxton.

That's what J.T. Barrett kept telling himself as Ohio State's season opener against Navy approached. The game would be played at the home of the Baltimore Ravens, M&T Bank Stadium. Barrett hadn't played a game in nearly 22 months, and now he would make his unexpected starting debut in an NFL stadium. It could have been overwhelming, but the reason J.T. Barrett had gotten even this far was that nothing overwhelmed him.

Joe Thomas Barrett IV grew up in Wichita Falls, Texas, which is near the Oklahoma border. His mother, Stacy, is a nurse. His father, Joe, is an electronics technician in the Army Reserves. The middle of three sons, J.T. was always mature for his age. When he was about six, he had a football in his hand when he told his parents that they wouldn't have to pay for his college. He was going to earn a scholarship, he said. "We just laughed at him," Joe said. "We looked at him like he was a little crazy. I said, 'Okay, son.'"

But J.T. proved early that he was willing to work for it. A summer of overeating while staying at a relative's house in Beaumont left him over the weight limit to be anything but a lineman on his sixth-grade Boys Club League. To avoid that fate, he begged to join his father at workouts at the local YMCA. The fact that Joe worked out around dawn didn't dissuade J.T. When people gave Joe dirty looks or accused him of dragging his son to work out at that ungodly hour, J.T. spoke up. "I'd say, 'He's not making me do it. It's something I want to do,'" Barrett said.

Barrett became a starter as a sophomore, and Rider went to the state quarterfinals after going 2–8 the prior year. The Raiders had a star senior running back who led the team, but Barrett showed that no moment was too big for him. In a tight playoff game against El Paso Andress, Rider had gotten a turnover. Raiders coach Jim Garfield told Barrett that he wanted to capitalize right away. The offensive coordinator called for a deep pass, and Barrett let it fly. "As soon as J.T. released the ball," Garfield said, "he just came running over to me—I don't think he even saw the pass completed—and said, 'How do you like that?!'"

That moment of bravado aside, Barrett was not a cocky player. He was, though, supremely confident, a product of the work he put in. Heading into his junior year, Barrett knew he had to become the team leader. He excelled that year and became a coveted recruit. Like many players in his state, he wanted to become a Texas Longhorn. But he didn't fit the Texas prototype. The Longhorns instead offered Tyrone Swoopes, a 6'4", 240-pounder who certainly looked the part. "I can't be 6'5". I'm going to be 6'1", 6'2"," Barrett said. "You can't teach 6'5". I didn't have the height and wasn't the pro-style quarterback they were looking for at that time."

Barrett had been invited to attend the Texas Junior Day event, but when Swoopes committed, the offer was rescinded. "I said, 'That's fine, but you could take two quarterbacks,'" Barrett recalled.

He had already gotten offers from LSU and Ohio State. Tom Herman's recruiting area is Texas, and he knew the state well from his days as a young assistant coach there. Herman talked to Garfield and others around Rider and got glowing reports about Barrett as a player and especially about his maturity. Asked how old Barrett acted during the recruiting process, Herman replied, "Forty-five. The kid is ridiculously mature. It's unbelievable—well beyond even what a college senior would be. Usually in recruiting, there's a lot of bullshit, so to speak, a lot of small talk, a lot of joking around. He didn't want any of that."

After Herman watched a lot of tape of Barrett, Ohio State decided to offer a scholarship. To the chagrin of Urban Meyer and many other coaches, recruits now expect offers to come in well before their senior season. If they don't, they often write off a program as uninterested. So schools sometimes have to offer scholarships to players before they'd prefer to, just to keep a kid feeling wanted. Commitments have become less iron-clad agreements than tentative reservations. "At that point, it was an offer to 'get in the game,'" Herman said. "We hadn't seen him throw in person, and we really weren't prepared to take it without ever having seen him in person."

Neither Herman nor Meyer had ever accepted a quarterback's scholarship commitment without personally having seen him throw. "It's nothing to take a wide receiver just off of film or a linebacker just off of film," Herman said. "But with quarterbacks, you want to physically see the ball come out of their hand, how fast it comes out, what kind of velocity. Some of those things you can't see on video."

So a week after Barrett took an unofficial visit in March 2012 and called Herman to say he wanted to commit to Ohio State, Herman was caught off guard. He didn't want to accept the commitment, but he also believed that if he turned it down, Barrett would feel rejected and sign elsewhere. Herman told Barrett he'd call him back in 10 minutes. Herman immediately called Meyer. They debated whether to accept Barrett's commitment.

"I started getting panicky," Meyer said.

They scrambled to call everyone they knew from different camps who'd seen Barrett throw. Meyer reached former NFL quarterback Trent Dilfer, who runs the prestigious Elite 11 camp that Barrett attended. They got good reports, but this was uncharted waters, essentially taking a quarterback unseen. Finally, Herman pleaded the case for Barrett. He knew Barrett had the personality, leadership skills, and athletic ability anyone would want in a quarterback. If there proves to be a problem with his throwing motion, Herman told Meyer, he'd fix it. Meyer went along but added a message to Herman. "It better work out," Meyer told him, "or we've got a problem."

A month after his commitment, Herman finally saw him throw. His verdict? "I was very relieved," he said.

After Barrett committed to Ohio State, Herman called him one day with a simple question: Why us? Barrett told Herman that he'd get a great education wherever he went. He said that staying close to home wasn't important, nor was the weather. He said that the only thing that was important to him was whether he could win a national championship there. "I was like, *Whoa!* That told me how serious this dude is," Herman said.

But Barrett's senior year at Rider did not go as planned when he tore his ACL. Barrett graduated early and enrolled at Ohio State in January. The Buckeyes had gone out on a limb accepting Barrett's commitment before they wanted. The guy who arrived in Columbus did not look the way they wanted. "He came into January fat and out of shape because he hadn't freaking done anything," Herman said. "Coach Meyer is looking at me like, 'Who the hell is this guy? He's going to play quarterback for us?' He'd kind of let himself go for the few months after surgery."

But if Barrett's body needed work, the leadership skills they loved quickly came to the surface. One day in early 2013, prospects James Clark and Dontre Wilson were passing through the weight room on their official visits. Mickey Marotti was talking to them when Barrett approached and asked if he could speak to them. Ohio State director of player personnel Mark Pantoni can almost recite what Barrett said. "If you come to Ohio State," Pantoni remembered Barrett telling Clark and Wilson, "Coach Meyer has proven he's going to win championships, and we're going to do it here, and I want you guys to be a part. We're going to make this run together. And if you don't [come to Ohio State], I'll be the

5

quarterback and I'll beat you no matter where you go. No one's going to work harder than us here, and we're going to get it done here."

Pantoni was floored. "You're like, *Wow, this kid gets it*," he said. "No one had any doubts about J.T. after we saw him do that."

Barrett spent his first year on campus rehabbing his knee and serving as the quarterback on the scout team. It wasn't until the moment that Miller reinjured his shoulder that anyone thought he'd be the starting quarterback in 2014. Barrett was standing right behind Miller on the fateful throw, and his first thoughts—his only thoughts—were concern for Miller. "You're looking at your friend and your brother on the field, and it hurts you," Barrett said.

It wasn't until the next day in the quarterbacks room, when Herman told them that someone had to emerge as the starter, that the enormity of the situation hit him. The battle was still close between Barrett and Cardale Jones. That day's practice, not surprisingly, was awful. But then Barrett realized that time was precious and he had to show he was capable. Each day, he had to improve. "My idea was just to focus on not taking everything in at once—not try to be like Braxton," he said. "The guys were telling me, 'You don't have to be Braxton. You don't have to run 90 yards and shake everybody on the team.' I could be myself and that's going to lead us to victory."

To Meyer, though, Barrett was still mostly a mystery. "J.T. is so quiet," he said. "To say I had a great relationship with him, I did not. I didn't really know who he was. To say that I knew he was a tough guy and a great leader—no idea."

*   *   *   *

EVEN BEFORE Miller's injury, the Navy game figured to be a challenging one. Openers are always a bit of a mystery. Unlike the NFL, college teams don't have preseason games to work out kinks. And

Navy is a particularly tricky opponent. The Midshipmen don't have the size or athletic ability of most big-time Division I programs. They do have the smarts, discipline, and scheme to overcome that. On defense, Navy plays an odd front, meaning that a defender lines up directly across from the center, complicating blocking schemes.

Herman worried how the new offensive line would handle that. "It kept me up at night," he said. "I was more concerned about that than I was J.T."

An even bigger challenge was on defense. Navy runs the triple-option offense, which is based on misdirection and precise blocking angles. A defense must be extremely disciplined. If a player is over-aggressive, the Midshipmen exploit it. Navy seldom passes, but its run game is so confusing that it often frustrates opponents. "It was very, very annoying," defensive tackle Michael Bennett said. "It's something you have to prepare a lot for, and you see it [only] once. It's so different than any other team we play."

Barrett just wanted to get back in action for the first time in almost two years. He couldn't wait for the first pass, the first time he got hit. "It was not really nerves," Barrett said. "I was just anxious to get out there. It had been a while."

On Ohio State's first play, Barrett completed a quick wide receiver screen to Devin Smith for 14 yards. A nice ice-breaker. Then the Ohio State offense stalled, as it mostly did throughout the first half. Dontre Wilson dropped a pass over the middle on Ohio State's first possession. Otherwise, Barrett's passes were short, safe ones. Ohio State's only scores in the first half came on field goals of 46 and 28 yards by freshman Sean Nuernberger.

Navy took a 7–6 lead into halftime thanks to a touchdown on which DeBrandon Sanders reached out to touch the pylon on a fourth-down play. Ohio State had a chance to score midway through the second quarter. But on first-and-goal from the Navy 8, Barrett spun out of a sack attempt and rushed an underthrown pass toward Wilson. Parrish Gaines intercepted the ball at the 3. "It was so silly," Barrett said. "I saw Dontre waving in the back and just got excited. I didn't see the guy underneath him and he simply dropped back and caught the ball. Coach Meyer was like, 'Okay, you got that simple play out of the way. Now it's time to play.'"

But it was the defense that finally created the spark. On Navy's first possession of the second half, defensive end Joey Bosa penetrated and hit Midshipmen quarterback Keenan Reynolds as he attempted an option pitch. Linebacker Darron Lee—or "DurRON," as CBS play-by-play man Verne Lundquist called him—scooped up the ball and ran unthreatened for the 61-yard score. "After I scored," Lee recalled, "I celebrated with the guys, and I was like, 'What did I just do? Thanks, Joey.' Right then, I was like, okay, I can play."

It would be the first big play in an All-America season for Bosa. "It's nice to make an impact early in the season," he said. "It gets rid of the butterflies. After all the hype and all the training, it's nice just to make a play."

The lead didn't last long. On Navy's next snap, Ryan Williams-Jenkins ran through a gaping hole in the Buckeyes' defense for a 67-yard gain. Three plays later, Reynolds scored from the 1.

Barrett then came up with his first big play as a Buckeye. Devin Smith got open deep. Though he had to slow down for Barrett's throw to get there, he was still able to outrun the coverage for an 80-yard touchdown. That gave Ohio State the lead for good. Navy kicked a field goal to make it 20–17 early in the fourth quarter, but the Buckeyes eventually wore down the Midshipmen. Ezekiel Elliott provided a needed cushion with a 10-yard touchdown run, and Michael Thomas scored on a nine-yard pass with two minutes left to wrap up the 34–17 victory.

Still, this was hardly a dominating win. Navy ran for 370 yards, averaging 5.9 per carry. Elliott, still feeling the effects of his broken wrist, ran for only 44 yards on 12 carries. The offensive line, still mixing and matching pieces, was inconsistent. Center Jacoby Boren sprained an ankle in the first half. He would seldom be healthy the rest of the season, though it wouldn't sideline him. As for Barrett, it was a solid but unspectacular debut. He completed 12 of 15 passes for 226 yards and ran for 50 yards on nine carries. He felt more relief than joy.

As for Meyer, he was glad to have survived with a win and somewhat reassured about his young quarterback. But not much else pleased him. "It was a very poor performance on both sides of the ball," he said.

It would get a lot worse before it would get better.

8

THE DEBACLE

IN HINDSIGHT, it was easy to see it coming.

Playing Navy was the first indicator that Ohio State's game the next week against Virginia Tech was going to be trouble. Teams that played the Midshipmen in 2014 were 3–8 the following week. One of those victories was by Temple over Delaware State, a Football Championship Subdivision team. That poor record was the continuation of a trend in recent years. Playing Navy, with its triple-option offense, is the football equivalent of facing a knuckle-ball pitcher. It can get a team out of sync. A team like Ohio State, with a new scheme and several new starters, including a redshirt freshman quarterback, was particularly vulnerable. The Buckeyes had to spend so much time in training camp preparing for Navy that their regular defense got short shrift.

"Overall, Virginia Tech was the first opportunity for us to play our defense," co–defensive coordinator Chris Ash said. Each year, the Buckeyes schedule one non-conference game against an elite program. Because the games are scheduled years in advance, the luster on that marquee opponent might have faded by the time they meet. California was Ohio State's big-name non-conference game the previous two years, but the Golden Bears' program had dipped badly since the teams agreed to play. Like California, Virginia Tech wasn't what it once was. Frank Beamer's glory days as coach seemed to be in the past. After eight consecutive double-digit victory seasons, the Hokies were a combined 15–11 in 2012 and

2013. They were unranked heading into 2014. A 10-point under-dog, this would be their chance to make a statement.

For the Buckeyes, something just seemed off all week.

"I didn't think we got out of Navy mode until Wednesday going into Thursday," linebacker Darron Lee said. "You could see it. People were playing a lot slower on film. I had a feeling in my gut that this is going to be an interesting game. I didn't think we were going to lose. But I thought it might be an interesting one because I didn't feel we were back in the swing of our defense."

*　*　*　*

THE BIGGEST CROWD in the 92-year history of Ohio Stadium filed in that cool September 6 evening. Stadium expansion in the South Stands, in what was once the open part of the Horseshoe, allowed 107,517 to watch Ohio State's first home game of the season. They arrived early to watch what's called "The Best Damn Band in the Land" perform "Script Ohio," with its typical precision, though the university's firing of band director Jon Waters for allowing what it deemed a culture of sexual harassment cast a pall over that. Certainly, the fans that packed the stadium didn't expect to see the Buckeyes lose to an unranked non-league visitor for the first time since 1982 (against Florida State).

If the Buckeyes felt a little off during the week of preparation, it turned into near panic when their offense took the field. Virginia Tech defensive coordinator Bud Foster is considered one of the top defensive minds in college football, known for his creative game plans. He had a doozy laid out for the Buckeyes—the so-called "Bear Zero" scheme. The "Bear" comes from the defense that defensive coordinator Buddy Ryan used with the overpowering 1985 Chicago Bears. Virginia Tech bunched its defenders at the line of scrimmage and used its safeties as extra run defenders or blitzers. The "Zero" refers to the number of safeties in deep coverage. It's a high-risk defense. Virginia Tech gambled that a young quarterback and Buckeyes receivers wouldn't be able to consistently beat Virginia Tech's superb cornerbacks.

The Buckeyes had tried to anticipate the wrinkles that Foster would throw at them. The Bear Zero wasn't one of them. "That's the worst feeling I've ever had as an offensive coach," Meyer said. "We didn't have an answer."

It wasn't as if Ohio State coaches hadn't seen that defense in their careers. They've coached long enough that they've seen everything. But the Buckeyes didn't expect to see that from Virginia Tech. "I think we had 14 games of film that we watched, and they never showed that defense from their game film," left tackle Taylor Decker said. "We always talk about our preparation, but we weren't prepared for that scenario."

Tom Herman understood what Virginia Tech was trying to do. "What they basically said was, 'You're not going to run the football,'" he said. "'We're going to play cover zero, or when we want to get really conservative, we're going to play with a free safety. But we're still going to play Bear and still going to play man coverage. We're going to blitz the ever-living shit out of the quarterback.'"

The spread offense is designed to create numerical mismatches against defenses by forcing them to cover the whole width of the field as well as the length. Virginia Tech's was designed to clog the middle and force Ohio State to throw deep. The run game was rendered ineffective. Barrett had some success running, especially on scrambles. He had consecutive carries of 25 and 20 yards on Ohio State's only touchdown drive in the first half. But Elliott ran for only 32 yards on eight carries. Buckeyes coaches knew they'd have to adjust on the fly.

"The talk was, 'Well, boys, we're going to have to throw it to win it,'" Herman said, "because there's not a run invented you can run against two extra people in the box and all the gaps inside covered.

We've been playing football for a long time, and nobody's invented one to account for two extra guys at the line of scrimmage."

Against Navy, Barrett threw mostly short passes so that he could gain confidence and get acclimated to the college game after not playing for so long. Now the Hokies were forcing him to beat them with his arm. Barrett had to do it with an offensive line with four new starters who hadn't come close to jelling and receivers who still had much to prove. "They were challenging a new quarterback to make quick reads and throws," Decker said. "It would have been hard for a veteran to make. They had an amazing game plan."

It didn't help that the defense couldn't get off the field. Virginia Tech converted its first five third-down situations, allowing the Hokies to take a 14–7 lead. To be fair, Virginia Tech made some hellacious plays. On the first of those conversions, Hokies quarterback Michael Brewer, a transfer from Texas Tech, avoided pressure from Joey Bosa. He rolled right with Lee approaching and threw across his body to the middle of the field—usually a cardinal sin—over safety Tyvis Powell to Bucky Hodges for an 11-yard gain on third-and-5. Eli Apple intercepted a deep pass later in that drive, but Virginia Tech scored touchdowns on its next two drives.

Ohio State had a chance to tie the game after Devin Smith finally made Virginia Tech pay for its man-to-man coverage by getting deep for a 58-yard catch to the Hokies 10. But Corey Smith dropped a pass in the end zone, and Sean Nuernberger's 27-yard field goal hit the left upright.

It was just one of several Buckeyes breakdowns on special teams. Nuernberger had already missed a 40-yarder. Punter Cameron Johnston shanked a punt 24 yards to give Virginia Tech the ball at the Ohio State 43-yard line for the Hokies' first scoring drive. Late in the first half, the Buckeyes allowed Greg Stroman to return a punt 35 yards to give Virginia Tech good field position for the drive that made it 21–7.

Ohio State appeared to have righted its ship when it scored twice to tie the game early in the fourth quarter. Michael Thomas scored on a 53-yard touchdown after breaking a tackle by cornerback Kendall Fuller on a short slant pass late in the third quarter.

The tying score came after a turnover caused by Bosa. The sophomore beat two blockers and drilled Brewer in the pocket. The hit jarred the ball loose, and defensive end Rashad Frazier recovered at the Virginia Tech 15. Elliott then finally found running room, taking an option pitch and scooting past three would-be tacklers for the touchdown.

But Virginia Tech had the final answers. Taking over at their 35 after Kyle Clinton's kickoff went out of bounds, the Hokies went 65 yards in six plays to regain the lead. Hodges caught a pass in tight coverage by Vonn Bell for the final 10 yards. Ohio State's offense couldn't respond. Virginia Tech turned up its pass rush, and it overwhelmed the Buckeyes. Barrett was sacked six times in Ohio State's last three possessions. "Every single pass, they brought more guys than we could block," offensive line coach Ed Warinner said. "There wasn't one pass that they didn't do that."

After one of the sacks forced the Buckeyes into third-and-18, Barrett threw a deep pass that was intercepted with five minutes left. Ohio State got one last chance after Virginia Tech missed a field goal. But on third-and-16 following yet another sack, Barrett tried to throw to the sideline to Corey Smith. The receiver, however, was nowhere in sight. "He obviously ran the wrong route," wide receivers coach Zach Smith said. "That's lack of preparation [by me]. I never gave him that look in practice."

That's because on that play, like so many others, Virginia Tech outsmarted Ohio State. "They ran a specific coverage that was very, very unique," Zach Smith said. "They're probably the only school in the country that runs it. On that route, they played the safety like 35 yards deep. [Corey] legitimately didn't see the kid because he was so deep. He thought the middle of the field was open."

So that's where he ran. Barrett, especially given his inexperience, didn't recognize that and threw to the sideline. The only player there was Virginia Tech's Donovan Riley, who made the easy interception and returned it 63 yards for the clinching touchdown in the Hokies' 35–21 win. Barrett finished with only nine completions in 29 attempts and three interceptions.

For Corey Smith, the early dropped pass and that last final play sent him into a spiral that almost ended his career. For the Buckeyes, it was a deeply humbling loss. "It was frustrating," Zach Smith said. "We really failed as coaches, obviously, in getting them ready for that and also having answers for that situation other than the wideout has to win and get open deep. It was kind of the perfect storm. When a wideout won, the left guard lost or the quarterback misthrew. When protection was great, the wideout was covered. When the quarterback made a great throw, the wideout dropped it. All units on offense failed at the wrong moments. The defense they played was high risk, and if you can just get all 11 to execute on one play, that whole game is different. But we couldn't get it done—all 11—at any time."

For the players, it was almost a surreal feeling. Ohio State had not lost a regular-season game under Meyer. The Buckeyes had come to expect victory as surely as they knew the sun rose every morning, even among players who weren't on the field for those 24 straight wins. And that might have been part of the problem.

"There was always that feeling that we were going to win," Barrett said. "At Northwestern [in 2013], not once did I think we were going to lose. Even against Michigan State in the Big Ten championship, I always had that confidence we weren't going to lose. In that game, it just felt different. I just didn't have that feeling deep down. The way the environment was, I don't know, it just didn't feel right. On the sideline, there was not a lot of energy, even when there were good plays for us."

Ohio State's loss was the final blow of a disastrous day for the Big Ten. Michigan had been shut out by Notre Dame, 31–0. Michigan State led in the third quarter at Oregon, only to collapse in a 46–27 loss. Purdue and Northwestern lost to Mid-American Conference schools. Nebraska barely escaped a challenge from McNeese State. That Black Saturday had many critics already dismissing any chance for a Big Ten team to get into the inaugural four-team College Football Playoff.

What would Meyer have said if he'd been asked that night about his team's chance to make the playoffs? "I wouldn't even have answered it," he said. "[The possibility] was so remote. If someone's thinking that, then I'm going to escort that person out of the facility. We better learn how to play much better defense, and offensively we were just a mess."

Virginia Tech's victory over Ohio State was the high-water mark of the Hokies' season. Injuries and close losses reduced them to a 6–6 team in the regular season before they won the Military Bowl over Cincinnati. But that wasn't the Virginia Tech team that came to the Horseshoe.

"They were very good," Meyer said. "I didn't study [what happened to] them afterward. But I have a lot of respect for that coach and defensive staff. When I left the field, I thought, 'That's a top-15 team that just beat us.'"

When Meyer got home that very late night, Shelley was stunned at the equanimity with which her husband had taken the loss. "He felt better than I did," she said. "I really didn't think we could lose and get to the playoffs. After the game, he said, 'We're going to be totally fine. We're going to be better. I can see it in these kids. They're going to mature and we're going to get better. We're going to be fine.' I'm like, 'Really. We really are?' I couldn't believe how well he took that loss because I thought it was awful, and I'm usually the positive one. He made me feel better because he knows the team better than I do."

As Virginia Tech's struggles wore on, the loss became magnified. But while the defeat looked like an albatross in the College Football Rankings, the truth is that it became a springboard for the Buckeyes' improvement. The optimism that surprised Shelley would be borne out.

Quarterback J.T. Barrett was thrust into a starting role when Braxton Miller reinjured his shoulder less than two weeks before the season began. (Kyle Robertson)

Early in the year, Urban Meyer had little reason to think that the 2014 season would produce his third national championship. (Jonathan Quilter)

Evan Spencer (6) caught only 15 passes all season, but his blocking and ability to contribute in other ways caused Urban Meyer to call him the team's MVP.
(Eamon Queeney)

Center Jacoby Boren (50), guard Billy Price (54), left tackle Darryl Baldwin (76), and Pat Elflein (65) teamed with Taylor Decker (68, above) to form "the Slobs," who grew into a dominating line.
(Kyle Robertson [*bottom*], Brooke LaValley [*above right*])

Vonn Bell (11), seen with Curtis Grant (14), led the team with six interceptions. (Chris Russell)

Defensive coordinator Luke Fickell (left), congratulating freshman Raekwon McMillan, personified the selfless nature of the 2014 Buckeyes with his acceptance of a new defensive system. Defensive tackle Michael Bennett (right), harassing Penn State quarterback Christian Hackenberg, became a dominating player in the second half of the season. (Chris Russell)

Joey Bosa (97) was a unanimous All-America pick after getting 13½ sacks and introducing the "Bosa Shrug."
(Kyle Robertson [*left*], Adam Cairns [*right*])

Safety Tyvis Powell (23) made several key interceptions during the 2014 season, including this one against Indiana.
(Eamon Queeney)

After a midseason lull, Devin Smith came up big against Michigan State, catching six passes for 129 yards and a touchdown in the Buckeyes' 49–37 victory. (Kyle Robertson)

On a bitterly cold day in Minneapolis, Adolphus Washington (high) and Joshua Perry (low) added to Minnesota quarterback Mitch Leidner's pain while Darron Lee (43) looks on.
(Kyle Robertson)

Ohio State struggled against Indiana until Jalin Marshall scored four second-half touchdowns to allow the Buckeyes to escape the upset bid. (Chris Russell)

Curtis Grant (14), cornerbacks coach Kerry Coombs, Joey Bosa (97), and Ezekiel Elliott (15) sing "Carmen Ohio" after the victory over Indiana.
(Chris Russell)

Nick Vannett (with ball) and Jeff Heuerman (86) celebrate during the Michigan game. Heuerman wore Braxton Miller's No. 5 in 2014 until going back to his original No. 86 on Senior Day. (Kyle Robertson)

arron Lee (43) came out of nowhere to win a linebacker job in the spring. Here, he clinches the in over Michigan with a fumble return for a touchdown. (Jonathan Quilter)

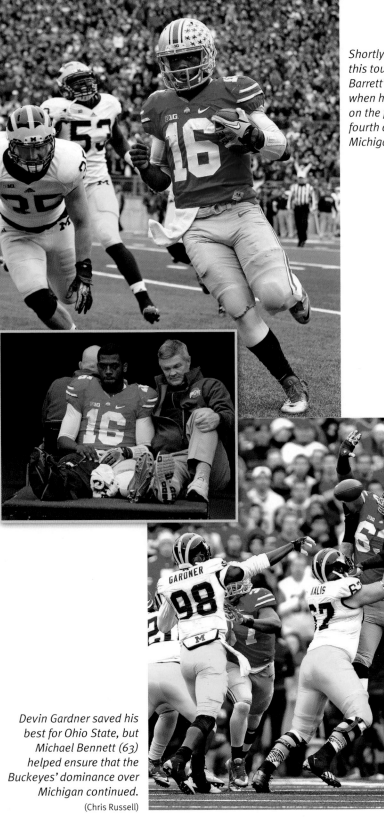

Shortly after scoring this touchdown, J.T. Barrett's season ended when he broke his ankle on the first play of the fourth quarter against Michigan. (Kyle Robertson)

Devin Gardner saved his best for Ohio State, but Michael Bennett (63) helped ensure that the Buckeyes' dominance over Michigan continued.
(Chris Russell)

9
FOR JACOB

THE LOCKER ROOM after Virginia Tech was a silent one. The Buckeyes were stunned. Introspection had already begun.

"I think it was good that nobody really said anything," J.T. Barrett said. "You were just looking at each other, figuring out, 'What does this guy bring to the table?' It wasn't like an evaluation period, but it was kind of like, 'If you're not doing your part, why not?'—whether you're a scout-team guy or the starting quarterback or a defensive tackle. Everybody's needed if we're going to do what we want. If not, you had to ask why. We're here to win games, and here we are. We didn't."

Barrett evaluated himself first. He knew he hadn't played well, though he was hardly the only culprit. He vowed to do everything he could to ensure such a performance didn't happen again. It was shared throughout the locker room.

"I think it was huge indicator of how everybody would respond," left tackle Taylor Decker said. "After that Virginia Tech game, it was going to be a fight-or-flight response. Are you going to get better or cave in?"

Doubters were everywhere. The Buckeyes dropped to No. 22 in the AP poll. People questioned whether Barrett could adequately fill in for Braxton Miller. The supposedly improved wide receivers had trouble getting open against Virginia Tech and holding on to the ball when they did. The offensive line looked overwhelmed late in the game when every dropback seemed to result in a sack. The defense had its moments but couldn't get stops when they needed them.

"Honestly, the thing I'll remember the most," Decker said, "was everybody throwing us under the bus, everybody selling us out, saying we have a bad team, we have all these problems. Everybody was saying, 'We can't, we can't, we can't.' The fact that people said we couldn't meant that we had to. That was the motivation. We realized we had to band together and become stronger as a team."

When the players came in Sunday, the coaches' tone was more reassuring than critical. "Coach Warinner didn't come in screaming and yelling," Decker said. "He basically came in and said, 'I love you guys. I believe in you guys. We just have to get better, and we will get better, and we'll move on to the next game.'"

But as the Buckeyes got back to business in preparing for Kent State, they were hit with some bad news. It came out late in the week that Noah Spence, the speedy pass-rusher who was expected to be the final piece to a dominating defensive line, had tested positive again for substance abuse. As a result, the Big Ten ruled him permanently ineligible. After the first violation, Spence claimed that someone had slipped ecstasy into his drink at a bar. It was on that basis that the Big Ten issued only a three-game suspension before the 2014 Orange Bowl. When Spence tested positive again, he confessed to his parents that he had a problem. Spence practiced with the Buckeyes briefly after that, but transferred to Eastern Kentucky after the season.

When Spence was a high-school star in Harrisburg, Pennsylvania, Larry Johnson tried to recruit him to Penn State. That's where Spence would have gone if not for the Jerry Sandusky scandal. When he reopened his recruitment, Mike Vrabel and Luke Fickell reeled him in with a persuasive pitch. The highlight of that came when Vrabel and Spence went toe to toe in the Spence's dining room simulating pass-rush drills. It got so intense that Vrabel emerged from the room with scrapes on his face. Spence had been the crown jewel of Ohio State's first recruiting class. Now he was gone.

"I knew Noah from the ninth grade," Johnson said. "I knew his family very, very well. It hit home. It was surreal. We had a really special relationship, and he was looking forward to having a coach-player relationship. Every day, my prayers have been with him and his family."

Spence's ban meant that senior Steve Miller would step into a starting role, with Rashad Frazier sharing time. The loss of Spence could have hurt the Buckeyes down the road. It had little effect against a team as overmatched as Kent State, coached by former Ohio State assistant Paul Haynes. Ohio State was a 32-point favorite over the Golden Flashes, who are usually one of the weaker teams in the Mid-American Conference. The Buckeyes were prepared for anything, including the Bear Zero defense that Kent State threw at them. If you're the Golden Flashes, why not try it? But Kent State didn't have the element of surprise in their favor, and they surely didn't have Virginia Tech's talent. The game was a mismatch from start to finish.

Meyer wanted to establish the passing game to give Barrett and the rest of the offense some confidence, and Kent State put up little resistance in a 66–0 rout. It was 24–0 after 16 minutes and 45–0 at halftime. Barrett tied a school record with six touchdown passes before ceding quarterback duties to Cardale Jones after the first possession of the third quarter. Freshman running back Curtis Samuel ran for 100 yards playing behind Ezekiel Elliott. Eleven Buckeyes caught passes. Defensively, the Buckeyes allowed the Golden Flashes to convert only 2 of 14 third-down chances.

What did it mean? Not much, other than allowing the Buckeyes to start ridding themselves of the bad taste from the Virginia Tech game. The Buckeyes could enjoy having a little time off during the upcoming bye week. Well, all but one of them.

Luke Fickell's wife, Amy, was pregnant with twins. It would be their second pair, giving them six children. The Fickells had planned to have the birth during the Buckeyes' second bye week, which was in early October. The stork had other ideas. The twins, sons named Laykon and Lucian, arrived on September 16, at less than 33 weeks. They were bigger than the Fickells' first set of twins, but they still spent five weeks in the neonatal intensive care unit. "We'd been through it one time, but the hard part this time is you have four kids at home," Fickell said. "My wife, obviously, had to do 95 percent of it."

Fortunately, three of Amy's nine siblings live in Columbus and were able to help out, especially with transporting the other Fickell children to activities. The wives of the other coaches delivered meals to the Fickells. Still, the stress of an all-consuming job and the worry about their newborns was immense. "Everything was good [medically], but not good enough for them to go home," Fickell said. "Having been through it once, we knew there was light at the end of the tunnel, but still there are a lot of unknowns, and it's frustrating and tough."

Fickell would often work past 10:00 PM and then drive to the hospital to visit his newborns. On home game days, aunts and uncles would take the other Fickell kids to the stadium while Amy spent it at the hospital. After the game, Fickell would go to the hospital and then take Amy home. She didn't attend a game that season until Michigan. "My wife and I prepared ourselves for it, but when you have a baby during the season, there's not a whole lot of things that can give you a break," Fickell said. "That's why you don't see a lot of coaches who don't have great wives. [Our lives] are not normal. During the season, there's not a whole lot of time for other things. Obviously, if there was a dire need, it would be different. But a lot of people are counting on you. That's why coaching is a way of life. It's not a part of life; it's a way of life."

* * * *

JEFF HEUERMAN didn't play against Kent State. Still recovering from the Lisfranc injury, Heuerman saw limited action in Ohio State's first two games without catching a pass. The Buckeyes didn't figure to need him against Kent State, and Meyer thought that taking that game off and the bye week before playing Cincinnati would be wise. For two weeks, he was not on his feet for more than 10 minutes at a time, per doctor's orders. "That was one of the critical decisions in getting healthy," Heuerman said after the season.

At the time, though, he was frustrated with how his season had gone. After Braxton Miller got hurt, the quarterback asked Heuerman if he would wear Miller's No. 5 as his jersey number in 2014. At first, Heuerman thought Miller was joking. Then he realized he was serious and was touched by the request and agreed to wear it. But early in the season, it looked like Heuerman might be as cursed by injuries as Miller. "Going to Week 5, and I don't have a catch," he said. "It's not how you planned your senior season, and we had a loss."

Heuerman would catch three passes for 38 yards against Cincinnati. That's not what he will remember from that week. It was Coach to Cure MD week at games across the country, and that had particular significance to Ohio State, especially Heuerman. At the 2013 Friday Night Lights camp, which is a major recruiting event, Meyer struck up a conversation with a 13-year-old boy, Jacob Jarvis, who was sitting in his wheelchair behind the end zone. Jarvis and his younger brother, Noah, have Duchenne muscular dystrophy, a genetic disorder in which muscles gradually weaken and degenerate because of the absence of a needed cellular protein. Noah, who's eight years younger than Jacob, is asymptomatic, which is common at his age. There is no cure for Duchenne and only limited treatment options. Most people with it live only into their twenties.

Jacob and Noah's parents, Chad and Tracy Studebaker, got an invitation to Friday Night Lights through connections with an Ohio State recruit, Kyle Trout. After saying hello to Jacob, Meyer found himself drawn to the boy. He showed Jacob how to throw a spiral and invited him and his family to attend practice. "Jacob is a kid who has such a spirit about him," Meyer said. "I knew that the first time I met him."

Jacob and his family became regulars at practice and sometimes even ate with the team afterward. As the relationship between his family and the Buckeyes' deepened, Jacob's attitude shifted from essentially "Why me?" to "Wow."

"He is so excited to be with them," Tracy Studebaker said. "I think it takes his mind off of, 'Yes, I have this stupid disease' to 'At least I have this.'"

Chad Studebaker said the family was careful not to overstep its bounds, yet Meyer constantly reassured them that the boys were always welcome. "I think about this a lot," he said. "Why would a team do this? It kind of restores your faith in humanity."

Meyer isn't normally regarded as the warm and fuzzy type, but he is when he talks about Jacob. "God's two greatest gifts to all of us are gratitude and compassion," he said. "When you're having a bad day or emotionally you're not in the right place, write down 10 things—I still do it to this day—that you're grateful for: your children, your wife, your opportunities in life, whatever it might be. It gets you emotionally in the right place.

"Compassion is the greatest of all, and I learned that directly from Tim Tebow. If you're having a bad day, go do something good for someone else and all of a sudden that bad day isn't bad anymore. To see Jacob's face, you can't have a bad day around that kid. Jacob is part of the team. He's a teammate now."

Jacob is close with several players on the team. Linebacker Joshua Perry, who attended the same Olentangy Shanahan Middle School as Jacob, attended his surprise birthday party. But nobody bonded with Jacob more than Heuerman.

On the surface, Heuerman and Jacob couldn't be more different. Jacob is an introvert. Heuerman is a life-of-the-party type who has had to learn to watch his mouth. In 2011 Ohio State had a news conference in which it allowed the incoming freshmen to introduce themselves. Most of the freshmen tentatively stood at the podium and uttered a few clichés. Then there was Heuerman. "We're going to kick some people's ass, I'll tell you that much," Heuerman declared. He ended his time by asking, "Can I play golf now?"

If he had dropped the mic, it would have been fitting.

"Coach Tressel left, and it was like all of a sudden everything went to shit," Heuerman explained. "Everyone was down. The seniors were down. Then the bowl ban came. We were all wondering, 'What the hell is happening?' People were saying we were going to get the death penalty. I think I was just trying to keep spirits up."

Heuerman was always a spirited kid. He and his two younger brothers were regulars in the emergency room because of various hijinks and mishaps. "We had a plastic surgeon who lived across the street," Heuerman said. "I can't tell you how many times he sewed us up at the house."

Even though he grew up in Naples, Florida, hockey was his first love. He was good enough to move to Michigan as an eighth-grader and play for the top-ranked team nationally in his age group. His roommate, Austin Watson, became a first-round NHL Draft pick. But Heuerman decided he didn't want that path and gave up the sport cold turkey the next year. He switched to football and soon was a 6'4", 150-pound quarterback. "I looked like a twig," he said. "I had size-16 feet. I was looking goofy as hell out there running around."

His high school coached preached to him the importance of the weight room, and Heuerman embraced it. He soon developed into a top prospect. Impressed by Tressel and the atmosphere at the 2010 spring game, Heuerman signed with Ohio State. He was a junior when he met Jacob Jarvis. They spoke briefly after a practice, and Jacob mentioned that his favorite player was Braxton Miller. Heuerman went into the locker room, had Miller sign a pair of cleats and returned to give them to Jacob. The friendship soon blossomed. For road games, Heuerman, as a co-captain, allowed Jacob to make the call on the coin toss. He always picked tails. They talked about everything, including the opposite sex. "I ask him sometimes how to play it," Heuerman said. "Girls are a tough subject. You never know their next move. He and I help each other and give advice and work it out together."

He said he gets more out of the friendship than Jacob does. "Football is a grind, man," he said. "It's tough. Throughout the grind, sometimes you get down or don't feel like doing something or get pissed off. Then you see Jacob, and you know he'd give anything to be out there for a day with us and do what we do. The same thing with coaches. We kind of feed off him. Some days you might not want to be doing stuff and you see him over there with a smile, and it really keeps you going."

The week of the Cincinnati game, Ohio State's players donated $10,000 to his Little Hercules Foundation. The Buckeyes made him an honorary captain for that game. For the pregame coin toss, Jacob and Noah accompanied Heuerman and fellow captains Curtis Grant, Doran Grant, and Michael Bennett to midfield.

*   *   *   *

UNLIKE THE Kent State game and most of Ohio State's games against in-state opponents, Cincinnati was no pushover. The Bearcats featured quarterback Gunner Kiel, a one-time five-star prospect whose vagabond college career didn't diminish his talent. Kiel originally committed to Indiana before signing with Notre Dame. Unhappy there, he transferred to Cincinnati. With the Bearcats, he was surrounded by talented receivers, the best Meyer said Ohio State had faced in his three years in Columbus. Even with a porous defense, Cincinnati had a puncher's chance to become the first in-state team since 1921 to beat the Buckeyes. "There's obviously tons and tons of pressure with that," wide receiver Evan Spencer said.

Meyer was well aware that he was 0–2 against Bearcats coach Tommy Tuberville from their time in the SEC when Tuberville coached Auburn. When Chris Moore beat safety Vonn Bell for a 60-yard touchdown catch less than two minutes after receiving the opening kickoff to take a 7–0 lead, the concerns seemed justified.

Then Ohio State's offense got rolling. The Buckeyes scored touchdowns on their first four drives, with none taking longer than three minutes and 15 seconds. After the second touchdown, Ohio State added a safety when Joey Bosa leveled Kiel and the beaten Cincinnati lineman swatted the ball out of the end zone. During the celebration in the end zone, Bosa extended his arms with his palms up. The "Bosa Shrug" was born. It would become his trademark gesture, one that even the president of the United States would come to know. "It really just happened," he said. "I've been asked 100 times how it started, and I don't really have an answer."

After UC's first touchdown drive, the Buckeyes' defense settled in. Ohio State allowed only 37 yards on the Bearcats' next four possessions. In fact, even assistant strength coach Anthony Schlegel got in on the hitting action. When an OSU student ran onto the field, Schlegel, a former Buckeye and NFL linebacker, body-slammed him and then forcibly removed him from the field. Video of the tackle became a YouTube hit.

Leading 30–7, the Buckeyes looked to be on cruise control. But then Curtis Samuel fumbled, and the Bearcats capitalized with a touchdown. When Cincinnati took its time after Cameron

Johnston's punt was downed at the Bearcats' 3 with 1:51 left in the second quarter, Ohio State figured to go into halftime with a comfortable lead.

But after Cincinnati got a first down, Kiel threw deep to Moore. Somehow, the Buckeyes had no help deep, and Moore beat Eli Apple for an 83-yard touchdown. That made it 30–21 at halftime. It got worse for the Buckeyes. After Ohio State kicked a field goal early in the third quarter, Moore took advantage of another breakdown in coverage. Moore beat Doran Grant off the line and caught a short slant pass. Safety Tyvis Powell had left the middle of the field to cover a receiver on the sideline, leaving Moore to run unthreatened for a 78-yard touchdown to make it 33–28.

After another Ohio State field goal, Cincinnati's next drive died after an offensive pass interference call, about which Tuberville was livid. From then on, the Buckeyes took control. Dontre Wilson scored on a 24-yard pass and Devin Smith added a 34-yard touchdown catch to make the final 50–28.

Barrett threw for 330 yards. Elliott ran for 182 yards on 28 carries, both career highs for the sophomore. Ohio State set a school record with 45 first downs and gained 710 yards. If not for a 20-yard loss when a snap went over backup Cardale Jones' head on the next-to-last play, the Buckeyes would have set a school record for yardage.

* * * *

MEYER IS A Cincinnati alum, but he said the game was not particularly emotional for him. His playing career for a struggling Bearcats program was forgettable. Other than the fact his family's roots are in Cincinnati and his older sister, Gigi Escoe, is a vice provost at UC, Meyer said it was just another game for him.

But two other Ohio State coaches with strong Cincinnati ties— offensive coordinator Tom Herman and cornerbacks coach Kerry

Coombs—left the game with vastly different feelings about the direction of their units. Herman was born in Cincinnati, where all of his relatives except his mother are from. Though Herman grew up in suburban Los Angeles, he would return to Ohio for six weeks in the summer to visit family. Herman was a passionate Reds fan, not easy to do back then in Dodgers country.

He played wide receiver for California Lutheran, a Division III school, and decided that he wanted to pursue coaching. Herman is exceptionally intelligent—a Mensa member—but coming from such a small school and with no contacts, he tried creative measures to get noticed. He bought shoes at Goodwill and sent them along with his résumé, explaining that he just wanted to get his foot in the door. His first job was at Texas Lutheran. He coached wide receivers for $5,000 and a meal card. He then became a graduate assistant at the University of Texas and worked his way up the coaching ladder, impressing his bosses with his work ethic, mastery of X's and O's and ability to relate to players. After having success with the spread offense at Rice and Iowa State, two programs not known for sustained success, he was regarded as one of college football's bright young coaches. Yet he also won points for not taking himself too seriously. If asked a question involving numbers, he might reply, "Eleventy-billion," to explain how hard something might be to quantify. "He's got old-man wisdom with teenager energy," Rice coach David Bailiff said. "That's a hard combination to find."

Herman became a devotee of the up-tempo, no-huddle offense out of the spread, which Meyer wanted to implement when he came to Ohio State. Herman had been a huge fan of Meyer's offenses, and he studied every tape he could find of Meyer's teams. But he had no idea that Meyer knew who he was, and thought that someone was pranking him when Meyer called to inquire about becoming Ohio State's offensive coordinator. In fact, he came close to hanging up the phone.

Certainly, Herman was not an obvious choice.

"I had some incredible, high-high-end offensive coordinators calling me who you wouldn't think would be calling me," Meyer said. "I had to really make a decision that, if I got back into it, would I want to just hand the offense to someone and be one of those CEO coaches? I kind of went through a period where I thought I might do that. Pay him a lot of money, let him run the offense, and I'll coach the kicking game."

But the more Meyer thought about it, the more he realized he had to be closely involved in running the offense. When he was working for ESPN, he would spend time on flights studying film of offenses from potential coordinators. The more he watched Herman's offense and did his research on him, the more impressed he got. When he interviewed Herman, he gave him his playbook and asked him to learn it. When they talked again, Herman knew it cold. Meyer told him that Herman would have to adapt to Ohio State's playbook, not the other way around, though the Buckeyes wouldn't huddle and added the quick-tempo element that Herman used.

Except for Braxton Miller, the Buckeyes were not a particularly dynamic offense in 2012, but they became that in 2013. They had hoped to continue the development in 2014, but Miller's injury and the growing pains of the new offensive line made that look iffy, especially after the Virginia Tech disaster. Though Cincinnati's defense was hardly stout, the ease with which Ohio State moved the ball allowed Herman to exhale a bit.

"I think our offense kind of gained its mojo back, even though Cincinnati is not tremendously well-known for their defense," Herman said. "We knew we'd have to score 40 or 50 to pull away from them, and we did. I think that's when guys started gaining a lot of confidence, especially J.T. He played pretty well in that game."

The same could not be said for the players under the other Buckeyes assistant coach born in Cincinnati. Except for his college years at the University of Dayton, Kerry Coombs spent his entire life in

Cincinnati. Almost with the sheer force of his energetic personality, he built Colerain High School into a power and then became an assistant at UC for five years before joining Meyer in Columbus. Coombs had recruited 24 Bearcats who took the field against Ohio State. His son Dylan attends UC.

"I don't think those games are fun, and you compound it with the fact they probably had the best receiving corps that we played against all year as a collective group," Coombs said. "We had a couple of huge coverage busts at the end of the first half and beginning of the second half. It was a frustrating night."

The touchdown pass on which Apple got beat right before halftime was particularly galling. "There were a lot of breakdowns on that play," Coombs said. "It was really bad from a lot of angles."

Until Cincinnati exposed the Buckeyes, Ohio State's defensive coaches had felt reasonably good about the progress the pass defense had made in its transition to a more aggressive scheme. The Bearcats showed that more tweaks were needed.

"It was still early in the year, where our guys hadn't really settled in to truly understand the package," Ash said. "We didn't have a lot of change-ups in the package, and Cincinnati exploited us on a couple things—maybe not the structure, but some individuals who hadn't perfected their technique or their responsibilities at that point. The issues we had in that game I kind of anticipated might come up because of my experience with this scheme. The issues we had against Cincinnati never came up the rest of the season because we were able to adjust and make some slight changes that made a difference."

* * * *

WHATEVER MIXED feelings Ohio State had about its performance was quickly set aside in the locker room. Two days before the game, Meyer told Heuerman that if the Buckeyes won, he wanted him to present Jacob Jarvis with the game ball. "My heart sank a little bit because of how emotional I am toward him and how special I knew that would be," Heuerman said.

He's not usually at a loss for words, but he lay awake the next two nights trying to figure out what to say. He decided he would speak from the heart when the moment arrived. "Honestly, it's one of the more special things I've gotten to do at Ohio State," Heuerman told Jacob, sitting in his wheelchair, and Noah, who was standing behind him. "What you do for us, I don't think we could ever repay you."

He told the boys that they were a part of the team and that the best part of winning that night was getting to present Jacob the game ball. "We've got a long journey ahead, so you've got to be there with us," he said.

Jacob was overcome with emotion. When Meyer asked Jacob if he wanted to say anything, Jacob choked up before finally saying, "Go Bucks!" Meyer gave him a hug and slapped hands three times as everyone in the locker room cheered.

"To see him tear up and me lose it a little bit was tough, but it was special," Heuerman said.

10

BIG TEN BECKONS

HEADING INTO Big Ten play, Ohio State did not look like a team headed for any kind of championship. It had struggled against Navy. It looked unprepared and overwhelmed against Virginia Tech. Kent State was so overmatched that the game's relevance was hard to deduce. Cincinnati showed that the Buckeyes' successful transition to a more aggressive pass defense was nowhere near complete.

Ohio State's conference opener was at Big Ten newcomer Maryland. The Terrapins have traditionally been a middling program. It looked like 2014 might be better for Randy Edsall's team. Maryland was 4–1 with a 40–37 loss to West Virginia as the only blemish. "I know Maryland," Meyer said. "They have good players. He's an excellent coach."

In College Park, the game was billed as the school's biggest in memory. In Meyer's mind, everything was stacked against Ohio State. It was a noon game on the road against a team with underrated talent. Meyer had instituted a 9:00 PM bedtime for the players the night before in hopes that the early start wouldn't be a factor. Even the cramped locker room at Byrd Stadium gave Meyer a bad vibe. "I'll never forget that Maryland locker room," he said. "Guys were on top of each other. Guys were getting taped outside. It was horrible. I couldn't change inside. I had to go sit outside by a garbage can just to get to my mind right. I'm a little claustrophobic."

All of Meyer's worrying was for naught. The Buckeyes dominated from the start in a 52–24 victory. Ohio State scored touchdowns on its first two possessions as J.T. Barrett was in full control.

After Maryland's Brad Craddock kicked a 57-yard field goal to give the Terps a little hope, Michael Thomas all but extinguished it. Barrett ran for 23 yards to move the ball to the Maryland 25. He then threw a ball to the deep left corner of the end zone. Thomas was tightly covered by William Likely. The cornerback would tie Ohio State safety Vonn Bell for the Big Ten lead in interceptions with six, but this was a mismatch. At 5'7", Likely is eight inches shorter than Thomas. Though Likely was draped around Thomas (and was flagged for pass interference), Thomas somehow caught the ball while managing to keep his feet inbounds. "Coach Meyer called the play on the sideline and was like, 'You've got to make this play. You better make it,'" Thomas said. "My uncle was there, along with my two cousins and my dad. I felt I needed to make a play."

The uncle that Thomas mentioned isn't just anybody. He's Keyshawn Johnson, the first pick of the 1996 NFL Draft of Just-Give-Me-the-Damn-Ball! fame. Thomas remembers being a young boy growing up in Los Angeles, watching his uncle play. "I always envisioned doing that," he said. At an early age, "I think I figured out what I wanted to do with my life."

That self-assuredness bordered on...well, let Stan Drayton explain it. The Ohio State running backs coach was in charge of Thomas' recruitment. "He'd tell me, 'Hey, I'm about to be one of the best receivers Ohio State has seen. I'm going to be the guy,'" Drayton said with a laugh. "He talked so much during the recruiting process that you'd have thought you had Randy Moss on the other line sometimes. But the kid honestly believed it. Who am I to tell a highly motivated individual that he's not Randy Moss? I want him to think he's Randy Moss, or die trying."

When Thomas enrolled at Ohio State, he got off to a promising start. In the spring game as a freshman, he caught 12 passes for 131 yards. That's no guarantee of success. A long line of Mr. Aprils never sniffed success again. He caught only three passes for 22 yards in 2012. Things went backward in 2013. For every good play he'd make in practice, he'd screw up another one. The week before the 2013 opener against Buffalo, wide receivers coach Zach Smith said, Thomas was "a mess" in practice. Smith didn't play him that week, figuring that was only a temporary setback. But the errors kept coming, and before long coaches decided to redshirt him.

"He was never disrespectful," Smith said. "He was just immature and needed to grow up. He needed 2013. When Michael Thomas is done playing football, the one year they'll never talk about is the one that was critical to his career, which is 2013."

Redshirting as a freshman is common. Sitting out as a sophomore is rare and often ominous. As hard as it was, Thomas accepted not playing that season. His family, including his dad and uncle, told him to stay at Ohio State and not consider leaving. "I could have transferred," Thomas said. "I could have cried. But I was taught growing up that you don't run from competition. There's no secret to success. All you've got to do is work hard and grind."

Even if he wanted to, taking the easy way out and returning to California was not an option. His family made sure Thomas understood that. "More support [for coaches] than I've ever witnessed," Smith said. "They were steadfast: 'You're redshirting for a reason. Don't complain to me. Do what they ask you to do.' If they hadn't been that way, it probably would have resulted in a transfer or a disgruntled kid."

Instead, the year on the sidelines fueled Thomas' fire. He said it taught him to be disciplined and level-headed. "There's so much stuff and so many people who can get you off track," he said. "I'm fortunate to have the great family I have."

After the Orange Bowl loss, though, Thomas couldn't contain himself. He sent out a series of tweets pointing out the lack of production of Ohio State receivers in the postseason and vowing to make a difference the next season. "It wasn't to point the finger at anyone or bring anyone down," Thomas said.

Zach Smith, however, was not amused. He told Thomas that his tweets were misguided. He reminded Thomas that he redshirted because he hadn't been able to beat out any of those receivers. The message was received. Thomas rededicated himself to his craft.

"The year he redshirted, you had to go get Mike to throw," Barrett said. "After that, it was Mike chasing me down. He wanted to help the team any way he could. I don't know how I'd be [redshirting as a sophomore]. That probably takes a toll on you mentally, thinking that I'm doing something wrong and I need to change. Mike Thomas made that change."

Thomas' touchdown made it 21–3. After a Buckeyes field goal made it 24–3, Maryland answered with a touchdown. When the Terrapins forced Ohio State to punt with 1:22 left, it looked like they would go into halftime with an upset within range. But the next 24 seconds would prove to be Maryland's undoing.

It started with a 69-yard punt from Cameron Johnston, the Australian who two years earlier had never seen an American football game. Johnston played Australian Rules Football before he was cut. He then joined Prokick Australia, a kicking academy that has become an assembly line for punters. Prokick alums Tom Hornsey from Memphis and Tom Hackett from Utah won the Ray Guy Award in 2013 and 2014, respectively.

Johnston became a Buckeye by accident. Ohio State expected to sign punter Johnny Townsend on signing day in 2013, but the Buckeyes found themselves out of scholarships to offer. They asked Townsend to walk on, but when Florida made him a signing-day offer, he took it. That left Ohio State in a lurch. Prokick coach and director Nathan Chapman had contacted the Buckeyes months earlier and sent them tape of Johnston's booming punts, which consistently went at least 65 yards. During spring practice, Meyer had senior place-kicker Drew Basil handle punting duties as well, hoping he'd prove able to do both. But it became clear that wasn't a great idea, and the Buckeyes decided to sign the 21-year-old Johnston.

"We had to take a leap of faith," Meyer said.

They would be glad they did. Ohio State was more interested in placement and hang time than raw distance, and Johnston proved to be a master at that. Buckeyes long-snapper Bryce Haynes marveled at Johnston's accuracy. He said that Johnston can kick as accurately as a quarterback can throw. "I could be 50 yards downfield, and he'll hit me on the run," said Haynes, a standout in his own right. He would be a 2014 finalist for the prestigious Wuerffel Award for community service and plans to enter medical school in 2016.

In 2013, 31 of Johnston's 49 punts were downed inside the opponent's 20-yard line, with only two touchbacks. He would be a huge asset in 2014 as well.

In this situation against Maryland, it was time to boom one, and Johnston did, a 69-yarder all the way to the Terps' 7. Instead of being conservative—and smart—Maryland elected to throw. With Joey Bosa bearing down on him, quarterback C.J. Brown underthrew his receiver and the ball went right into the hands of Darron Lee. The linebacker fumbled as he ran toward the end zone, but freshman linebacker Raekwon McMillan recovered it. On the next play, Barrett threw to Nick Vannett for a one-yard touchdown to make it 31–10.

The Buckeyes were never threatened in the second half. Against the same Bear Zero defense that Virginia Tech used, Barrett threw a perfect ball on a post pattern that Devin Smith caught for a touchdown to make it 38–10. Barrett completed 18 of 23 passes for 267 yards and four touchdowns. Elliott added 139 rushing yards.

The defense's performance was even more encouraging. Lee, Apple, Doran Grant, and McMillan had interceptions, with McMillan's returned for a touchdown for the game's final score. Bosa continued to dominate. He had 2½ tackles for loss, including a sack. Maryland star receiver Stefon Diggs, whom Meyer once coveted for the Buckeyes, did little damage. He caught seven passes for only 52 yards. Except for one 60-yard reception, Maryland's longest play was 25 yards.

"I thought Maryland was a game-changer," Meyer said. "That was a big one, one that doesn't get enough credit. That's when I started thinking we've got a chance. I thought the coaches did a brilliant job. It was coaches having their nine units ready, and I thought we played great."

The same could be said for the following week's game against visiting Rutgers, the other new Big Ten school. Like Maryland, the Scarlet Knights (5–1) entered with a gaudy record. Ohio State quickly exposed that as fraudulent as well in a 56–17 victory. The Buckeyes scored touchdowns on eight of their first nine possessions. Barrett threw for three touchdowns and ran for two more while gaining 107 yards on only seven carries. The defense also chipped in. Cornerback Eli Apple picked up a fumble caused by Rashad Frazier's hit on Janarion Grant and jogged in from four yards out for a touchdown in the second quarter to give the Buckeyes a 28–7 lead. The Buckeyes held senior quarterback Gary Nova in check, sacking him four times and limiting him to 192 passing yards.

"We had a very good plan," Meyer said. "You started to see the super sophs show up." Two sophomores established themselves on their way to stardom—Bosa and Elliott. Bosa had two more sacks against the Scarlet Knights. He'd finish the season with 13½ sacks and 21 tackles for loss to earn Big Ten Defensive Player of the Year honors. Both Bosa and Elliott came from athletic families. Elliott's parents starred at Missouri. Bosa's father, John, and his uncle, former Buckeye Eric Kumerow, were first-round NFL Draft picks. His mom, Cheryl, is also an Ohio State grad.

Raised in Miami, Bosa resisted becoming a Buckeyes fan. "Growing up, I always cheered against Ohio State, not because I didn't like them but because my brother and my mom rooted for them," he said. "I just liked to be that annoying kid who cheered against them."

Despite his family background, Bosa said he was never forced to play football. "I've loved football since the day I started it," he said. That love was tested when he was moved to offensive line in youth ball. Bosa hated it. When he was allowed to switch to defense, though, his talent quickly surfaced. He moved to Fort Lauderdale to attend St. Thomas Aquinas, one of the top prep programs in the country. Bosa was such a coveted prospect that Alabama offered him a scholarship when he was a sophomore. He'd gone to a camp in Tuscaloosa, and Nick Saban invited him to his office. Shirtless because he'd just finished a workout, Bosa recalled how awkward that was. "He has a button on his desk that closes the door behind people as they walk through," Bosa said. "I think I was only 15 then, so it was very intimidating."

He considered accepting the offer before deciding to weigh his options. Those didn't include Ohio State until the Buckeyes hired Meyer. "I didn't even talk to Ohio State until he came," Bosa said.

When he came on his official visit to Ohio State, the Buckeyes made the wise choice of having fellow Floridian Jeff Heuerman host him. "He was just a knucklehead from Fort Lauderdale, so they threw him with me," Heuerman said. "We went out that night till 1:00 or 2:00 AM. We were doing what college kids do and had a good time. When he got done, he said, 'I'm committing to Ohio State University.'"

When Adolphus Washington got injured early in the 2013 season, Bosa took over at his defensive end spot. Bosa played so well that coaches moved Washington to tackle when he healed. "Freshman year, when you watched him, you knew he had ability," Michael Bennett said. "But everyone at Ohio State has ability. What he had was the ability to learn. When he was coached, he learned quickly. Even when he wasn't coached, he learned from his mistakes. That's what I noticed most about him."

Bosa set his goals high. "My goal my freshman year, once I earned my starting spot, was to be a freshman All-American," he said.

He was.

"My goal my sophomore year was to be an All-American," he said.

He was, a unanimous one.

And in 2015? "Be the best player in college football," Bosa said.

The "Bosa Shrug" gave a glimpse into his personality. He loves electronic dance music and is irreverent on social media. "He's different in a good way," defensive line coach Larry Johnson said. "You're a great player and you could walk around not wanting to talk to anybody. But that's not his style. I think it's kind of neat that he has a personality. I think that's good. He doesn't mind saying what he feels. But at the end of the day, he wants to be a great player. He works at being a really great player. He's all ears, he's all mouth, and he's all listening. Our relationship is really special."

The same went for Elliott and his offensive coaches. Unlike Bosa, Elliott's private high school in St. Louis didn't have an elite football program. The Buckeyes had mild concern that he might be a little soft. In truth, Elliott's family actually lived in blue-collar Alton, Illinois. In any case, Elliott quickly put coaches' concerns to rest. Drayton recalled a play his freshman year when Elliott kicked it into an extra gear to make a tackle against Purdue in kickoff coverage. Elliott took as much pride in blocking and carrying out fakes as he did running the ball.

"His mom and dad raised him right," Tom Herman said. "From the day he walked on campus, he was the hardest-playing running back without the ball in his hands that I've ever been around. There is nothing asked of him that he ever had a sour look on his face [about]."

Herman said there'd be times when Elliott would sprint 30 yards downfield trying to throw a block on a bubble screen. "Normal human beings don't do that," he said. "He's got a fanatical work ethic. There are guys who play hard at that position when you put the ball in their hands. But he does it every single snap."

Elliott said that work ethic comes from his mom, Dawn. "She was kind of like a drill sergeant when I was younger," he said. "Perfection—that's what she demanded. Kind of like Coach Meyer." Even his handwriting had to be meticulous, thanks to his mom. "My mom did a great job raising me and giving me a great foundation to build on," he said.

As rugged as he is on the field, he has a much softer side off of it. Drayton said that Elliott found out while on summer break in St. Louis after his freshman year that a young boy from New Jersey would head there for cancer treatment. Elliott, Drayton said, visited the boy in the hospital and then invited him to an Ohio State practice. Sure enough, the boy and his father came to a Buckeyes practice during preseason camp.

"To see that kid light up..." Drayton said, "Zeke took charge and brought the whole running-back corps and myself over there to hang out with that kid. Those are the kinds of things that make you understand when he makes it big, the reason why."

During Elliott's recruitment, Drayton said, he heard stories of how Ezekiel would seek out the smallest or least-talented players on his team and develop friendships with them. That's just his personality, which he admits includes a healthy dose of goofiness. "I kind of describe myself as a good time," Elliott said. "One of my purposes in life—I always joke about this, but I really believe it—is to brighten people's day. You never know who you can affect. I'm always smiling, and that wears off on people. I'm not the type of guy to be in a bad mood. I like to have fun."

There is one person Elliott does like to torment—Bosa. They have been best friends since their arrival in Columbus, and they lived together their first two years. Their parents described them as "an old married couple" for their bickering.

"My goofiness sometimes gets under his skin," Elliott said. "I think I'm maybe the only person on earth who's not afraid when Joey's mad at him. He's a fun, outgoing guy, [but] he can go zero to

100 pretty fast. You can push his buttons pretty easily. I keep poking at him. You keep poking at the caged tiger. If you keep poking,
he's going to get you eventually."

Bosa moved out of their apartment three months after the season ended, though they remain close friends.

*   *   *   *

OHIO STATE eventually stretched its lead over Rutgers to 56–10 on
a touchdown significant only because of the player who scored. The
Buckeyes' play-calling philosophy on passes isn't usually designed
for one specific target. The quarterback and receivers make their
reads, and the pass goes to the best option. But at that point in
the Rutgers game, Meyer wanted to reward Evan Spencer. Wide
receivers crave catching passes, and the senior was no exception.
Yet he accepted that his value came doing other things, particularly
leadership and blocking. "I think we all did," Spencer said of the
receivers. "We all accepted the notion that to be a great receiver
you have to be able to do everything, and blocking is a part of it."
Nobody quite embraced it as willingly as Spencer, whom Meyer
would repeatedly describe as the team's most valuable player.

Spencer is the son of former Buckeyes star running back Tim
Spencer, who became an Ohio State assistant coach. "I probably
came out of the womb wearing a Buckeye helmet," Evan said.
A young Evan would accompany his dad to Ohio State practices.
Mischievous and energetic, sometimes he'd sneak into huddles, to
the amusement of Buckeyes players but less so to his father. Even
when he moved to Chicago when his dad became an assistant for
the Bears, Spencer's love for the Buckeyes didn't fade. Though he
was open-minded during his recruiting process, it seemed a given
he'd end up a Buckeye.

In his career debut against Akron in the 2011 opener, Spencer
made a spectacular one-handed sideline catch of a Braxton Miller

pass. But Spencer caught only 37 passes in his first three seasons and had only five his senior year entering the Rutgers game. "He's not a guy who lights up the stats sheet because they keep stats on catches and yards [only]," wide receivers coach Zach Smith said. "In the film room, he lights the film up."

Against Rutgers, Spencer's only prior catch was one that lost a yard. So when Ohio State got the ball to the Rutgers' 11 on a 42-yard catch by Devin Smith, the Buckeyes targeted Spencer. He thought he was held on first down, but it wasn't called. On the next play, Spencer lined up from the slot and got a step on the Rutgers defender. At first, it looked as if Barrett's lob was too far. But Spencer reached out with his right hand and made the one-handed grab for the touchdown. "I realized I wasn't going to get it with two [hands]," Spencer said, "so I went up with one, and it stuck to my hand."

Spencer's touchdown pushed the Buckeyes past the 50-point mark for the fourth straight game, tying a school record. As glittery as that offensive stretch had been, Ohio State hadn't exactly been facing stout defenses. The next week, it would.

11

THE TURNING POINT

FOR ALMOST EVERY championship team, there is a moment of truth, a pivot on which the season turns. For the 2014 Ohio State Buckeyes, it came on October 25 in front of 107,895 fans at Beaver Stadium in State College, Pennsylvania. There would be bigger games against more accomplished opponents. They could become bigger games against more accomplished opponents only because Ohio State survived the Nittany Lions that night in Happy Valley.

On paper, the Buckeyes had the advantage. Penn State lacked dynamic playmakers, and its offensive line had been a sieve, unable to protect star quarterback Christian Hackenberg. Ohio State's defensive line figured to have a field day. The Nittany Lions' defense was ranked sixth nationally in points and yards allowed and first against the run. But that had come against inferior competition. Penn State started 4–0 under first-year coach James Franklin before losing 29–6 to Northwestern in Happy Valley a month earlier and then at Michigan, 18–13. Oddsmakers made the Buckeyes a two-touchdown favorite. Penn State hadn't been that big an underdog at home since joining the Big Ten in 1993. But Beaver Stadium is a different venue playing Ohio State at night in front of a frenzied white-out crowd than playing Northwestern at noon.

"I knew it was going to be that way," Larry Johnson said. "Whenever it's a white-out, it's real. It's the loudest thing that our players had ever gone through." Johnson knew his return to Beaver Stadium would be emotional. You don't coach somewhere for 18 years without planting deep roots, and Johnson certainly had. Now he would be on the visitors' sideline. "I was very emotional pulling in on the bus," he said.

During pregame, he stayed in the locker room rather than walk on the field and see all those familiar faces. Only when the whole team came on the field did he join them. "People were saying, 'Coach, everybody wants you to come out,'" Johnson said. "I knew I couldn't do that. I knew I couldn't stand around and shake hands with people."

Ohio State had not played in a truly hostile stadium up to this point in 2014. Though the Naval Academy in Annapolis, Maryland, is close to Baltimore, Ohio State fans made it, at worst, a neutral site game. Maryland's Byrd Stadium holds half of what Beaver Stadium does, and the Buckeyes silenced that crowd quickly. Penn State was a different story. To get from the visitors' locker room to the field, players must walk along a chain-link fence. Nittany Lions fans packed that area and weren't shy about expressing their rancor toward those in scarlet and gray. "They're yelling and banging on the fence, trying to hit us and knock the fence into us," left guard Pat Elflein said. "They just have crazy fans."

The night before, Ohio State players were awakened in the middle of the night at the team hotel when airhorns blared. That was nothing compared to the noise once the game started. Strands from fans' white pom-poms blew onto the field, creating a snow effect at times.

"You couldn't hear anything," Ezekiel Elliott said. "I couldn't hear J.T. calling the plays. I'd have to go up, and he had to scream in my ear."

Even so, Ohio State jumped ahead early, albeit with the help of a couple of blown calls. On the game's fourth snap, Hackenberg was pressured by a blitzing Darron Lee and threw toward Matt Zanellato. Safety Vonn Bell stepped in front of the receiver and tried to cradle the ball as he fell to the ground. Officials ruled it an interception, perhaps aided by a convincing selling job by Bell. "It was an interception," Bell maintained months later. "I will go to my grave saying it will still be an interception. My hand was under the ball."

It will always be an interception in the record books. Whether it should have been is another question. Replays clearly showed the ball hit the ground. The call was not overturned, however, because of a glitch with the replay system. For some reason, the ABC broadcasting crew announced, the proper feed was not sent to the replay booth.

Seven plays and 39 yards later, Ohio State took a 7–0 lead on a 10-yard run by Elliott. The Buckeyes made it 10–0 early in the second quarter on a 49-yard field goal by Sean Nuernberger. The kick should have been disallowed because the play clock expired before the ball was snapped. A delay-of-game penalty would probably have prompted Meyer to punt rather than try another field goal. The 49-yarder was Nuernberger's longest attempt of the season.

Ohio State again took advantage of favorable field position to make it 17–0 late in the first half on a one-yard touchdown catch by Jeff Heuerman, his first score of the season. The Buckeyes figured to be in good shape.

On the next-to-last play of the first half, though, Barrett sprained the medial collateral ligament in his left knee. "On a scale of 1 to 10, I was hurting probably a 7 or 7.5," he said. But Barrett was determined to continue, and the team's medical personnel allowed him to, with a brace. The knee would be tested early in the second half, though not in a way Barrett or the Buckeyes wanted.

Ohio State got the ball to open the third quarter. On third-and-6, Barrett dropped and threw a short slant toward Michael Thomas. But Penn State used a zone blitz and Anthony Zettel dropped back in coverage. Barrett didn't read the blitz properly and threw right to the defensive tackle, who ran 40 yards for the touchdown. Barrett was the only Buckeye who had a chance to prevent the score and chased down Zettel, but not before Zettel dived and hit the pylon. At least Barrett showed that he could still run.

The touchdown gave Penn State a needed spark, and the crowd noise rose a notch or 10. Buckeyes coaches decided to play conservatively, partly because of Barrett's knee but also because the offensive line, particularly left guard Billy Price, had become shaky. "He gave up a sack in the second quarter on a spin move, which I don't think anybody on our team the last three years would have blocked," offensive line coach Ed Warinner said. "But he lost confidence that he could [pass] protect in that game."

The Buckeyes didn't pass much the rest of the game. Their longest completion after halftime was an eight-yarder to Devin Smith. Part of the credit goes to the Penn State defense, which, led by linebacker Mike Hull, was "way better" than offensive coordinator Tom Herman anticipated. "Both from a personnel standpoint and a schematic standpoint," he said. "They've got good players and are well-coached. They knew where to be and when to be there. And they're, I would imagine, a lot better with 110,000 screaming right behind them in white."

The cautious offensive approach looked like it might pay off. Ohio State's defense was stout, led by a player who, despite impressive statistics, flew largely under the radar in that game and all season. Weakside linebacker Joshua Perry had 18 tackles, 12 in the second half.

The junior was the only remaining linebacker from his recruiting class. Truth be told, he wasn't sure he would survive, either, as a freshman in Meyer's first year. "It was awful," he said. "It was sooo bad. I was 17 years old and really didn't have an idea what this was going to be like. I was not very tough. Physically, I was not very big. I could run fast, but conditioning was awful for me. The coaching staff wants to bring the best out of you, so they back you against the wall and put you in those situations, and I wasn't ready for that at all."

That wasn't exactly true. Perry's upbringing helped prepare him for a lot. He's the middle of three brothers, between Wesley and Jahred, who has Asperger's Syndrome on the autism spectrum. As the boys grew up, Joshua and Wesley were protective of Jahred. Joshua is naturally mature for his age. That added another layer to it. "You have to be mature to handle situations where your brother might be getting bullied and people might not understand," Perry said. "You might have to step in and tell people, 'Leave him alone. That's my brother. You don't know what's going on. Don't judge him.' You're not going to be popular for doing that. But at the end of the day, it doesn't matter because I'm going to have my brother with me the rest of my life. That's my blood, and I love him to death and I'm going to do whatever I have to do to stand up for him."

All three Perry brothers enrolled at Ohio State. Wesley is a jazz musician, primarily a saxophonist, and his band has released an album. Jahred is a student in the TOPS (Transition Options in Postsecondary Settings) program for students with intellectual disabilities. He is also a manager for the men's lacrosse team.

After his difficult freshman year, Joshua became a starter as a sophomore, gradually bulking up from work in the weight room. His development continued as a junior. His hallmark was steadiness rather than highlight-reel plays. He would finish the season with 124 tackles, 32 more than any other Buckeye.

"You remember Darron Lee, and Curtis Grant and his leadership, and Vonn Bell and his picks," defensive coordinator Luke Fickell said. "Oh yeah, who was the most consistent guy? Who led the team in tackles? Joshua Perry. That's just who he is. He's a great example in our room. He's one of the guys who's a true pro."

Head strength coach Mickey Marotti called him "the face of Ohio State football."

Meyer said he had his doubts about Perry early in his career. He pegged him as a guy who was merely using a football scholarship to get his education paid for. Perry's work ethic and leadership changed Meyer's opinion. "He's one of my favorites of all time," Meyer said. "He's built himself into an NFL player."

With Perry leading the way, it looked as if the Buckeyes defense would be stout enough to win, even with a close-to-the-vest offense. Lee sacked Hackenberg to end Penn State's next possession. On the Nittany Lions' next drive, they moved the ball from their 24 to the Ohio State 44—one of their best drives to that point. On the next play, Hackenberg rolled out and threw toward Chris Godwin, who ran a crossing route. But Ohio State safety Tyvis Powell read the route and intercepted the pass. It was a beautiful play, especially considering that Powell was playing with a broken bone in his wrist. Against Rutgers, he fractured the scaphoid bone when he landed on his arm while making a tackle.

"When I got up, it was just dangling," Powell said of the injury. "I'm like, yes, it's broke. I didn't miss any plays. After that series was over, I came over to the sideline and said, 'It's broke, y'all, because I can't move it.' They taped it up real tight and checked it after the game."

Powell wasn't going to allow a little thing like a broken bone keep him out of the lineup. He'd worked too hard just to get his shot at Ohio State. Powell grew up in Bedford, Ohio, near Cleveland. After his junior season in high school, his coach, Sean Williams, asked him about his goals. Powell told him that his dream, since watching Ohio State win the 2002 national championship was to play for the Buckeyes. Williams told Powell that he had the ability, but he would need to work for it. Whatever it took, Powell said.

"He said, 'Tyvis, I'm telling you it's going to be so hard that you'll quit,'" Powell recalled. To test his resolve, he told him that their workouts would start at 6:00 AM every day. Every weekday and some Saturdays until he graduated, Williams put Powell through grueling drills, particularly in the weight room. Nothing could break his spirit, but that's just his nature. No Buckeye smiles and laughs more than Tyvis Powell.

"I think a lot of people focus on negative things," he said. "I'm one of those people who really tries to see the good in every situation, no matter how bad the situation may be. I'm just a very positive person."

He earned the scholarship offer from Ohio State and became the nickel cornerback as a redshirt freshman. His interception of Michigan's two-point conversion attempt preserved Ohio State's 42–41 victory in 2013. Now, his interception against Penn State was the second biggest play of his career to that point.

But the game was far from over. In the fourth quarter, Ohio State's defense finally began to crack. Barrett threw another interception, this time to Hull, who had 19 tackles for the Nittany Lions. Penn State's offense finally cashed in, going 45 yards for a touchdown to make it 17–14. The drive was aided by a roughing-the-passer penalty on a second-and-20 by Joey Bosa, who rolled into Hackenberg's knees after being pushed by a beaten blocker.

Ohio State had a chance to run out the clock but was forced to punt from midfield with three minutes left. Cameron Johnston's punt was fair-caught at the 9. The Nittany Lions needed to have their longest drive of the game, and that's exactly what they put together against a tired Ohio State defense. The longest play of the drive was 11 yards, but Penn State converted three short third downs and moved the ball to the Ohio State 14. Fortunately for the Buckeyes, some game mismanagement—a foolish timeout and an unneeded spike by Hackenberg—forced Penn State to settle for a tying field goal that sent the game to overtime.

Penn State got the ball first. Despite a holding call on the first play, the Nittany Lions got in position to score on 18- and 12-yard completions to DaeSean Hamilton. On third-and-goal from the 1, Bill Belton pounded into the end zone. Now Ohio State's offense, silent in the second half, would have to go 25 yards into the end zone by the whipped-up Penn State student section.

"All I remember [thinking] is the script was written: we just lost," Meyer said. "You're up by 17. You lose the lead. You play good defense, but when you have to, we didn't. In overtime, we're down by 7 jogging into one of the toughest environments I've ever been in."

Barrett knew he hadn't played well in the second half. His knee clearly was limiting him. But he knew what was at stake. His message to the team was simple. "Get the ball into the end zone," Barrett said. "It didn't matter what it was going to take. Let's make sure we get the ball in the end zone."

The Buckeyes caught a huge break on their second play. After Elliott gained three yards on first down, Barrett faked a handoff to the running back, raced to his left, and found running room for a 17-yard gain. Months later, Hull said that the Nittany Lions had a miscommunication on the play. "The backside safety didn't hear the call to come down to be the force player on the edge, so we were short a guy," he said.

The gain to the Penn State 5 revitalized the Buckeyes. Barrett scored on a run to the left side on the next play. On Nuernberger's extra-point kick that tied the game, Hull was hit with a personal-foul penalty for stepping on a teammate to launch himself in a failed effort to block the kick. That allowed Ohio State to start the second overtime from the Penn State 12. On third-and-2 from the 4, Barrett appeared to have been stopped but kept churning and bulled into the end zone. Actually, he was pushed from behind by right guard Pat Elflein. "I was blocking my dude and kind of fell off the block," Elflein said. "I saw J.T. running, and he got stuck at like the 1-yard line. I just grabbed him and kept driving my legs until he was in the end zone."

Now it was the Buckeyes defense's turn. Perry and Raekwon McMillan stuffed running back Akeel Lynch for no gain on first down. After a five-yard completion, Hackenberg threw an incompletion to Hamilton at the goal line with Bell in coverage. Bosa provided the coup de grâce on fourth down. Somehow, no Penn State lineman attempted to block Bosa, leaving Lynch to keep Hackenberg protected. He had no chance. Bosa plowed Lynch into Hackenberg for the game-clinching domino sack to seal Ohio State's 31–24 victory.

He felt more relief than exhilaration. "That was probably one of the toughest games I've ever played, how long it was and the physical toll on my body," Bosa said.

Running on fumes, he decided that the best path was a straight line through Lynch to Hackenberg. It was the Point A–to–Point B mantra in its purest form. "Being tired of trying to go around people, I just went right through him, and the outcome ended up being good," Bosa said.

The rest of the team, like Bosa, was exhausted. But the Buckeyes knew instantly that they were a team transformed. They hadn't played particularly well, but they had survived in hostile conditions. Meyer said it was the second-toughest environment he'd ever coached in, just behind LSU against his Florida Gators in 2009.

"There are certain characteristics of a great team," Meyer said. "Beating an inferior opponent badly isn't one of them. I don't think people truly appreciate Penn State's environment. We did something great teams usually do—survive."

If there was any doubt about Barrett having what it took, that ended. "I didn't really know who J.T. was [before Penn State]," Meyer said. "He did well against Kent State and did well against Maryland. He'd never been in a situation like this. That's to me when the true character of that kid showed up. That was phenomenal."

Taylor Decker said he wasn't even aware that Barrett had sprained his knee. "He's a poised guy," he said. "He handled himself in a manner that he wasn't going to let this team down. Most guys would have been out of the game standing on the sideline with the degree sprain he had. That's leadership right there."

Three days later, the first College Football Playoff rankings were released. Ohio State was No. 16, barely an afterthought. The Buckeyes had a tall hill to climb. But the Penn State game made them believe that anything was possible. "The changing point of last season was Happy Valley," Elliott said. "Being able to go into that type of environment against a good Penn State team and pull it out in double overtime showed how resilient we were as a team and how close-knit we were. Only a team with great chemistry could come in to an environment like that and win."

12

THE SLOBS

THE PENN STATE GAME was a turning point not only for Barrett. The defense didn't allow a long touchdown drive. Yes, it gave up 10 points in the fourth quarter and then a touchdown on the first overtime possession. But it played rock solid for the first three quarters and then stuffed the Nittany Lions in the second overtime. "I think the Penn State game was when the defense crossed over," safety Tyvis Powell said. "People didn't think they were good, but they were actually a really, really good team."

In that environment, Powell said, players knew that their teammates were all they had. They had to trust in each other. "Because if you don't, we were going to be embarrassed, and our chances of going to the championship are gone," he said.

But no unit pivoted more from the near-death experience at Penn State than the Ohio State offensive line, which was exposed earlier in the game. Right guard Pat Elflein said it was his worst game of the year. Left guard Billy Price struggled badly at times. But in overtime, the offensive line answered the challenge, particularly Price. "On both touchdowns in overtime," offensive line coach Ed Warinner said, "we ran right behind him, and he totally dominated the guy in front of him."

At that moment, the unit that calls itself "the Slobs" came of age. The term was coined in 2013 by Andrew Norwell, and for him, it probably fit. The three-year starter created an alter ego he dubbed the Great White Buffalo. Norwell had, Jack Mewhort said affectionately, "a touch of insanity" in him. Even after Norwell left and became a starter for the Carolina Panthers, his nickname for the unit stayed.

But the 2014 version of the Slobs had to create their own identity, and that took time. In the first three games, Warinner fiddled with combinations in the interior of the line. Elflein opened the season at left guard, next to Taylor Decker, so the Buckeyes could have one side of the line that had some starting experience. Joel Hale and Chase Farris saw some time at guard, though Price got most of the snaps. The configuration that would last the rest of the season was first used against Cincinnati. Price settled in at left guard, between Decker and center Jacoby Boren. Elflein returned for good at right guard, to the left of Darryl Baldwin.

More than any unit on a team, the offensive line must work together as one. One improper step or hesitation because of lack of confidence or trust can sabotage a play. Each line establishes its identity over time, and that develops through both harmony and friction. That was certainly the case for Ohio State's 2014 line.

Much of the friction was provided by Boren. Meyer considers the center to be the apex of the line. That position has the critical job of calling out the final blocking assignments before the snap. He has to be the brains of the unit. Boren certainly has that, though none of the Buckeyes' starting linemen were lacking in that department. Decker was the only lineman who wasn't All-Academic Big Ten in 2014, and he was the year before. A zoology major, Decker just missed the 3.0 GPA threshold after taking a whopping 19 credit hours in advanced animal-science classes in the fall semester.

At 6'1" and at most 290 pounds, Boren has been described as undersized so often that it might as well be his first name—Undersized Jacoby Boren. "That's something I heard pretty much every day, whether it was coaches, players, media," Boren said. "It's something people held against me."

Boren is the youngest of three brothers who've played at Ohio State. Their father, Mike, played at Michigan for Bo Schembechler and Jacoby's eldest brother, Justin, started his career as a Wolverine before transferring to Ohio State. Middle brother Zach famously switched from fullback to linebacker during the Buckeyes' 2012 undefeated season and became one of Meyer's favorite players. In the Borens' home in the Columbus suburb of Pickerington, the older brothers did not spare young Jacoby. "Justin and Zach were always beating on me," he said.

What Jacoby lacked in size, he compensated for with feistiness. "No matter how outmatched I was, whether it was Justin, who outweighed me by 100 to 150 pounds, or Zach," he said, "I would never back down and always went against them even if I knew I wasn't going to win."

If skeptics said he was too small to play at Ohio State, he'd show them. Even Meyer acknowledged that he didn't know if Boren's size issue would be insurmountable. But Boren pushed himself to the brink to compensate and demanded the same of others. If Boren believed a teammate needed to be chastised, he wouldn't hesitate. "Jacoby is a prick," Mickey Marotti said. "I don't know how else to say it. That's who he is. He's the youngest of three boys, and he got his face kicked in."

Boren didn't disagree.

"Off the field and outside the weight room, I feel I'm a pretty nice guy," he said. "On the field and in the weight room and anything with football, I can be kind of a dick, I guess. It's kind of the way I am and the way I play and how I train. In training when we're going up against other guys, I'll call them out and talk shit to them. It's more competitiveness. Some of the younger guys, you kind of have to get on them. They're not used to the way things work or our workout program. You go off on guys to get them to work harder."

Price got the worst of it from Boren. Price said it got so bad on occasion that he wanted to put Boren's face through a wall. In some ways, Price would seem an unlikely target. He is from Youngstown, where toughness is a fact of life. An exceptional student academically, Price also is unanimously regarded as the strongest Buckeyes player. "No question," Marotti said. "He's a freak. He trains harder than anybody."

Price was recruited as a defensive lineman. It took all of four days in his first Ohio State training camp for him to realize he needed to switch to offense. "I was continuously getting beat all the time, and I was like, 'Hey, enough is enough,'" Price said. "It was overwhelming."

He said he was so overmatched that he would have quit football if he couldn't switch sides of the ball. Fortunately, Meyer was receptive when Price asked him to move to offense. He spent 2013 as a redshirt, learning from the original Slobs. After the Orange Bowl loss, when he had that early-morning conversation with Darron Lee, he resolved to earn a starting job. He competed with Boren at center in the spring. About three weeks before the opener against Navy, Warinner told him he'd won a starting spot at guard.

Still, he had much to learn, and sometimes he was his own worst enemy. "He's just kind of goofy," offensive coordinator Tom Herman said. "He's a super smart kid, but he says and does some dumb things on the football field. But he does it very innocently, so I guess it makes him an easy target."

Early in the 2014 season, Price was the weak link on the line. Virginia Tech, in particular, exploited his inexperience. "My talents," he said, choosing his words carefully, "were not demonstrated properly in that game. There were a lot of bad things in that game."

He admitted that he was discouraged after Virginia Tech. Seeing derogatory comments on Twitter and the like didn't help. He deleted his account after that game. "Yeah, there was a lot of doubt," Price said. "People on social media are just nasty. I was getting 'You suck,' 'You shouldn't even be on scholarship,' 'You're just a big old bunch of expletives.' It was one of those moments where you have to find the confidence within. [I thought], *Hey, I messed up, but I need to grow from this.* You can't just look at it as a negative."

Price gradually improved, but it wasn't until he endured the hiccup against Penn State and came through in overtime that he gained the full trust of his linemates and coach. Push had come to shove, and shove he did. On Barrett's first touchdown run, he manhandled the Penn State defensive tackle, pushing him several yards before bulling him to the ground. On Barrett's game-winning score, Price simply tossed aside the lineman.

"At that point, we could walk in and say, 'You are a good player and can get it done,'" Warinner said. "It was a process of getting him to understand that for the offensive line to work, all five guys have to work together. It's not five independent contractors. It's one general contractor—that's me—and five guys who are there to do whatever the contractor says. We had to get Billy to rip his chest open, which our guys had done in 2012. Billy wasn't a part of us then. Let us show you the way and use all your talents and intelligence to change your way of thinking and doing business to our way, and life will be really good."

Two years earlier, Meyer had exhorted his team before it played Michigan State in 2012 to rip its chest open and shed the skepticism about the new coaching staff. At the time, Darryl Baldwin was a recently converted offensive lineman who still pined to play defense. But coaches saw more potential for him on the offensive line. He was an understudy for two years at right tackle behind Reid Fragel and then Decker. He played in 2014 as a graduate student in sports management after earning his undergraduate degree in business marketing with a 3.2 grade-point average.

Like Price, Baldwin struggled with confidence early in the year. "It was a long process with him," Warinner said. "I saw signs in him the year before in practice. He had all the tools to be really good. But because he had no experience, he had no confidence."

In the offensive line room, Baldwin stood out because of his reserved nature. "We would go through meetings for one and a half or two hours, and he wouldn't say a damn word," Boren said.

"He's a really smart guy, but he wouldn't talk at all during the meetings."

But behind his laid-back disposition was a fierce competitiveness. Baldwin's Solon High School team made the playoffs his senior year. In the first game, he badly sprained his ankle. "It was black and blue and swollen," Solon coach Jim McQuaide said. "It was huge. I didn't see how he could walk on it."

Solon won and Baldwin was determined to play the next week. "When I saw it in the training room, I thought, *No way anyone could play [on that]*," McQuaide said. "We made it to the regional finals, and he played the whole time. He worked as hard as any guy I've been around to come back from an injury."

Baldwin was the only 2014 Buckeyes player who was on the Ohio State roster when Jim Tressel was still Ohio State's coach. He redshirted as a freshman, then was asked to move to offense. While he slowly developed, he watched and soaked in everything from Warinner and the veteran linemen. "Darryl's always been a good kid, but he was a bad player," Meyer said. "He turned out to be an excellent player for us and a great leader. Incredible credit to Ed for creating the culture in that room [of], 'For you to survive here, this is the way it is.'"

Baldwin had four years to prepare himself to play in pressure situations. Pat Elflein had about 30 seconds. He was on the bench in Ann Arbor in 2013 when Marcus Hall had his infamous meltdown and got ejected after fighting and delivering the ol' double-bird salute to the Michigan faithful.

All of a sudden, he was thrust into action against Ohio State's archrival. The offense didn't miss a beat with Elflein in. "It happened so fast, it was hard to take it all in," Elflein said. "After the game, I saw my family and realized what had happened, and it was just incredible."

Like Boren, Elflein grew up in Pickerington with two older brothers—and in Elflein's case, an older sister. He credited his brother Matt for instilling in him as a high school freshman the work ethic he'd need. He starred at Pickerington North (Boren attended rival Pickerington Central), but was not considered a blue-chip recruit. In fact, Elflein was dead last in Ohio State's 25-member 2012 recruiting class in 247sports.com's composite rankings. It didn't take long for Elflein to show how flawed such rankings can be. He quickly began turning heads and then proved able against Michigan and then in the Big Ten title game versus Michigan State.

No one reveled in being one of the Slobs more than Elflein.

How does he define them? "Big, nasty, mean, tough linemen who love to eat, tell good jokes, and love ranch," he said.

Ranch?

"Yeah, we all love ranch dressing."

Their self-given nickname gave the line some notoriety. Because offensive linemen are often overlooked and have such a grueling job description, any little bit helps. "It's fun to play around with," Elflein said "You have to have fun when you're at the facility. Playing football is hard. You go there every day and work out and have school. The lifestyle is challenging. We like to have fun with it to keep our spirits up."

Ohio State's game against Illinois wasn't so challenging, and for the Illini, not much fun. Illinois had shown some signs of progress in Meyer protégé Tim Beckman's third season in Champaign but were overwhelmed 55–14 by the host Buckeyes in a prime-time game. Ohio State led 31–0 at halftime and 48–0 midway through the fourth quarter.

Before the game, the Buckeyes encountered some more adversity. Senior Rod Smith was dismissed from the team after failing a drug test. "Heart-breaking," Meyer said. "It's devastating. There are certain guys who get kicked off the team for being a bad guy. He's not a bad guy. He's got a problem."

That wasn't the only change involving the running backs. Freshman Curtis Samuel got the start over Ezekiel Elliott at running back and ran for two early touchdowns. "I thought Stan Drayton really did a good job," Meyer said of the Buckeyes' running backs coach. "He shut down Zeke [for] not taking care of his business off the field. That's power of the unit. That wasn't my call. That's the sign of a good football coach, and Stan Drayton is a great football coach. That's building culture."

Playing only in the first half, J.T. Barrett showed no ill-effects from his knee injury against Penn State, though he was uncharacteristically off-target with some early throws. It didn't matter. Ohio State's defense shut down Illinois' offense until the Illini scored a couple of late touchdowns against Buckeyes reserves. Darron Lee and Curtis Grant each had an interception. Joey Bosa had two more sacks.

Cardale Jones took over in the second half and got the most playing time in his career to that point. His first possession included both the first touchdown pass of his career and the first tackle. The latter came when the ball slipped out of his hand as he started his throwing motion. It looked like an incompletion, but no whistle blew after Illinois cornerback V'Angelo Bentley picked up the ball. So Bentley, a high school teammate of Jones' at Cleveland Glenville, began to return it. Out of nowhere, Jones leveled him, immediately popping up with a big smile on his face.

The fumble was overturned on replay review, and Jones finished the drive with a 27-yard touchdown pass to Dontre Wilson. Jones later hit Michael Thomas with a 19-yard score for Ohio State's final touchdown.

After the game, the Buckeyes took little time to reflect. Usually in a victorious Ohio State locker room, coaches take time to single out deserving players for praise in front of their teammates. That tradition was deemed unnecessary in light of what the Buckeyes faced next: Michigan State.

13

ON A MISSION

THE OHIO STATE BUCKEYES waited 11 months for another shot at Michigan State. Eleven long months. "I want to play right now, honestly," Darron Lee said right after the Illinois game.

Nothing will ever surpass in importance the Buckeyes' rivalry with Michigan. It would be sacrilegious within the walls of the Woody Hayes center to suggest otherwise. But truth be told, the rematch with the Spartans is what drove Ohio State players in the off-season ever since that crushing December night in Indianapolis. The Spartans had ripped away everything the Buckeyes savored and sought. Gone was the Big Ten title and the 24-game winning streak under Urban Meyer. Gone was a date for a national championship game against Florida State. Meyer said the loss was so painful that he hasn't watched a replay of it.

"Every single person on that football team had a vivid, disgusting picture painted in our brains of what happened the year before," wide receiver Evan Spencer said. "I'm getting chills thinking about it now. That was the toughest loss I think I've ever been a part of. Props to them. They played better than us that day. But it was so crushing. All throughout the off-season, I told myself, *Evan, when we play them again, you're going to do everything in your absolute power to beat this team. You are not leaving that field without beating this team.*"

Much was at stake beyond the revenge factor. With the addition of Maryland and Rutgers, the Big Ten changed from its much-mocked Legends and Leaders divisional format—really, what were they thinking?—to one based on geography. Ohio State and Michigan State were in the East. Unless the winner somehow lost twice in their last three games, whoever prevailed in East Lansing would play in the Big Ten Championship Game. Only the winner would stay in contention for one of the four spots in the College Football Playoff, though that still looked like a longshot, especially for the Buckeyes. National respect was also on the line for Ohio State. For all the success Meyer's Buckeyes had in his three seasons, they hadn't beaten a team ranked in the top 15.

Since its loss at Oregon, Michigan State had rolled. Its only scare came against Nebraska when the Spartans nearly blew a 27–3 lead. In their previous game, they'd crushed Michigan 35–11. Ranked No. 7, the Spartans returned the core of the team that beat Ohio State and then Stanford in the Rose Bowl. Their offense, led by quarterback Connor Cook, running back Jeremy Langford, and wide receiver Tony Lippett, ranked ninth nationally. Their defense ranked fifth, featuring defensive end Shilique Calhoun, safety Kurtis Drummond, and cornerback Trae Waynes, who'd be a first-round 2015 NFL Draft pick.

Not only did the Spartans have home-field advantage, they also had the benefit of being off the previous week to prepare and get healthier. Michigan State was a four-point favorite. BTN.com senior writer Tom Dienhart surveyed Big Ten and national writers for predictions. Twenty-five of 29 picked Michigan State. ESPN provocateur Skip Bayless tweeted that the Spartans would "annihilate" Ohio State.

None of it went unnoticed among the Buckeyes. Football coaches often use war analogies with their players, and Meyer trotted out plenty that week. During spring practice, Meyer had invited Marcus Luttrell to speak to the team. Luttrell is the author of the book *Lone Survivor*, which was later made into a movie. It's the story of his escape after an ambush in Afghanistan that killed the other three members of his Navy SEALS team. Luttrell preached to the Buckeyes the necessity of selflessness and being able to push beyond normal limits. Meyer reminded his players of that talk during Michigan State week.

"Our whole theme that week," he said, "was that the most prepared team will win the game, number one; and number two, we're sticking together like Special Forces. One of the things about Special Forces is that when contact is made, you resort back to your training. You're facing a very good team, a very talented adversary."

Meyer has much respect for the Spartans program built by Mark Dantonio, the Buckeyes' defensive coordinator on Ohio State's 2002 national championship team. Under Dantonio, the Spartans have shed their reputation as underachievers. Now the results matched the talent, and they oozed confidence. Their swagger was partly expressed in their defensive scheme, superbly orchestrated by Pat Narduzzi. Michigan State plays what's known as a "quarters" scheme. The Spartans crowd the line of scrimmage, and their cornerbacks mostly play man-to-man coverage. That allows safeties to be active in the run game. The scheme contains risk. It can leave them vulnerable to the deep passing game. The Buckeyes had their chances to exploit that in the 2013 Big Ten Championship Game but couldn't. Virginia Tech's success against Ohio State was based on a similar approach.

But the Buckeyes were a different team offensively since losing to the Hokies. Barrett had thrown 20 touchdown passes and only three interceptions in his previous six games. He had become a confident and effective runner. It also helped that Ohio State had become used to facing a Michigan State–style defense in practice. Ash helped install a quarters scheme, though the Buckeyes vary it more than the Spartans do. "When we brought Chris Ash in and kind of made the philosophical change on defense, we learned a lot as an offensive staff about how to beat quarters coverage," Tom Herman said. "Then it became a matter of finding a weak link, if you will. We wanted to go after the field corner [Darian

Hicks], not the boundary guy, Trae Waynes. We felt we had a much better grasp of the intricacies of that defense. Not to say we didn't a year before, because at the end of the day their philosophy is you've got to throw it over their head, and it didn't change from '13 to '14."

All week long, practices were even more intense than usual. For one Buckeye who'd been teetering on the edge for most of the season, things came to a head. Corey Smith had been in a funk since dropping a pass in the end zone against Virginia Tech. Smith had bounced around since his high school days in Akron. He attended two junior colleges before signing with Ohio State in 2013. He was seen as a high-risk, high-reward signing. Now it was looking like the gamble wouldn't pay off.

"You just saw the disappointment and pressure consume him," wide receivers coach Zach Smith said. "He just spiraled downhill as a player and how he approached everything in his life. That Sunday [after Virginia Tech], I came in and told Tom Herman, 'What happens in the next three weeks is going to dictate this kid's entire life. If I can get him back, we've got a chance, but it might be over.' A lot of stuff happened over the next five weeks, and he was one foot out of the door of the program because he wasn't operating the way he should have been."

Buckeyes coaches don't whitewash issues, from Meyer on down. Zach Smith had been blunt with Corey Smith about his deficiencies, and Meyer was fed up. "You've got to live by a certain standard, and he wasn't doing it," Meyer said. "[Including] academics, his lifestyle wasn't conducive to what it takes to be a major-college player."

On Wednesday of Michigan State week, Corey Smith left practice. Zach Smith went to Corey's apartment, believing it was a lost cause, that Smith was done. "He was a defeated kid," Zach Smith said. The coach was able to persuade the receiver to give it another chance. He pleaded with him to do what he was asked. Corey agreed. But how long would he stick it out? There was little reason to be optimistic.

"You cut the kid open and he's got a great heart and is a great kid," Zach Smith said. "He wants to be a great kid and do great. He just didn't know how. I took on the task of teaching him how, which is a process and is not done. I didn't know if he had the mindset and the resiliency to change. To really change, there's nothing harder to do. You look at people who have heart attacks and can't change their eating habits. You look at people who get lung cancer and can't stop smoking."

It wasn't just Corey Smith whose emotions overheated that week. In the Wednesday practice, wide receiver Michael Thomas and cornerback Doran Grant jawed at each other so much that they almost got into a fight. "It was all the frustration going into the game," Grant said, "because we were ready to get it on. I remember Coach Coombs pulled me aside and said, 'What's going on? Are you going to be all right?' I told him, 'I know my team. We are ready to play.'"

For Grant, Michigan State was personal. His father, Ted Jones, had been a star receiver for the Spartans, and Michigan State unsuccessfully recruited Doran. A five-star recruit, Grant was so discouraged after seeing only limited time as a freshman in 2011 at Ohio State that he considered transferring to his father's alma mater. To do so would have required losing a year of eligibility because of a Big Ten rule that discourages intra-conference transferring. "I was willing to sit down that year," Grant said.

He decided to stay because of loyalty to the players in his recruiting class, who'd endured a difficult first year and faced an uncertain future under Meyer. Grant became a starter as a junior and an eager leader in 2014. "Whenever guys needed to get extra work, he grabbed them and got it done," Ash said. "Whenever guys needed to watch extra film, he grabbed them and got it done. Whenever he was asked to go all out, he went all out. He was a 4 to 6 [seconds] dude. Without him doing that, I don't think we would have made the improvements we made. He set the tone, and he was consistent with what he did, and everybody else followed."

It helped that Grant embraced the new aggressive, press-style scheme right away. That's what he'd always wanted to play. Against Michigan State, Grant was at the center of the defensive game plan. Usually, Ohio State corners don't cover specific receivers. One covers the boundary—the short side of the field. The other is the "field" corner—the wide side. In 2014 Grant was the boundary corner and Apple the field corner. But Apple had injured his hamstring and was doubtful to play against Michigan State. Gareon Conley would start in his place. Coaches decided to have Grant cover Michigan State's Lippett wherever he went. It was a challenge he relished.

*   *   *   *

THE LAST TIME Ohio State went to East Lansing, it transformed the program. In 2012 the Buckeyes began the Meyer era with four unimpressive non-conference victories. In the team hotel before playing Michigan State in the Big Ten opener, Meyer pleaded with his players to "rip open their chests" and stop doubting their coaches. He raised a glass of water—championship water, he called it—and asked them to join in a toast if they would commit to the cause. They did. By the time the Buckeyes got to the locker room at Spartan Stadium, they were practically frothing, complete with chairs being thrown around the place. Ohio State's 17–16 victory was the true spark that led the Buckeyes to their undefeated season.

Nothing got thrown in the locker room in 2014, but the intensity was palpable.

"It was more like, 'We *have* to do this,'" linebacker Joshua Perry said. "This is going to determine the direction of the team. It's one of those defining moments. We were under the lights, a hostile environment, where people didn't necessarily give us a chance. It was kind of, 'Backs against the wall. What do you do?' You come out swinging, and let's go get it."

The Buckeyes spent most of the first half having to counter-punch. After Sean Nuernberger's 47-yard field-goal attempt fell short on Ohio State's opening possession, Michigan State wasted little time trying to exploit Conley. Cook threw a perfect pass to Keith Mumphery, who'd gotten a step behind the cornerback and safety Tyvis Powell for a 44-yard gain to the Buckeyes' 19. Three plays later, Cook threw a swing pass to Mumphery, who shed a high tackle attempt from Conley and ran into the end zone for the game's first score.

After that, Ohio State's plan to keep Apple on the sideline ended, even though he hadn't practiced all week. "They said, 'We need you. You've got to toughen up and get in there,'" Apple said. "I didn't know exactly what I could do, but I just gave it a shot."

Ohio State's offense answered the Spartans' opening score with a quick 71-yard drive, all on the ground. Ezekiel Elliott followed a 19-yard carry with a 47-yarder aided by relentless blocking by Michael Thomas. The latter run was Elliott's longest run of the season to date by 19 yards. "We spent an off-season, an entire spring, and an entire fall preparing for that defense," running backs coach Stan Drayton said. "He understood that defense inside-out. So, when he got in that game and was able to put all that study into action, it was great to see. It was really the first sign and true growth of him starting to anticipate what defenses are doing. That's when you started to see the big plays take place."

After Elliott's runs, Barrett then tied the game on a five-yard keeper. The Buckeyes held Michigan State on its next possession before one of their several special-teams blunders cost them. On Michigan State's punt, the ball bounced off of the Buckeyes' Jeff Greene, and the Spartans recovered. Langford scored from 33 yards on the next play.

Ohio State had to punt on its next possession and, on the one after that, faced a third-and-23 after a penalty and a sack. "Okay, what are we going to call on third-and-23?" Barrett said. "Is there anything in the playbook for third-and-23? Of course not. But we knew we wanted to attack their field corner."

Devin Smith got a step on Hicks, but the ball came at him from a difficult angle. Smith, though, has a rare ability to maintain body control on deep throws. He made the 43-yard over-the-shoulder catch look easy. Three carries by Jalin Marshall got the ball to the Spartans' 2. On fourth-and-goal, Barrett bulled in to make it 14–14. Michigan State answered with a 66-yard touchdown drive to regain the lead.

Then came the most pivotal sequence of the game. On the ensuing kickoff, Dontre Wilson fumbled. It had already been a tough game for Wilson. He dropped a pass on Ohio State's first possession and fumbled on an earlier kickoff return, which was recovered by teammate Cam Burrows. Now Michigan State had the ball at the Ohio State 18. On third-and-3, Langford took the handoff and ran off tackle into the end zone. But there was a reason Langford was able to score. Center Jack Allen, attempting a pulling block, tackled Apple as he got to him. The official saw it and threw a flag on Allen. The holding penalty nullified the touchdown. On the next play, Curtis Grant had tight coverage on an incompletion in the end zone. Michigan State had to settle for a field-goal attempt, and even that went awry when Michael Geiger's 39-yard kick missed left.

On the next play, the Buckeyes made the play that permanently changed the momentum of the game. It had been in the works for a long time. The Spartans dub their secondary the "No Fly Zone," and it lived up to its billing in the Big Ten title game. Wide receivers coach Zach Smith and his unit, which calls itself the "Zone 6 Bomb Squad," took it personally. Smith had video cutups made for each of his receivers against every Michigan State defensive back so that they would know exactly what each defender's tendencies were.

"That week, because of 2013, game preparation—probably from myself, which permeated throughout my group—was on a level I've never seen," Smith said.

One matchup he really liked was a slant to Thomas against Hicks on the field side. Smith once had Hicks, who's from Solon, Ohio, in a camp, so he knew a little about him. The timing was perfect. Thomas noticed that his teammates were downbeat on the sideline after Wilson's fumble. They perked up when the defense held and Michigan State missed the field goal. Now the offense needed to capitalize. "We needed someone to start the fire," Thomas said. "Devin came out real good that game, but he couldn't win it by himself. We needed a team effort, and I felt I needed to do my part."

He'd caught a pass on a slant pattern for a 53-yard touchdown against Virginia Tech. That was mostly forgotten because Ohio State lost, but the Buckeyes remembered. "We knew that Mike runs probably the best slant in the country," Barrett said.

Now it was time to go back to it.

"That wasn't one of those plays where there are reads," Smith said. "It was, 'Let's throw the slant to Michael on the field [side].' Everyone else operated to keep the defense away from him or to give the quarterback an option if they changed coverages."

Barrett used play-action to freeze the linebackers and then made sure he hit Thomas in stride. "It was all about coming off the line, being physical, getting on the defender's toes to make him panic and trusting in my coaching and technique," Thomas said. "I ran my route just like I was coached all week."

Thomas set up Hicks perfectly. He broke to the outside and then cut inside, opening space on Hicks, who wasn't able to close enough to bring down Thomas, who is five inches and 30 pounds bigger. After Thomas shed Hicks' tackle, he outran Kurtis Drummond for a 79-yard score. "Everything went kind of blurry, and it was tunnel vision to the end zone," Thomas said.

A couple minutes earlier, before the flag on Allen, it looked like Michigan State had taken a two-touchdown lead. Now the Buckeyes had forged a 21–21 tie with three minutes left in the half. Ohio State allowed only one first down on Michigan State's next drive. Jalin Marshall, increasingly becoming a factor on special teams, caught Mike Sadler's punt at the 10 and broke four tackles on a 26-yard punt return to give Ohio State solid field position. Barrett completed a 12-yard pass to Spencer on third down to keep the drive alive at the Michigan State 44. One minute remained. It was time to take another shot, this time to Devin Smith. He ran a post pattern, flying past Drummond and R.J. Williamson, and caught Barrett's perfectly thrown pass in stride for the touchdown.

"I had trouble in spring and in camp when I wasn't getting my deep balls out there [to Smith]," Barrett said. "I threw deep balls in high school, but I didn't throw to guys running 4.4s and 4.3s. I would underthrow Devin. With Devin, it was throw it to the grass and let him go get it."

Ohio State had its first lead. The Buckeyes never relinquished it. Michigan State kicked a field goal to open the third quarter. Ohio State overcame a drop by an open Wilson at the Spartans' 2 to score anyway, with Elliott capping the 13-play drive with a one-yard touchdown run.

Leading 35–24, the Buckeyes defense needed to maintain the momentum, and it did. On fourth-and-5 from the Ohio State 35, Apple tackled Nick Hill for a one-yard loss on the last play of the third quarter. By then, Apple's hamstring had really started to flare up. "The second half, I started cramping up in the hamstring," he said. "It affected me a ton. I couldn't do the things I wanted to do. I had to play a little more off on man-type stuff. When I did press, my technique had to be perfect because if I let them past me a little bit, I wasn't catching anybody."

On the other side of the field, Grant was rewarding coaches' faith in him. Shadowing Lippett all over the field, the senior caught only five passes for 64 yards, none longer than 17 yards.

After Apple's fourth-down tackle, the Buckeyes' offense all but put the game away. A 14-yard run by Elliott along with a late-hit penalty by Michigan State started Ohio State's drive. Marshall then caught a 20-yard pass to the Spartans' 10. On third-and-goal from the 7, the Buckeyes turned to an unlikely target. Dontre Wilson had suffered through a miserable game, with the two fumbles and two drops. That wasn't the worst of it. At some point, he'd also hurt his right foot. "What I distinctly remember is when he got hurt, they're telling me, 'He's out. He can't play,'" Zach Smith said, referring to the OSU medical personnel. "Finally, they said if you have to use him, we don't know if it's broken but it's not good."

Smith said Wilson told him he was available.

"He kept saying, 'I'm good if you need me, but I'm telling you this shit really hurts. I just can't plant on it,'" Smith recalled. Well, in Smith's view, the Buckeyes did need Wilson. Marshall was winded after catching the 20-yard pass. The alternative was freshman Noah Brown, and Smith didn't yet have enough trust in him. He knew that the pass pattern Wilson would be asked to run required him to plant on his left foot, not his right. "I said, 'Dontre, I need you to make this play. If the ball comes to you, I need you to make this play.'" Smith said.

Wilson lined up in the right slot against Williamson, ran into the end zone, made his break and made a tough catch near the sideline for the touchdown. It was 42–24 Buckeyes. Teammates mobbed Wilson, as did Smith on the sideline.

"I gave him a huge hug," Smith said. "I told him I was proud of him. The emotions kind of took over. It was essentially a kid who was defeated, made a bunch of mistakes, broke his foot, then went out and made a play because I'd looked him in the eyes and told him, 'Dontre, I really need you to make a play.'"

It would be the last significant play of Wilson's season. He had, indeed, fractured a bone in his foot.

Michigan State scored on its next possession, but Ohio State ended any suspense by doing the same. Sprung by blocks from Billy Price, Pat Elflein, and Elliott, Barrett broke a 55-yard run. Elliott then ran for a 17-yard touchdown off a block by Taylor Decker to make it 49–31 with seven minutes left. The Spartans scored quickly to make it 49–37—their two-point conversion failed—but then the Buckeyes milked almost all of the remaining time with a 10-play drive.

That final march allowed one particular Buckeye to exorcise a lingering demon. On third-and-3 at the start of the drive, the Buckeyes called for a quarterback keeper around the right edge. Tight end Jeff Heuerman's assignment was to make the seal block to allow Barrett to get free. It was the exact same play—"deuce left up yak 28 lead C," according to Heuerman—on which he failed to block Denicos Allen on the critical fourth-down run by Braxton Miller in the Big Ten Championship. This time, he wasn't denied. He got to the outside shoulder of Shilique Calhoun and shielded him from Barrett, who ran for the first down. "Reached him, kicked his ass, did my job," Heuerman said. "I set the edge for J.T., and he got the first down. You couldn't have sealed it any better."

Ohio State gained 568 yards, more than double what Michigan State had yielded per game. In the biggest game of his career, Barrett threw for 300 yards. "I said after the Penn State game I thought we had something unique or special as a group," Herman said. "After that game I said, 'Wow, we've got a unique, special dude at quarterback, too.'"

The same was becoming true at running back. Elliott ran for 154 yards. With six catches for 129 yards, Devin Smith became the first Buckeye in 2014 to have 100 receiving yards. It was the first time since 2006 that Ohio State had a 300-yard passer, 100-yard runner, and 100-yard receiver in the same game.

"That was the best anybody had prepared all season," Evan Spencer said. "Once we got it done, we saw for the first time what we were capable of. We were like, 'Hey, there's no team in the country that can beat us.'"

14

FROZEN ESCAPE

IT WAS TIME, Urban Meyer believed, for The Talk.

Before beating Michigan State, Meyer dismissed any discussion about where the Buckeyes stood for the postseason. Even after that win, he still believed a berth in the College Football Playoff was a longshot. Did he think at the time, he was asked after the season, that a national championship was possible?

"No," he said.

But he thought for the first time that a "legitimate, big-time bowl game" was realistic. Besides, he knew the chatter about where the Buckeyes stood would only grow. They shouldn't ignore it. So Meyer had what he called a "state of the union address" with his players. "Because they deserved it," he said. "Up to that point, what would you talk about? They earned the right to have the conversation. 'On a national scale, where are we?' It wasn't very long. But they're going to hear it from uncles and family, and [reporters] are going ask, so I wanted to prepare them."

That Tuesday, the Buckeyes moved up to No. 8 from No. 14 in the College Football Playoff rankings. It would still be a steep climb to get to the top four. The Virginia Tech loss loomed ever larger. The Hokies had lost three straight games to fall to 4–5. Ohio State would need any juice it could get from its remaining schedule. In the College Football Playoff rankings that week, it got a little bit. Its next opponent, Minnesota, entered the rankings at No. 25. But the Buckeyes would be going from the East Lansing frying pan to the Minneapolis freezer.

Jerry Kill had resurrected the Golden Gophers from the nadir they'd sunk to during the disastrous Tim Brewster regime. Kill didn't become coach of a Football Bowl Subdivision team until Northern Illinois hired him at age 47 in 2008 after he coached Saginaw Valley State, Emporia State, and Southern Illinois. He overcame a bout with kidney cancer, and then his career was threatened by epilepsy. Kill took a leave of absence during the 2013 season after having his fourth game-day seizure in three years. Not much was expected from the Golden Gophers in 2014, but their only losses had been a 30–7 loss at Texas Christian and a 28–24 upset by Illinois. Minnesota crushed Iowa 51–14 the week before the Buckeyes came to town. Kill, in fact, would be named Big Ten Coach of the Year ahead of Meyer, much to the disbelief of Ohio State fans, though not their coach. "Jerry Kill was very deserving," Meyer said. "I think I voted for him."

Meyer viewed the Minnesota game with trepidation. He worried about a letdown after Michigan State. It would be the second of back-to-back road games, and it would start at 11:00 AM local time. And as the week progressed, the weather forecast looked ominous. Most of all, he recognized that Minnesota was a dangerous team. The Gophers didn't have the talent that Ohio State had, but they had enough, and they played well as units.

Tom Herman said Minnesota had "probably the second- or third-best defense" in the Big Ten. "I don't remember personnel-wise a whole lot," he said, "but schematically and from an overall 11-guys-playing-as-one standpoint, they were very similar to Penn State. They maybe had only one or two draft picks on the entire defense from freshmen to seniors. But they understood what they were doing, played hard, were fundamentally sound, and tackled well."

On offense, the Gophers did have some star power. Running back David Cobb emerged as a star in his senior season. Entering the Ohio State game, he'd already run for 1,205 yards behind a physical offensive line. Tight end Maxx Williams could make acrobatic catches and would be a first-team All–Big Ten pick.

When the Buckeyes landed in Minnesota, it became clear this would not be just another road game. The weather was brutally cold, and it wouldn't get any better on game day. The temperature at kickoff was 15 degrees, the coldest Ohio State had played in since at least 1960. A steady snow would fall all game. "I don't know if I've ever been cold in a game because I don't think about [weather]," Meyer said. "But that was brutal."

Many of the Buckeyes chose to go sleeveless anyway, including the entire offensive line. The coaches on the field wore appropriate clothing, with a notable—and predictable—exception. Cornerbacks coach and special teams coordinator Kerry Coombs has the energy of someone with caffeine in his veins, and he must have had hot coffee in them in Minneapolis because wore a short-sleeve shirt. "Yeah, I did," he said sheepishly. "That's kind of embarrassing. I've got to quit doing that."

Coombs had never worn a jacket since becoming head coach at Cincinnati Colerain High School. He eschewed wearing anything other than his shirt to show his players they have to be tougher than they really are. Now it had become a bit of a badge of honor. Meyer reminded him before an earlier 2014 game that was to be played in chilly weather that he expected him to go without a jacket. Even Shelley Meyer mentioned it to him. "It's kind of a bad thing I've got to figure out a way to get out of now," Coombs said.

But Coombs said he really is impervious to the cold during the game. "I don't know how to explain that," he said. "I usually get pretty cold right after the game, but during the game I don't feel it. Now if you come to practice, I'll be bundled up. But games are different."

As for Meyer, he wore a jacket. "I don't have to prove to anybody that I'm tough," he said.

At least the benches on the Buckeyes sideline were heated, and they took refuge in that. But on the field, the cold only magnified the pain from contact. "Every hit hurt," Eli Apple said. "That's the thing about the cold. Every hit, you could feel it times 10. And that running back was physical."

Not everybody was miserable. Herman, as always, was among the coaches who worked from the warmth of the press box. He felt not a bit guilty about it. "I was eating hot dogs and popcorn," he said. "It was a good day."

It helps when your quarterback makes you look like a genius. The Buckeyes got the ball first and went three-and-out for the first time in 30 possessions. Ohio State faced third-and-1 from its 14 on its next possession.

"I was just trying to make the first down, bro," Herman said. "Then our short, slow quarterback with a knee brace decided he was going to outrun everybody to the end zone."

J.T. Barrett, who because of the cold was wearing gloves for the first time ever in a game, took the snap and ran through a hole created on the left side by center Jacoby Boren and left guard Billy Price. It looked like defensive back Eric Murray had the angle on Barrett from the quarterback's left, but he couldn't chase him down.

"In my mind—I'm not lying—I'm thinking, 'Don't get stripped of the ball. Then keep on running to open grass,'" Barrett said. "I had to curve it to the right, or I would have gotten caught."

From the press box—the warm, cozy press box—Herman couldn't believe what he was watching. "I can still picture that play in slow motion from my vantage point in the press box," Herman said. "I was like, 'Surely, they're going to catch him.' I was getting ready to call the next play. Okay, they're going to catch him. They haven't caught him. They're going to catch him. Okay, they haven't caught him yet. Surely, they're going to catch him. And they didn't catch him. It was unbelievable. I was shocked that nobody caught him. I mean, shocked."

Barrett could barely catch his breath because of the length of the run and the cold. "I wasn't really that tired until I actually passed the goal line," he said. "When I actually took that deep breath, I couldn't even talk trash like I wanted to. I was by the student section, and they were talking trash. But I couldn't talk trash. I was just trying to get off the field and get some Gatorade."

Ohio State scored again on its next possession. On third-and-7 from the Buckeyes' 43, Barrett dropped back to pass. No one was open right away, so Barrett stepped up in the pocket. He then spotted Jalin Marshall on a crossing route being covered by linebacker Cedric Thompson. Barrett's throw was right on the money. Marshall caught the ball in stride, broke Thompson's attempted tackle and breezed into the end zone.

It was 14–0 and the Buckeyes seemed to be on their way to a comfortable victory. Then the game turned, for Ohio State and for Marshall. After a three-and-out by the Buckeyes' defense, Barrett threw deep to Corey Smith. But Briean Boddy-Calhoun had a step on Smith and easily intercepted the pass and returned it 56 yards to the Ohio State 39. The turnover jolted the Gophers' offense to life. Cobb ran five straight times, scoring on a five-yard run.

Ohio State was poised to go back ahead by 14 when it drove to the Minnesota 7. Barrett threw to Marshall, but he fumbled at the 2, and the Gophers recovered. "It was going to be my second touchdown, and I got really excited," Marshall said. "I tried to run the guy over, and he made a perfect tackle and knocked the ball out right at the goal line."

Minnesota then went 80 yards to tie the game with 1:24 left in the first half. Cobb went the final 30 on third-and-15, running through a big crease up the middle before breaking a tackle by Tyvis Powell.

Powell was an inconsistent tackler for most of 2014. It turns out there was an explanation. In practice before the Michigan State game, Powell separated his shoulder. "Every game I had to have the shot in my shoulder to let me play," he said. "Coach Ash was like, 'Tyvis, I don't know. You're not healthy right now. Do you really want to play?' I'm like, 'Coach Ash, I ain't missing no games and I'm not missing any plays.' People were like, 'Why is he missing so many tackles?'" he added with a bemused laugh. "My shoulder hurt."

But he didn't blame it all on the shoulder—or the pinkie finger he dislocated in practice before Minnesota. "For some reason, I would start off games tackling well, and then as the game went on, I would start missing tackles," Powell said. "As much time as we spend on tackles, how do I keep missing tackles? Toward the end of the season, I kind of figured it out. I was lunging early. I needed to take a couple more steps instead of shooting early."

A game that the Buckeyes seemed to have under control was now tied. Even though a field goal on Ohio State's last drive gave the Buckeyes a 17–14 lead, their mood was deflated at halftime. The weather was not improving and figured to favor the Gophers, who were used to such conditions. The Minnesota crowd had come alive at the prospect of an upset. (Meyer noted that alcohol was served at TCF Bank Stadium.)

While the Buckeyes thawed out in their locker room, Michael Bennett took the opportunity to put the heat on his teammates. He had prided himself on being a positive leader in 2014. But he decided this was time for fire and brimstone. "I told them it was not okay that they were running it down our throats," Bennett said. "That's not what our defense is about. It's probably the first time I was that angry in the locker room. But I talk to the team when I need to. That's the first time I really got after them. I think we were all kind of embarrassed by how they'd scored, especially me and Adolphus [Washington]. That's our area. You don't do that. We say before every game that the game is decided by me and you."

Minnesota got the ball to start the third quarter, and it almost turned into a disaster for the Gophers. Doran Grant intercepted a Mitch Leidner pass and returned it for an apparent touchdown, but he was called for pass interference. As receiver Isaac Fruechte made his cut, he slipped while Grant was jostling him. A questionable call, but not a blatantly bad one. Minnesota had a chance to tie the game when Ryan Santoso attempted a 52-yard field goal. His kick bounced off the left upright. The Buckeyes needed only six plays to go 65 yards for a touchdown to make it 24–14. The final 30 came on an easy toss to Michael Thomas, who was wide open because of a busted coverage.

Meanwhile, Bennett's speech at halftime might have done the trick. The Buckeyes tightened their run defense. Bennett and Washington provided the anchor in the middle of the line, as they would the rest of the season. A key in that late-season surge was a little-noticed change that the two interior linemen made a few games into the season. Bennett started the season as the nose guard with Washington at the other tackle position, called the three technique. The nose guard typically lines up across from the center. His primary job is to be stout against double-team blocks so that others can make the tackle. The three-technique tackle lines up farther away from the center and is expected to make more tackles and be an effective pass-rusher. Washington started the season as the three-technique, a more natural fit given his history as a defensive end. But neither Bennett nor Washington lit it up early in the season, and defensive line coach Larry Johnson decided to have them switch spots. "Adolphus wasn't quite ready yet," Johnson said. "Our three-tech has to be our best pass rusher because he gets so much one-on-one blocking."

Playing nose guard can be a thankless job, but Washington took to it with grace. Part of that was that he didn't take a starting spot for granted. A year earlier, he lost his defensive end spot when he first tore a groin muscle and then hurt his ankle. His replacement,

Joey Bosa, quickly became, well, Joey Bosa. Washington was moved inside, where his father had predicted he'd end up in college back when his son was in high school.

To Washington, if his father says something, he's going to accept it. Adolphus and his dad share a first name, the same nickname ("DeDe"), and a bond. Adolphus Sr. raised him as a single father in a tough neighborhood in Cincinnati, determined that he would not become another statistic. Sports became Washington's outlet. Basketball was his first love, and he led his AAU team to numerous titles as a post player. But when he stopped growing at 6'4", he realized football might be his future.

Washington had all the tools—intelligence, girth, quickness, and strength. "Ridiculous athletic ability," Bennett said.

But there was one issue. Washington is a genuinely kind-hearted, easy-going guy, and he hasn't always been able to transform his personality on the field. "He has such a big heart," Bennett said. "He's not very naturally mean. I take it upon myself to turn him into a nasty, aggressive, mean defensive lineman."

As Washington transitioned to nose guard, that was essential. He made the move willingly, largely out of respect to Bennett. "It's his senior year, and he was considered one of the top defensive tackles in the country," Washington said. "It wouldn't be right to make him take on double-teams all the time."

Though Washington played reasonably well at nose guard for most of the season, he wasn't consistently dominating. Each week after a victory, coaches designated players who played at a high level "champions." Each week, Washington thought he'd get that honor. Each week, he'd be disappointed. His confidence sank. Finally, he went to Meyer and asked if they could watch film together to analyze how he could improve. Meyer showed Washington video of himself compared to that of the best NFL players at his position. "Some of my plays were as good as theirs, but some weren't," he said. "Coach Meyer told me, 'Whenever you learn how to do this every play, you could be a first-round draft pick.'"

At practice, Meyer spent extra time with Washington to motivate him when the defense went against the scout team. "It actually worked," he said. "My confidence went up. When you hear it from the head duck, it just makes you feel so much better. I wouldn't say my [statistical] production went up, but my disruptiveness went up."

Against Minnesota, his production was just fine. He had eight tackles, including six unassisted ones. As for Bennett, he flourished with the move to three-technique. His calling card is his quickness and relentlessness, and he admitted that he played tentatively early in the season. After the move, he became much more aggressive and productive.

"That's where I'm comfortable at, especially in college," Bennett said of three-technique. "I don't feel I'm told to just go eat blockers. I'm told to just go get the ball."

* * * *

THE BUCKEYES didn't entirely shut down Minnesota's run game in the second half, but they did enough to force Leidner to throw, and that produced the results they wanted. Doran Grant got his retribution for the pass-interference call on the would-be pick-six when he intercepted a pass on Minnesota's next possession. Vonn Bell did the same thing the next time the Gophers got the ball. The Buckeyes took over at the Minnesota 32 after Bell's pick, and Barrett threw a 22-yard touchdown pass to Evan Spencer to make it 31–14.

That should have been enough to seal the victory. But Minnesota got a glimmer of hope when Jalin Marshall muffed a fair catch on a punt. The Gophers recovered at the Ohio State 14. Two plays later, Cobb scored from the 12 to make it a 10-point game with seven minutes left. Ohio State got three first downs on its next possession to bleed the clock before punting. Minnesota got into field-goal position on a 31-yard run by Leidner, and Kill elected to get the three points right away. But Jeff Heuerman easily recovered the ensuing onside kick to seal Ohio State's 31–24 win.

It wasn't pretty, and Ohio State could have used the style points for the College Football Playoff rankings. But the Buckeyes had survived in brutal weather conditions.

"You out-toughed a team that was very tough," Meyer said. "Some reporter said to me, 'You only won by seven.' But we kind of controlled the game. I said that I challenge any team in America to get on a plane and do what we just did, including teams from the South or West. We'll charter a plane for them. I meant that. I don't want to take away from Minnesota. It wasn't just weather. It was a very well-coached team with good players. A top-25 team."

15

RESCUED BY MARSHALL

THE INDIANA HOOSIERS did not figure to require heroics by any Ohio State Buckeye.

But the Hoosiers did, and that Jalin Marshall was the one who provided it was a sort of poetic justice. After his two costly turnovers against Minnesota, Marshall could have gone in the tank. He didn't come close.

"A lot of negative things were said toward me, but I didn't pay it any mind," Marshall said. "My teammates and my family had my back, and it allowed me to focus on the next game. I was fine because they allowed me to be fine. They didn't pressure me about the game. They moved on, just like I did. It allowed me to be confident in my game."

The support from the Buckeyes came in part because of Marshall's likeable disposition. "There are certain kids who are the personality of the team," Zach Smith said. "He is one of them. He is loaded with personality. That kid will be successful in football and more successful out of football. He'll be legendary, one of those Joey Galloway–type of guys where the janitor will say, 'Jalin is my favorite player because he's always nice to me.' He's crazy intelligent, I don't mean school-wise, which he is, too, but street-smart. You don't want to rag on him because he's relentless and hilarious. They always say, 'I will flame you.' He will flame you, whatever that means."

But Marshall's talent and personality didn't prevent him from having a bumpy transition to college. He comes from a close-knit family in Middletown, and he acknowledged that he struggled living on his own for the first time. A 3.5-GPA student in high school, he'd sometimes show up late to class. Typical college freshman stuff, but it didn't go unnoticed. "He was a knucklehead his first semester," Meyer said. "Was lazy. Didn't work hard. But he comes from a great family. He's a wonderful person."

The football side didn't start well, either. He had to make the transition from high school quarterback to college receiver. In the third day of training camp, Marshall suffered a concussion. The Buckeyes eventually decided to redshirt him in 2013. Marshall performed well during off-season conditioning, only to tear the meniscus in his left knee early in spring practice. After arthroscopic surgery, Marshall didn't start running again until June. He was full-go in training camp, and his talent quickly emerged. In addition to his speed, Marshall has soft hands, the shiftiness to avoid tacklers and the strength to run through them. He shared time at the hybrid position with Dontre Wilson at the start of the season. Marshall was getting more playing time even before Wilson broke his foot against Michigan State. Then in his first game as the full-time hybrid, he had those turnovers. In practice before the Indiana game, Marshall went outdoors in the brisk November weather and caught punt after punt.

"I felt like I had to get my reputation back, as far as people calling me this or that," he said.

* * * *

INDIANA HAS long been one of the Big Ten doormats. It looked like things might be different early in 2014 when the Hoosiers went on the road and stunned eventual SEC East champion Missouri. But Indiana reverted to being Indiana. In some ways it was beyond the Hoosiers' control. Injuries decimated the quarterback position. Nate Sudfeld was lost for the season with a shoulder injury. Tre

Roberson, once considered a potential star, had transferred to Illinois State after being beaten out by Sudfeld. Other injuries followed, leaving one-time fifth-string freshman Zander Diamont to take the snaps. Indiana did have one legitimate star—running back Tevin Coleman, who had run for 307 yards against Rutgers the previous week. But the weak passing game and a sieve-like defense left the Hoosiers 0–6 in Big Ten play.

Indiana, which had lost 18 straight times to the Buckeyes, was a five-touchdown underdog. With that kind of mismatch on paper, not even the fact that Ohio State would clinch the Big Ten East Division title with a victory gave the game much juice. The weather contributed to the feeling that this would be a forgettable game. An ice storm hit Ohio that morning. Ohio Stadium had large pockets of empty bleachers at kickoff as road conditions delayed spectators.

Ohio State opened the game as if this would be the blowout most expected. On the third play from scrimmage, Ezekiel Elliott took a handoff and ran untouched through a gaping hole opened by Pat Elflein and Jeff Heuerman for a 65-yard touchdown. After a three-and-out by Indiana, Ohio State faced little resistance until a sack and penalty forced a third-and-15 from the Hoosiers' 16. Barrett threw to Heuerman for a 12-yard gain. Meyer then chose to go for it rather than kick a field goal, and Barrett and Heuerman made that decision pay off with an easy four-yard touchdown pass. Less than seven minutes into the game, it was 14–0.

Then it happened. The letdown that Ohio State fought happened anyway, thanks to three turnovers. "I think our guys just let off the gas," Tom Herman said. "*Hey, it's Indiana. We're going to blow them out*. The next thing you know, they're playing damn good defense. We knew they could run the ball, so they were controlling the clock."

The Buckeyes knew about Coleman. But it was Diamont who made the play that shifted momentum. On third-and-11 from the Indiana 45, the quarterback dropped back to pass. He was quickly pressured out of the pocket and found a hole. When Tyvis Powell was blocked and Doran Grant overran the play, Diamont had nothing but green in front of him. Vonn Bell finally dragged him down at the 2. On the next play, Coleman scored.

Indiana kicked a field goal to make it 14–10 after its defense stripped Michael Thomas of the ball on the first play of Ohio State's ensuing possession. On Ohio State's next drive, the Hoosiers' Antonio Allen intercepted a deep ball intended for Devin Smith at the Indiana 18. Allen picked off another pass later in the second quarter, this time from a deflection off of Thomas. Indiana kicked a field goal after Diamont connected with Shane Wynn for a 49-yard gain to make it 14–13 at halftime.

"Probably the worst thing that could have happened is that we scored early on the first drive," Herman said. "Human nature says, *Oh, this is Indiana. We blew them out last year. Their record isn't very good. This is going to be another Kent State or whatever.* Certainly, it wasn't."

The Buckeyes were struggling even though they'd contained Coleman. He had only 50 yards on 15 carries in the first half. He would almost double that on one carry midway through the third quarter. After the teams traded punts, Indiana took over at its 10. Coleman took a handoff, waited for a hole to present itself, and boy, did it. Joshua Perry and Curtis Grant got blocked, and Coleman outran Tyvis Powell down the left sideline for a 90-yard touchdown.

"They said he was fast, but I didn't know he was *that* fast," Powell said. "Coach Ash had said, 'Tyvis, I'm telling you right now that the man is fast. He broke a run against Michigan State and he's still running.' That was the joke."

All of a sudden, Indiana was no joke. Who would have thought the Buckeyes would be trailing 20–14 late in the third quarter? Ohio State had to punt on its next possession, but Cameron Johnston gave the Buckeyes a lift when his line-drive punt hit at the 5 and somehow died at the 1. If he hadn't done that kind of thing all season, it might have been dismissed as a fluke.

The punt helped shift momentum. Jalin Marshall then seized it for the Buckeyes. Ohio State's defense forced a three-and-out. Marshall caught Erich Toth's punt at the Buckeyes' 46, broke left, got key blocks from Curtis Grant and Armani Reeves and broke upfield. Toth was the last Hoosier with a chance to make a touchdown-saving tackle, but Marshall juked him easily. "Once I cut back and saw it was just me and the punter, I knew I had to score," Marshall said. "Earlier in the season, I got tripped up by a punter."

For a kick returner, nothing invites barbs more than getting tackled by a kicker. Marshall wasn't going to let that happen again. "Once I got one-on-one with the punter, I knew it was a touchdown," he said.

Marshall was just getting started. He took a shovel pass from Barrett and ran through two Hoosiers for a six-yard touchdown to make it 28–20. Indiana still had a chance when Sean Nuernberger missed a 46-yard field goal with eight minutes left. But the Buckeyes forced a punt on one possession. On the next, Tyvis Powell intercepted a Diamont pass and returned it 20 yards to the Indiana 15. On the next play, Barrett threw to Marshall, who made a one-handed catch in the end zone to give the Buckeyes some breathing room. Marshall wasn't done. When Ohio State got the ball back with three minutes left, he took another shovel pass and ran around left end for a 54-yard touchdown.

Coleman scored on a 52-yard run for the final score in Ohio State's 42–27 win. Coleman finished with 228 yards on 27 carries. "I think their running back is a first-round draft pick," Meyer said. (Coleman went in the third round.) "That was a bad day. I was very disappointed with our performance on defense. But we had back-to-back prime-time games and then Minnesota. I felt the wear and tear a little bit on our team."

The victory clinched a spot for Ohio State in the Big Ten Championship Game, and that was a big deal, even if another victory over Indiana wasn't. But the Buckeyes would get terrible news after the game. The sister of wide receiver Devin Smith's girlfriend was killed in a car accident on an icy road in Minerva, Ohio, the morning of the game.

"It was real tough," Evan Spencer said. "We just provided all the support we could."

Unfortunately for the Buckeyes, a tragedy that would hit all of them hard was just ahead.

16

RIVALRY AND TRAGEDY

ON PAPER, this did not look to be the most consequential of Ohio State–Michigan games. The Buckeyes had already clinched a spot in the Big Ten Championship Game as the East Division representative. They had edged up to No. 6 in the College Football Playoff standings, but their chances of moving into the top four looked unlikely. Michigan was just playing out the string. The Wolverines were 5–6 and needed an upset just to qualify for a bottom-tier bowl game. The Buckeyes were a 20-point favorite. During the season, Michigan athletic director Dave Brandon, who hired Brady Hoke in 2011, resigned under pressure. Already, the obituaries were being written for Hoke's coaching career in Ann Arbor.

Meyer took no glee in Hoke's fate. Michigan's defensive coordinator Greg Mattison coached at Michigan with Hoke in 1995–1996 before going to Notre Dame, where Meyer was an assistant. The three of them would occasionally drive together on recruiting trips. Mattison later coached under Meyer at Florida for the first of the Gators' national titles. "I think the [Michigan] players loved him," Meyer said of Hoke. "I like Brady a lot. He's a friend. I hate that part of the job. Families get displaced."

That did not diminish the intensity of the week one bit. On Meyer's orders, the LL Cool J song "It's Time for War," blared at the Woody all week. As is recent custom, the letter "M" was crossed out all over campus. After all, Ohio State's players and coaches are forbidden from saying "Michigan" by name all year.

J.T. Barrett may be from Texas, but he'd been in Columbus long enough to know how different Michigan week is. "I knew how much of a big deal it was not just to the team, but also fans and alumni and guys that played at Ohio State," he said. "It's not an Indiana or even a Michigan State. This is The Team Up North. Everything is kicked up a notch. If you're a defensive guy, when you hit a guy, you want extra sting to it. When you're someone blocking on the O-line, make sure they feel it. Leading up to that game that week, it hit me how much it meant. Fans carry that on their shoulders."

Despite their mediocre record, Michigan had enough talent to worry Meyer, especially given the emotion that the Wolverines figured to play with in Hoke's finale. Meyer had respect for Devin Gardner, a turnover-prone but talented quarterback. Michigan's defense had improved dramatically from a year earlier. Led by linebacker Jake Ryan, the Wolverines ranked ninth nationally in yards allowed and 21st in scoring defense, though the late-season dismissal of defensive end Frank Clark because of a domestic-violence charge hurt.

"They could have lost every game by 100 and had 32 players when we play them, and it'll still be a dogfight," wide receiver Evan Spencer said. "We were prepared for it. The Ohio State–Team Up North game is going to be a battle from now until eternity."

*   *   *   *

AS PASSIONATE as the rivalry is, it is not life and death. That distinction became more and more clear as the week went on. On Wednesday morning, walk-on defensive tackle Kosta Karageorge didn't show up at practice. That was puzzling, but Karageorge sometimes was absent from the football team because of his obligations with the Ohio State wrestling team, for which he was a backup heavyweight. But when no one on the team or his family heard from Karageorge and he was absent the next day, concern turned to worry. His family reported him missing and his sister Sophia sought help in finding Kosta. She told a reporter that her brother was last seen leaving his off-campus apartment at 2:00 AM that Wednesday morning. Shortly before that, he texted his mother, Susan, "I am sorry if I am an embarrassment, but these concussions have my head all fucked up."

Sophia Karageorge told a reporter that Kosta had a history of sports-related concussions and the family was worried that his thinking might have been affected by one she said he sustained a month earlier. Karageorge did not take his motorcycle or have his wallet or any form of identification. Police traced his phone to a nearby neighborhood, but the phone wasn't found. As news spread of his disappearance, 5,000 fliers were posted near his apartment and its vicinity. His former wrestling coach at Thomas Worthington High School, Jeremiah Webber, organized a search party of more than 150 people. They could not locate him.

In the midst of preparing for their archrival, Karageorge's teammates coped as best they could. "It was hard for everybody," Michael Bennett said. "We all kind of expected the best because Kosta was the toughest of all of us. We came up with a bunch of fantasies for what he was probably doing and kind of found solace from that."

This was not just concern over a walk-on teammate. Karageorge had truly bonded with his teammates. "Kosta wasn't just like a new guy, a walk-on, just on the team working out," cornerback Doran Grant said. "Everybody knew who Kosta was. He was a great guy, good to talk to, very enthusiastic. You knew he knew a lot about life. He cared a lot."

Karageorge wasn't the most polished player, given his background as a wrestler. But he proved with his physical strength and relentlessness to be valuable as a scout-team player preparing starters for each week's game. "I used to go against him," center Jacoby

Boren said. "He was a tough player. He was a guy who would give it his all. Those guys on scout team never really get a break. He'd be going hard every play no matter if it was the first period or the final period. He never played football, but he used his wrestling techniques. There'd be moments when you'd be blocking and he'd use some wrestling move, and you'd be like, *What the hell just happened?* His work ethic was through the roof."

Karageorge never got into a game. At one point, Ohio State erroneously listed in its participation chart that Karageorge played against Penn State. He did not make that trip. He dressed only for home games.

"It was weird because he looked up to me because I was the leader on the defensive line," Bennett said. "I looked up to him because he was a positive dude and a tough guy and one of the most interesting persons I'd ever met. There was such a mutual respect. I always wanted to meet him at dinner and hang out with him. He always had a story. He sounded like a person out of a movie."

None of Karageorge's teammates had any clue that he was troubled. Bennett said that his personality was as upbeat as anyone's on the team. Yes, he was hard on himself about football, but the same could be said for practically every player on the team. They held out hope that Karageorge would be found safe.

Meanwhile, they had Michigan to get ready for. "Preparing for it with that in the back of your head is difficult, but you have to do it," Bennett said. "If they had postponed the game, that would have been great, but we knew it wouldn't happen."

Home games against Michigan, as the regular-season finale, are always Senior Day for the Buckeyes. One by one, starting with walk-ons, they walk onto the field, exchange greetings with Urban Meyer and then join their parents on the field. Karageorge would have been one of the 24 seniors so honored. Meyer consulted with the Karageorge family to see how they wanted it handled. When Karageorge's name was announced, his picture with the word

MISSING above it was shown on the video board asking for information about his whereabouts.

"I was still hopeful," Bennett said. "I was hoping he was safe, doing his thing. At that point, I was still in denial."

*   *   *   *

THAT THIS Ohio State–Michigan game lacked some of the excitement of vintage games in the rivalry was reflected by a few empty areas of the venerable Horseshoe at the start of the game. One of the most conspicuous was in the north end zone of C Deck—the top section—where many of the visiting team's fans sit. The way Michigan started, it looked like the absent Wolverines fans knew what they were doing. On the game's opening possession, Gardner, under pressure from Joey Bosa, sailed a pass that was easily intercepted by Vonn Bell. The Buckeyes quickly cashed in. Ezekiel Elliott's 17-yard carry set up a six-yard touchdown pass from J.T. Barrett to Nick Vannett. It was the 43rd touchdown that Barrett had run or thrown for, breaking the Big Ten record held by Drew Brees.

But the rout that oddsmakers expected did not materialize. Not that the Buckeyes themselves expected to roll over Michigan. They'd been big favorites the year before in Ann Arbor and needed Tyvis Powell's interception on a two-point conversion attempt to escape with a 42–41 victory.

Sure enough, a Wolverines offense that had scored more than 24 points in Big Ten play only once—34 against Indiana—came alive. Michigan put together touchdown drives of 80 and 95 yards to take a 14–7 lead. Ohio State's offense had to punt on its next three possessions, gaining only 28 yards total. The Wolverines were particularly effective in preventing the Buckeyes from running to the perimeter.

"I think I learned from my sophomore season that that game truly is always going to be a battle," Taylor Decker said. "I knew better than to overlook them or think we would blow them out. Playing for Ohio State, I think it's the greatest rivalry in sports. I think their players acknowledge that, too. It's a cliché to say it, but you can throw the records out the window. That game is going to be a battle."

The Buckeyes got the ball back with 2:15 left at their own 17 and faced first-and-24 when Boren was called for a face-mask penalty. Ohio State escaped that when Michael Thomas broke a tackle on a 16-yard reception and Barrett scrambled 12 yards for a first down. Corey Smith, who'd worked his way back into the coaches' good graces after nearly quitting the team before the Michigan State game, then made a nifty catch of a low pass for a 16-yard gain. The Buckeyes were at the Michigan 25 with 17 seconds left when Barrett dropped back to pass. Not seeing anyone open, he darted upfield, juked Jake Ryan at the 20 and had an open path to the end zone for the tying touchdown.

Ohio State got the ball to start the second half and finally got its deep passing game going. The Buckeyes didn't complete a pass longer than 16 yards in the first half. After one first down to the Ohio State 46, Ohio State took a shot. Barrett hit Devin Smith on a post pattern for a 52-yard gain. On the next play, Barrett scored on a two-yard keeper. But Michigan tied the game with a 75-yard drive. Running back Drake Johnson went the final four, though he tore the anterior cruciate ligament in his left knee as he scored.

Furious that Ohio State was allowing what had been a feeble Michigan offense to mount three long touchdown drives, Bennett assembled the defense on the sideline. In the 2013 Michigan game, the Wolverines had unexpectedly moved the ball so effectively with misdirection and screen passes. This was worse. So as he had done at halftime of the Minnesota game, Bennett unleashed quite the tongue-lashing to his teammates.

"They were just straight-up beating us," Bennett said. "They were driving down the field on us. That's not okay. I wanted to bring it to the forefront and eliminate all confusion. We were just getting beat and we had to go out there and beat the man lined up from us on every play. There were some descriptive words."

While Bennett was chewing out his teammates, Ohio State's offense began an 81-yard touchdown drive to regain the lead. Barrett withstood pressure to throw a dart to Michael Thomas in tight coverage on third-and-6 to keep the drive alive. Barrett then threw to Nick Vannett for 22 yards, aided by a devastating block by Corey Smith.

A week earlier, Jalin Marshall scored four second-half touchdowns against Indiana. Somehow, he hadn't touched the ball against Michigan other than as a kick returner. Now he finally got a shovel pass from Barrett and went eight yards for a first down. After a pass-interference call, Elliott ran the final two yards for the 28–21 lead. The defense forced a three-and-out, and Elliott gained nine yards to start Ohio State's next possession on the last play of the third quarter.

* * * *

THE BUCKEYES had the lead, the ball, and the momentum as they got set to play the final 15 minutes of the regular season. Then it happened. Tom Herman called for a zone-read run. Barrett had the option of keeping it or handing to Marshall. But Barrett saw that Marshall was too far away to give him the ball, so he kept it. "I thought, *Well, let me stick my foot in the ground and get the first down,*" Barrett recalled.

But as he planted, defensive end Mario Ojemudia grabbed him. Barrett's legs crumpled underneath him. "He's got my jersey and he's dragging me down, and I felt kind of dead weight and my leg go underneath me," Barrett said.

It wasn't immediately apparent to him or anyone else what had just happened. Jeff Heuerman walked over and extended his arm to help Barrett up. Then the tight end glanced at Barrett's right leg and turned away in horror. "He was like, 'No, no, no. You've got to stay down,'" Barrett said. "Then I looked and my ankle was all the way to the right and my leg was straight. It was like, 'Yeah, it's probably messed up.' The adrenaline was still running, so the pain wasn't crazy."

Meyer realized almost instantly how serious this was. When some players go down, he said, he thinks they might be milking it. Barrett wasn't one of them. "I knew he was done," Meyer said.

Medical personnel immediately put an air cast on his leg. Devin Gardner came from the Michigan sideline to console Barrett, as did numerous Ohio State players before he was carted off. X-rays confirmed that he had fractured his ankle. Cardale Jones came in and was stuffed on the third-down play. Not only had Ohio State lost its quarterback. It now was in real danger of losing to their biggest rival.

"Like it was in training camp [with Braxton Miller], you have to have such split emotions," Herman said. "You're sad for the kid, but you've got a game to win. You can't allow yourself to think about ramifications of what just happened. You've got a job to do and have to serve the other 109 kids on the team and call a good game."

Ohio State appeared to have forced a three-and-out on Michigan's next possession when Gardner was stopped, but Joey Bosa ripped the quarterback's helmet off at the end of the play and was penalized for unnecessary roughness. "Sometimes, things like that happen," Bosa said. "I never intentionally try to hurt anybody or be a dirty player. It's not easy sometimes to pull up."

Michigan couldn't take advantage. Darron Lee tackled De'Veon Smith for a one-yard loss, and Vonn Bell broke up Gardner's third-down pass to force a punt. Though Ohio State's defense had righted its ship, the Buckeyes needed something from their offense. Marshall took a couple of snaps as a wildcat quarterback, running for a first down. After a false-start penalty, the Buckeyes called for their first pass since Barrett went down. It did not go well. Jones' quick sideline pass to Michael Thomas sailed way over his head.

"It looks like he never threw a ball before in his life," Meyer said. "It comes out of his hand and he almost hits me with it. I thought, *How are we going to win this game without throwing a pass the rest of the game?*"

Jones did complete a short pass to Corey Smith for a six-yard gain, leaving the Buckeyes with fourth-and-1 at the Michigan 44 with five minutes left. Meyer called timeout, needing to decide whether to go for it or punt.

"Coaching 101 is punt that ball," Meyer said.

He leaned toward calling for Cameron Johnston, knowing he'd probably pin Michigan deep. But he remembered conversations he had with Florida athletic director Jeremy Foley back when he coached the Gators. Foley preached that if a team had the chance to deliver a knockout blow, it should go for it. Given Meyer's innate aggressiveness, it wasn't a tough sell. Meyer kept the punt team on the sideline.

Smart move. Jones handed the ball to Elliott as Marshall went right and two Michigan defenders followed him. Elliott broke left. Taylor Decker sealed Ojemudia, and Billy Price and Jacoby Boren double-teamed defensive tackle Ryan Glasgow. Jake Ryan attempted a diving tackle at the line of scrimmage, but Elliott brushed him off. The seas parted and he ran unthreatened to the end zone.

If there was any doubt about the outcome, it was erased on Michigan's next possession. On first-and-10 from the Wolverines' 38, Bosa swatted the ball from Gardner as the quarterback double-pumped in the pocket. Lee, who was blitzing, scooped up the ball and ran 33 yards for the touchdown to make it 42–21. Lee probably shouldn't have been in position to make the play. He said that he and freshman linebacker Raekwon McMillan miscommunicated, and Lee wasn't supposed to blitz off the edge. But it worked out anyway. Lee had started the season with a fumble recovery off a Bosa forced fumble against Navy. Now he had bookended his regular season with a similar play. Michigan added a meaningless touchdown with 1:15 left to make the final 42–28.

Throughout the week, the Buckeyes' thoughts had been with Kosta Karageorge. They'd persevered against an inspired performance against their rivals and after the loss of their quarterback. "I knew that he'd want for us to go out and get that W," Elliott said of Karageorge. "He hated Michigan as much as anybody. He'd want us to use him as motivation to go achieve something for him, and that's what we did."

As for Barrett, he handled the injury the way people who knew him well expected. He had gotten to the fringes of Heisman Trophy contention. Though Oregon's Marcus Mariota had all but secured winning college football's most prestigious individual award, it looked like Barrett might do enough to earn a trip to New York for the ceremony. Now that was likely gone.

Barrett lived in an apartment with several teammates, including senior walk-on Russell Doup. Doup's parents visited the apartment the night of the Michigan game to check on Barrett. "The first thing he said was that the team will be just fine because Cardale is really, really good," said Doup's father, Kelly. "There was no 'woe is me' about the injury or 'I'm not going to get to New York.' It was team and Cardale."

*   *   *   *

USUALLY, OHIO STATE players who've just beaten Michigan feel untempered joy. Every one of them will receive a gold-pants trinket, which is as treasured as any championship trophy to a Buckeye. This Michigan game, though, was different, and not just because of Barrett's injury. Ohio State had played with a heavy heart as hopes dimmed for a happy resolution to Karageorge's fate. In the first couple of days after he disappeared early Wednesday morning, his teammates remained hopeful. That nothing had been heard from him and he wasn't at the Michigan game was ominous.

On Sunday afternoon, the worst fears were confirmed. A woman rummaging for recyclables found a body in a dumpster in the University District section of Columbus near Karageorge's apartment and called 911. A gun was discovered near the body, which had a single gunshot wound to the head. Soon, Twitter was abuzz with the discovery of a body. Though the identity wasn't confirmed right away, everything pointed to it being Karageorge. Darron Lee, whose mother, Candice, is a local news reporter/anchor, was among the first players to hear about it. Meyer said he couldn't remember who told him that the body was in fact Karageorge's, but he knew before that day's late-afternoon practice.

The players met in their positional groups before practice. As the defensive linemen sat down in their room, Larry Johnson remained in his office briefly. Then he silently walked into the room. "I guess he was trying not to show it," Adolphus Washington said. "We were about to watch film. Halfway through the first play, he paused and dropped his head. I was like, 'Damn, man. It's true.' You could see tears dropping to the ground. He stood up. That's all I remember."

The whole team assembled for practice, and Meyer gathered the players at midfield. He told them that Karageorge's body had been found. "When he said it, chills shot through my body," Washington said. "It was so hard for me to believe. It was so hard for me to believe because he was such a joy to be around. When I say he was happy at all times when he was around us, he literally was smiling every time. You could just look at him and he would start smiling at you. It was ridiculous."

There is no playbook for a football coach to consult in such situations. This, unfortunately, wasn't the first time Meyer had to deal with such a tragedy. When Meyer was at Florida, Michael Guilford, a 19-year-old walk-on nicknamed "Sunshine" after a character in *Remember the Titans*, was killed in a motorcycle accident. Another player died of a drug overdose.

Meyer relied on the only thing he could in that moment when he informed the team. "A faith-based approach," he said. "There's no other answer. All focus went immediately to the family. Whether people want to admit it or not, or you're allowed to admit it or not, there's a big spiritual element in our program. Huge. In that kind of situation, there's no other answer. Is there some speech you're going to give or a speaker you're going to bring in? No. It's the power of prayer and the power of your faith. That's in our core, and I'd have to say it's in the core of our program—not because of me but because of the people we've got."

Ohio State had counselors present after practice for players. A vigil was held that night at the Oval on campus, attended by about 400. "It's hard," Mickey Marotti said. "A lot of times, kids that age have never had anyone pass away."

The funeral was Wednesday morning. Meyer, with Shelley, met with the Karageorge family in the morning before the service. He had texted the parents saying that the team would make sure that Kosta would get a championship ring, though he realized how trivial that was in the scheme of things. For the Meyers, Karageorge's death—it was later confirmed by the coroner to be a suicide—wasn't the only one they had to cope with that week. A friend of their family had just died the same way.

"You're like, 'What is going on?'" Meyer said. "You talk to your kids about it and pray hard about it. I prayed hard about what to say because I know they're all listening. This is so much bigger than a college football game."

Karageorge's teammates could not understand why he committed suicide. They wracked their brains wondering if they'd missed signs of trouble, only to conclude that Karageorge hadn't displayed any.* "The biggest thing that I took away from that is you don't know what people are going through," left tackle Taylor Decker said. "They might be struggling with things in their personal lives or internally. You have to be sensitive to that. You have to be gracious and respectful to people and if you can, reach out and say, 'How's your day going?'"

That it was Karageorge, of all people, who'd committed suicide shook his teammates to their core. He was the last guy they would suspect. "If you saw him on the street, you'd definitely notice him," Ezekiel Elliott said. "He was a loud guy, always smiling, having a good time."

Even though he was a walk-on who never got into a game, Karageorge would start each practice by yelling, "Yeah, baby!" energizing the whole team. "Everyone respected what he did, not only playing football but doing it on top of his wrestling regimen," Elliott said. "He was a big part of our team, even though he didn't get to shine on Saturday. He was out there grinding Sunday through Friday."

An overflow gathering packed Annunciation Greek Orthodox Cathedral for the funeral. Elliott was a pallbearer. "It was good being there as a team and getting to see his family and checking in with them," right tackle Darryl Baldwin said. "I think it really brought the team together, especially the defensive line."

Unfortunately, the calendar did not allow for an extended break to grieve. The Big Ten Championship Game against Wisconsin was three days away, and Ohio State had to break in a new quarterback.

---

*Police later revealed that he'd sent suicidal texts after breaking up with his girlfriend. An autopsy revealed no evidence of chronic traumatic encephalopathy, the brain disease caused by repeated concussions.

17

CARDALE

TED GINN SR. had told Michelle Nash about Cardale Jones' smile before she met the 15-year-old that August day in 2008. Cardale had a huge smile, the Glenville High School football coach told her, but behind it was a lot of pain.

Nash would see how true that was. That Jones ever made it to Ohio State was a victory against steep odds. Jones grew up in Cleveland as the youngest of six children. He does not know who his father is, nor does he want to. His mom, Florence, supported her kids by working as a home-health aide and by braiding hair. "In my opinion, she was a hell of a mom because she always tried to make sure we had what we needed," Jones said.

But it was a constant struggle to have even the bare minimum. Jones often went to bed hungry. His clothes and shoes were hand-me-downs, if he was that fortunate. His mom couldn't afford to buy her kids boots for the long, snowy Cleveland winters, so Cardale would tie bags around his shoes to try to keep his feet dry. The Joneses didn't have a washing machine or dryer. Sometimes, he would have to wear the same shirt multiple days, turning it inside out or wearing it backwards to hide stains. Jones was a tall kid, which presented its own problems when it came to clothes. As he outgrew pants, sometimes he'd cut them and wear them as shorts.

With his mom out scrambling to make ends meet, Jones spent a lot of time on his own.

"I'm sure guys on the team came from worse situations than I did," he said. "But just like any inner-city kid coming from a rough city, dealing with the same issues and same problems—drugs and gang-infested neighborhoods and not knowing where your next meal is coming from or who it's coming from—it was pretty rough. But I was always taught not to let anything make for an excuse for myself. So I didn't let it hold me down or limit me."

Sports became a refuge for Jones. He began playing football when he was eight. His team practiced at a field adjacent to the one for Glenville High School. "So I used to go there probably an hour before practice," Jones said, "just watching a little bit of practice and just watching how they do it. You always hear about guys saying, 'Ted Ginn Jr.' I had no clue who he was."

Ted Ginn Jr. was a star receiver for the Buckeyes who played with fellow Glenville graduate Troy Smith, the 2006 Heisman Trophy winner. Ginn's father, Ted Ginn Sr., is the legendary coach at Glenville. He's known not just for producing a pipeline of talent to colleges, especially Ohio State, but for molding players off the field. Ginn knew the maternal side of Jones' family, the Murphys. So Ginn took an interest in the skinny kid with the ever-present smile when he would come to practice.

"Throw a pretty ball," Ginn would say to Jones day after day, then playfully shoo him away. That struck Jones as funny because he started his career as a lineman. He couldn't figure out why Ginn wanted him to throw. Then he heard the coach say, "That's going to be our quarterback."

Jones did have quite an arm. As a baseball pitcher, he claimed to have thrown an 85 mph curveball as a freshman. Ginn's prediction proved true. Jones did become a quarterback at Glenville. Ginn did everything he could to nurture him on and off the field. "He was more than a father figure, a mentor," Jones said. "He always made sure that everything he taught us we can apply to football and life."

But Ginn has an entire team to lead. He recognized that Jones needed more guidance than he alone could provide. That's how Nash entered the picture. Her cousin is married to Ronnie Bryant, the father of former Glenville and Ohio State star Christian Bryant, now with the St. Louis Rams. Nash has always had a soft spot for children—she was unable to have her own because of ovarian cysts—and told Ronnie that she'd be willing to help if he knew a kid who needed guidance. Some time passed before Ginn suggested that Nash meet Jones. For Nash, it was a difficult time. She had been raised by her grandparents, and her grandfather had just died, so she was still in mourning. She went to Glenville, where Ginn called Jones over to meet her.

"He never took his helmet off, but he kept looking at me," Nash recalled. "He was just smiling. Coach Ginn said, 'This is Miss Michelle. She's going to be your mentor. She's going to be assisting and helping you.' He just kept smiling. It was just something about the smile that was like, 'Here's somebody to help.' I don't know if I took that wrong, the smile that he gave me, but that's how I felt."

But she remembered the words that Ginn had shared about the pain behind the smile. The first day she spent with him, she noticed his ill-fitting shoes. She took Jones to buy new shoes after practice that night, a first for him. "I knew that's not a thing you're supposed to do when mentoring, but he didn't have a decent pair of shoes on his feet," Nash said. "I was just like, 'Lord, what should I do? Lord, shouldn't I?' It didn't sit well with me to allow the child to walk around with nothing on his feet, so I took him to the mall."

When Nash told Jones to call her anytime he needed anything, he told her that he didn't have a cellphone. She bought him one. "It was the coolest thing in the world to me because I finally had a phone," Jones said.

Nash said that she wanted to develop a relationship with Jones' mom, but that Florence showed no interest in it. "She always used to drop me off and ask, 'Is your mom in the house?'" Jones said. "I'm like, 'I don't know. I don't know where she's at.' She always used to try to see my mom and introduce herself to my mom and let her know, 'This is where he's been.' She offered my mom many times, 'Come over and see where he's at. Know that he ain't at a frigging crack house or something like that.'"

Not long into their relationship, Jones was at his home after Nash dropped him off. He was in bed late at night after playing a videogame. An acquaintance visiting the house was in the bathroom and had a gun.

"It's an automatic," Jones said, "and it has a hairpin trigger."

The guy touched the trigger and six shots pierced the wall. One of them narrowly missed Jones. In fact, if he hadn't leaned over to check for his phone charger, it might have hit him. There was a hole in the wall right where his head had been.

"It's literally a big-ass hole," Jones said. "I'm like, 'This is where I've been sitting!'"

Jones called Nash. It was 2:00 AM. "He said, 'Miss Michelle, I don't want to live like this no more. Would you come get me?'" Nash said. "I was in my pajamas and I got up and picked him up. He was standing on the corner with a little bag in his hand. He has been with me ever since."

Nash and Jones bonded quickly. She provided structure. He was to go to school and do his homework. After football practice, he was to come home. His room was to be kept clean. He could not have sleepovers at other friends' homes, with two exceptions because she knew the parents well. Only once did Jones disobey the rules and stay out on the street. Nash temporarily confiscated his cellphone, among other consequences.

Nash and Jones genuinely enjoyed each other's company. Nash laughed at Jones' silly sense of humor. When they'd approach a door, he would run ahead as if to be chivalrous and open the door for her. Then he'd pull it closed so she couldn't get in. Another time, she took Cardale and Christian Bryant's younger brother, Coby, to buy a suit at Men's Wearhouse. She looked over, only to see the boys play-wrestling on the floor. Jones was amused by Nash's penchant for tearing up at anything remotely emotional. He nicknamed her "Crybaby." Mostly, though, he came to call her by another name: Mom.

"I don't look at me as his mentor," Nash said. "I don't look at me as his guardian. I look at him as my child. I look at Cardale and I say, 'He's my God-given. Not being able to have kids, I was blessed with Cardale. To me, he is my child.'"

And Cardale thinks of himself as having two mothers, though his relationship with Florence is complicated. "It's hard to explain," he said. "It's almost cordial on my part because it's my mom. I've got to respect her. I've got to have a relationship with her. That relationship ain't where I want it to be, and her and Michelle's relationship ain't where I want it to be. She doesn't understand that Michelle has my best interest at heart. She just feels like Michelle just wants to take credit for everything, which has never been the case. Ever."

* * * *

Under Ginn's tutelage, Jones became a star quarterback at Glenville. He grew to 6′5″ with a big arm. He was in the same recruiting class as Braxton Miller, though, and the Buckeyes under Jim Tressel wanted to create some separation between Miller and Jones. So Jones attended Fork Union Military Academy in Virginia for one semester where he roomed with Michael Thomas.

Jones enrolled at Ohio State in January 2012. To say that Jones did not make a strong first impression at Ohio State would be wrong. He did. It just wasn't a favorable one. "A bona fide idiot," Meyer said. "A guy who was immature. A guy who truly didn't belong at Ohio State. A guy who had one foot out the door."

Mickey Marotti may have had even harsher words. The strength coaches began working with the freshmen earlier than the veterans in January 2012 because the older players needed a short break after returning from the Gator Bowl. Jones not only couldn't get through the first workout, Marotti said, he couldn't get through the *warmup* for the first workout. "Like it was the hardest thing in the world, like someone was torturing him," Marotti said. "It was pathetic. That's the word. His physical fitness level when he was a freshman was pathetic. I was embarrassed for him. I thought this guy was a bum. Where'd this guy come from? He ain't going to make it. Not in this program."

From Jones' point of view, he was being punished for someone else's sins. He wasn't a part of the 2011 team. He was just a freshman trying to get acclimated to college life and Ohio State. "They inherited a lot of problems, a lot of inner-program problems that I'm glad people weren't able to see," Jones said. With a laugh, he added, "They just treated us so bad. They just broke us. They broke us quick. And I was like, 'I didn't sign up for this. I didn't do anything bad. I shouldn't be getting punished the way these guys are getting punished. I was like, 'Wow, I really don't want to be here.'"

Jones redshirted in 2012, with his only notoriety coming when he posted that infamous tweet about not coming to Ohio State for academics.

"That wasn't a joke," Meyer said of the tweet. "He was living his life that way."

What was not known during the uproar about the tweet was the reason he sent it. It wasn't as if Jones had just flunked a test and was showing his disdain for school. He said he had a 3.3 grade-point average at that time and was angry because he'd gotten a B+ on a sociology exam, which lowered his grade from an A to an A-.

"So for anyone who thinks that I don't take academics seriously, or I was just a dumbass, they're sadly mistaken," Jones said. But Jones acknowledges that he was immature. He wasn't a hard worker. He didn't carry himself the way a quarterback is supposed to. Then again, Jones knew that Braxton Miller was the established starting quarterback. In 2012 and 2013, Kenny Guiton was the able and revered backup. He knew that Meyer and Tom Herman had recruited J.T. Barrett, not him. What was his path to a meaningful role? He couldn't see it. So Jones continued to drift, and his coaches grew increasingly exasperated. As frustrated as they may have been, though, they weren't willing to give up on him.

"When I hear the media or fans or someone say, 'Just get rid of the guy,'" Meyer said, "[I think], *Get rid of your son, then.* I hear that and, first of all, I think it's a joke. I've been criticized for many years. 'You give kids too many chances.' I like to look at the person saying that and ask, 'Is that right?' You're giving a human being a second or third chance. If our biggest knock is that we give our guys second or third chances, I'm good."

Even in the worst moments, coaches could see potential in Jones as a player and a person. He was immature, not disrespectful. "Off the field, he was a child," Herman said. "He was not a bad kid and never has been a bad kid. You're not talking about a guy that was doing drugs or beating women or getting in fights or saying "F— you" to the establishment. He was just a kid who was perpetually a step behind. Late for a workout. Missed a tutor because he forgot. Overslept this. It was constant reminding of the gravity of the position he was in. He plays quarterback at The Ohio State University. Not just a prestigious position, but one that comes with an enormous amount of responsibility. I don't know that for the first couple years he grasped that. I think he saw himself floating in the wind like a third-string guard."

Jones' lack of responsibility was deemed so much of a problem that one day in 2012 Tom Herman made him wear a cardboard dunce cap that he had interns and graduate assistants make. The word "Dunce" was actually written on the cap, so there'd be no misunderstanding. For an hour in the quarterbacks' room, Jones had to sit in front wearing that makeshift cap.

"A fairly regrettable decision by me," Herman said. "I was just searching for motivation. To be honest, I wanted to shame him in front of his peers."

Jones said he didn't take offense to Herman's ploy. He knew his lackluster work habits called for consequences. But when Jones sent a picture of himself in the dunce cap to Michelle Nash, she became livid. She called Herman to give him a piece of her mind and demand a meeting. That was fine with Herman. "I said, 'Okay, great. I'm glad you have an issue with it. Let's all meet with Coach Meyer, and we'll talk not just about that incident but the entire saga that was Cardale Jones at that point,'" he said.

Nash, accompanied by her father, drove from Cleveland and met with Herman and Meyer. She asked the coaches how they would feel if a teacher put dunce caps on their children. Nash said that Meyer did most of the talking. "He apologized for it and tried to tell me some of the things that were going on with Cardale and how sometimes Cardale would come to practice and not really give his all, that it seemed like his mind was somewhere else," she said. "I understood all of that. I was fine with that. You can call me and talk to me about that. If we have to have another pow-wow and come down here to try to talk to him, that's fine. But to put a dunce cap on him? Absolutely not."

Cardale believed the coaches didn't like him, and the feeling was mutual. One night he texted Nash, saying that he didn't think he could make it at Ohio State. "That's what bothered me," Nash said. "I felt that his spirit was being broken."

She tried to bolster his confidence. She sent him affirmations and positive quotes. Nash told him that the road is not always going to be easy, and that he'd regret it if he didn't stick it out. Slowly, things began to improve. Nash began a dialogue with Ryan Stamper, who played for Meyer at Florida and had become the coordinator of player development for the Buckeyes. Jones' relationship with Herman, with help from Herman's wife, Michelle, gradually got better.

But Jones remained an enigma. He had a likeable, endearing personality. His teammates were amused by all the nicknames

Jones gave himself, the most popular being "12 Gauge," based on his uniform number and strong arm. Yet he almost preferred to hide his intelligence.

"There probably was not a meeting that went by when he did not crack the whole group up," said Herman, who himself has a better sense of humor than the typical coach. "He likes to disguise himself in this simple, almost dumb character and say some things that are really funny, that only a simpleton would say. But I think they're calculated by him and maybe he knows the right thing to say, but chooses the simple/dumb way to say it to get a rise out of people. He's really smart."

J.T. Barrett said he is continually amused and amazed by things Jones would say because they often come out of left field. "He just says things that normal people don't think about," Barrett said. "He's going to say whatever pops into his head and say it out loud like it was nothing. It's like, 'Don't you think sometimes about what you say? Who thinks of that?' He's just silly."

Then there'd be times he'd seem like a sage.

"In meetings," Barrett said, "he'd ask questions almost like a coach was in there asking questions, deep-thought football questions. "I'd be sitting there like, 'Uh, yeah, I was thinking that, too.' But I was lying."

*   *   *   *

LIKE BARRETT, Jones thought of himself as no more than a backup in 2014. Braxton Miller's training-camp injury changed that. For Jones, that meant more discouragement. He didn't believe he got a fair shot in the 11 days before the opener to retake the job from Barrett, who'd edged ahead of him just before Miller's injury. Jones said that for the remainder of preseason practice, Barrett got almost all of the reps with the starting offense, which typically went against the second-team defense. Most of Jones' snaps came with the second team against the first-team defense. That was no way to overtake Barrett.

"I'm getting sacked literally every play," Jones said. "I've got guys running the wrong routes. I've got guys getting D'ed up by Doran Grant. How do you expect me to have an opportunity to push him for the starting spot?"

Jones said that Herman told him to be ready to play against Navy. Jones didn't play a snap.

"I was just like, 'Fuck this shit. Whatever,'" Jones said.

When Barrett and the rest of the offense struggled in the Virginia Tech loss, Jones thought he might get a chance. When he didn't, his spirits sank even lower. He figured that the coaches had committed to Barrett, sink or swim. With Miller returning in 2015, Jones was already thinking about transferring at year's end. He told Herman as much a few weeks later.

"I'm like, 'Dude, I'm outta here after the season,'" he said.

But though Jones' heart may not have been in it, he had matured to the point where he did practice and prepare diligently. He said that the change began after the Purdue game in 2012. Miller got hurt that game and Guiton rallied the Buckeyes to an overtime victory. But there was a point in the game when Guiton had an equipment issue and it looked like he'd have to sit out a play. The next man up was Jones, redshirt or not. Playing Jones was the last thing Meyer wanted, especially since this wasn't long after "The Tweet."

"Coach Meyer, out of nowhere, found me," Jones said. "He turned directly to me and gave me the meanest stare ever, like, 'You've got to be shitting me. Your ass is going to have to go out there and take a snap.' That's probably the most scared I've ever been in my life. I was all silent. My helmet was strapped and my mouthpiece was in. I was just shaking, like, *Oh, my God. Please don't make me have to go in.*"

Guiton didn't have to miss a snap, but Jones had been scared straight. He hadn't prepared for Purdue that week. He never wanted to feel that way again. Whatever his feelings, he would at least try to be ready if he was called on.

*   *   *   *

THE PURDUE GAME was the start of a turning point for Jones. But the real transformation came the weekend of the 2014 Michigan State game when his daughter, Chloe, was born. She was due in mid-December, but her mother, Jones' girlfriend and Ohio State student Jeaney Durand, had a doctor's appointment in Cleveland that Thursday and was told she had already started to dilate. In that day's practice, which is a light one with the game only two days away, Jones neglected to get his ankles taped, as is Ohio State's rule.

"I still had that attitude like, 'Well, I'm not gonna play, so...'" Jones said.

Sure enough, he sprained his ankle. Herman, understandably, was furious. A trainer taped his ankle, and coaches forced Jones to continue practice. Jones got treatment that night and was ordered to show up at 5:30 AM the next day to get additional treatment before the Buckeyes headed to East Lansing. When he checked his phone after Friday morning's treatment, there were about 40 missed calls from his family saying that Durand was in labor. He rushed out after treatment, got in his car and rushed up to Cleveland. His phone battery died on the way, and he didn't know where to go when he got to the hospital.

"I'm limping," Jones said. "I've got crutches. I throw the crutches somewhere in the hospital. I'm running around, limping around in every wing of the hospital trying to find her. By the time I get there, I'm in full-blown sweat, so much pain, ankle done swelled back up. They've got ice on my ankle, and I'm holding [Jeaney's] leg while she's [pushing]. I'm like, 'This is the craziest shit ever.'"

Jones left shortly after the birth to return to Columbus for the trip to Michigan State. He drove up to Cleveland on Sunday morning after the game, then back to Columbus that day for practice and then returned to Cleveland that night.

"Sixteen hours of driving in three days," he said.

It was all worth it to watch Chloe enter the world. "I understood when she was pregnant, it's not about me anymore," he said. "But just seeing that—this is what my life is about now. This is what I have to work for."

The Wisconsin game would be his chance to show it. His roommate, safety Tyvis Powell, was accustomed to returning to their apartment after class and seeing Jones playing videogames. Not this week. Jones was at the Woody whenever he wasn't in class.

"He was not going to let that moment get by him for lack of preparation and/or readiness," Herman said. "He was great. He was almost to the point where he was mad with everyone asking if he was okay or if he could do it. It was like, 'Fuck you, I'm good. I'm trying to prepare for the game,' which was cool. I admired that his approach where he was almost annoyed by the attention and almost put off by it."

But Herman knew that some of that had to be a façade. On the inside, he figured, Jones had to be a nervous wreck, knowing the fate of the season rested on his shoulders. As his coach, Herman knew he had to instill confidence in Jones. It was positive-reinforcement week. No dunce caps were anywhere in sight. As the week progressed, Herman's confidence grew as he came to believe that Jones was up for the moment.

"I asked if he was nervous," Powell said. "He said, 'I'm not nervous at all. I'm ready. I want to prove it to the world that I can do this.'"

He would.

18

BLOWOUT

BEFORE THE BIG TEN switched to the East-West configuration with the addition of Maryland and Rutgers in 2014, the rivalry with Wisconsin had probably become Ohio State's most heated aside from Michigan. The rivalry was replete with recent examples of one team ruining the other's season. In 2011 the biggest highlight of the Buckeyes' dreary season was their dramatic upset of the Russell Wilson–led Badgers at the Horseshoe. With 20 seconds left, Braxton Miller threw a 40-yard touchdown pass to Devin Smith, who was somehow left open in the end zone. The year before, Wisconsin jumped on No. 1 Ohio State early, winning 31–18 in Madison. Buckeyes fans detested former Badgers coach Bret Bielema, considering him a whiny oaf. The Badgers won three straight Big Ten championships. It chafed Ohio State that their last one was in 2012 when the Buckeyes, who had beaten Wisconsin in overtime in Madison, were ineligible to play in the conference title game. With Wisconsin in the Big Ten West and Ohio State in the East after geographical realignment, the rivalry would inevitably cool. In 2014 the teams didn't play in the regular season for the first time since 2006. But for players in the Big Ten Championship Game, the rivalry remained fresh enough.

It was personal on the coaching front as well, though friendlier. Wisconsin coach Gary Andersen was the defensive line coach under Meyer in 2004 for Utah's undefeated season. They remained close friends. So were Tom Herman and the guy with whom he'd be matching wits, Wisconsin defensive coordinator Dave Aranda.

They were teammates at Cal Lutheran. Herman said they were roommates for a semester. "Actually, maybe I just slept on his couch a bunch of weeks in a row and that counted as being a roommate," Herman joked.

Ohio State co–defensive coordinator Chris Ash coached at Wisconsin from 2010 to 2012 under Bielema before going with him to Arkansas. "Just about all those 22 starting players were there when I was there," Ash said, "and I either coached or recruited them."

Wisconsin's identity for the last 25 years has been to try to bludgeon opponents into submission with its running game. It was as if the Badgers wanted to make Woody Hayes proud. With Melvin Gordon carrying the ball, that made perfect sense. Gordon would finish second the next weekend in the Heisman Trophy voting behind Oregon quarterback Marcus Mariota. Gordon entered the Big Ten Championship Game with 2,260 yards in 2014, the fourth-most in NCAA history and a single-season Big Ten record. Against Nebraska on November 15, he shredded the Cornhuskers for an NCAA-record 408 yards, though his mark was broken the next week. Displaying speed, power and agility, Gordon averaged 8.0 yards per carry. As always, Wisconsin had a beefy offensive line to maul opponents, though center Dan Voltz was questionable with an ankle sprain.

All week long, Buckeyes players heard about Wisconsin's running game. Ohio State's redesigned locker room had a wall of televisions. To hear the Buckeyes' defensive players tell it, every talking head on every TV spent the week predicting that Gordon would run roughshod over the Buckeyes. "All they were talking about was how our defensive line was not big enough and strong enough to handle Wisconsin's running game," Adolphus Washington said. "All of us took that personally. We went into the game focused and knew that we had to stop the run because they were a pretty one-dimensional team."

The weak link in Wisconsin's offense, as it often is, was at quarterback. Neither Joel Stave nor Tanner McEvoy had seized control of the job. Stave had recovered from a case of the yips during preseason camp and played well enough to take most of the snaps during a seven-game winning streak following a loss to Northwestern. Ohio State didn't fear the Badgers' wide receivers, either. Jared Abbrederis, who'd had a big game against the Buckeyes in 2013, was in the NFL. Ohio State felt comfortable putting its cornerbacks on an island against Wisconsin's receivers and have Buckeyes safeties help in the run game.

On defense, the Badgers lacked stars, but they were effective. Wisconsin had lost all seven starting linemen and linebackers from the 2013 team. Even so, the Badgers ranked second nationally in total defense and fourth in scoring defense. Wisconsin disguised its alignments and coverages well, which would pose a challenge to even an experienced quarterback, let alone one making his first career start. Ohio State's offensive game plan was designed to keep things simple for Jones and give him easy reads in the passing game early until he settled in and gained confidence. Meyer was adamant about one thing. He did not want Jones throwing over the middle. When Meyer was an assistant at Notre Dame in 1998, starting quarterback Jarious Jackson was injured. Against Southern California, the Fighting Irish had to use a backup, who threw two interceptions over the middle in USC's win. Meyer has a long memory. "I kept having visions of that," he said. "Even on third downs, keep the game on the outside. We had to work hard to game-plan it. That ball would not be down the middle of the field."

Because of the questions about Jones, Wisconsin (10–2) was a four-point favorite. That just added another dose of motivation to a Buckeyes team that didn't need any more. Jones couldn't wait to prove he was worthy. Just as they had when Miller went down, his teammates girded themselves to playing even harder. The Buckeyes craved the championship that had eluded them the previous two years. They also knew they had to make a statement if they were to sway minds and have any chance to earn one of the four spots in the College Football Playoff. The Buckeyes had moved up to No. 5 that week after Mississippi State lost to Ole Miss.

Perhaps most of all, they drew inspiration from the death of Kosta Karageorge. Such tragedies can fracture a team or unite it. For the Buckeyes, it added to their sense of purpose. The leadership training they'd been through had trained them for such moments. A terrible event—the worst imaginable—had happened. They couldn't control that. They could only control their response. "That just brought the team closer together," middle linebacker Curtis Grant said, "showing us that life is short and stick together and do as much as you can together while you have the chance. It was a totally different feeling around the team, how everybody went about their business and how hungry we were as a team."

Several of Karageorge's defensive linemates asked to wear his No. 53 in tribute. Larry Johnson gave the honor to Michael Bennett, the senior captain. "It meant a lot just to be able to bring glory to him and help people remember him," Bennett said.

*　*　*　*

GAME DAY ARRIVED, and the Buckeyes were hoping to get good news from the earlier games with College Football Playoff relevance. They didn't get it. No. 2 Oregon had already won the Pac-12 championship the night before with a 51–13 victory over No. 7 Arizona, avenging an earlier loss to the Wildcats. The Ducks were clearly in. No. 3 Texas Christian had an early-afternoon game against 2–9 Iowa State. The Horned Frogs couldn't afford to slip. They didn't. Leading 17–3 at halftime, TCU rolled up 31 third-quarter points in a 55–3 victory. Other top contenders won as well. No. 1 Alabama pulled away late in a 42–13 victory over Missouri in the SEC title game. The Crimson Tide's ticket was punched.

The Big 12 picture became even more muddled. No. 6 Baylor took care of business at home against No. 9 Kansas State, 38–27, to keep itself in the CFP picture and stay tied with TCU atop the Big 12. Baylor had edged TCU 61–58 in October. Because the Big 12 has only 10 teams, it cannot have a league championship game. So the conference's motto of "One True Champion" became ironic when commissioner Bob Bowlsby declared TCU and Baylor to be co-champs. The other team playing at night was No. 4 Florida State. The Seminoles had narrowly escaped upsets all season to remain the country's only undefeated team. The defending national champions would do it again against Georgia Tech, 37–35, in the Atlantic Coast Conference championship.

Without any of the teams ahead of or just below them losing, Ohio State's chances of earning its way into the top four spots looked dim as the team bus pulled up to Lucas Oil Stadium on Saturday night. Something dramatic would have to happen for that to change.

"I think we all went in there realizing we had to make a statement," Taylor Decker said. "We had some good wins—beating Michigan State, Minnesota, winning our rivalry game. But people were talking about, 'Well, they lost their Heisman candidate at quarterback. What are they going to be like? Are they going to keep up their level of play?' We had to put an exclamation point on our résumé for the selection committee. We definitely were conscious of that going into the game."

But what were the odds of winning convincingly enough to sway the committee? The more realistic goal was to win and capture that elusive Big Ten championship. Certainly, Meyer wasn't obsessed with making the playoffs. "I wasn't even thinking that way," he said. "I thought we'd have a chance if the game was a rout. But I never expected that. Win the game, win the Big Ten championship. No one was thinking about the College Football Playoffs at that point. We had to win with a new quarterback, and we're facing a Heisman Trophy[–caliber] tailback."

And how confident did he feel in that quarterback?

"So-so," Meyer said. "He'd never done it before. I thought he had the talent. I just didn't know if he could sustain it for a whole game."

*   *   *   *

TO THE BUCKEYES, the first clue about the way the night would go came during warmups. Ohio State's players were enthused and loose. Jones grabbed the crossbar of the goalpost as if dunking a basketball and shook it, leaving it reverberating for seconds. As the Buckeyes looked across the field, Wisconsin looked tight.

"We're hopping around and we're dancing, getting all hyped down," left guard Billy Price said. "You look down there, and they're just solemn. There's no energy, nobody bouncing around, almost like a funeral-home feel to it. At that moment, it's over. You could tell which team was going to win just based on looking at pregame warmups. I've always believed that, even in high school."

After what happened, Price shouldn't be doubted. After a moment of silence for Karageorge, the Buckeyes received the opening kickoff. On the first snap, Jones rolled to his right and completed an eight-yard pass to a diving Michael Thomas near the sideline. Ezekiel Elliott ran for first downs on the next two plays before Jones completed a curl to Corey Smith.

The Buckeyes then unleashed what would become a potent combination during the postseason. Ohio State had Devin Smith in the slot. That wasn't his normal spot, but the Buckeyes wanted to take an early shot to him on a long pass. "Devin Smith is as good a deep-ball guy as there is, and I felt we matched up well," Meyer said.

To disguise the route and try to get Smith one-on-one coverage, the Buckeyes put Elliott in motion. Jones dropped back in the pocket and threw to the end zone. Wisconsin cornerback Sojourn Shelton had good coverage on Smith. But as the ball approached, Smith shielded Shelton like a basketball player boxing out for a rebound and made the catch. The only thing that went wrong was that Elliott blew his assignment and also ran toward the end zone, almost allowing the defender covering him to get in on the play. Jones ran to the end zone to celebrate and high-stepped it back to the sideline with his ever-present smile.

For the Buckeyes, Smith's touchdown boded well. In the 20 games during his career in which he had caught a touchdown pass, Ohio State was undefeated. Wisconsin's coverage on the touchdown revealed something about their defensive strategy that played into the Buckeyes' hands the rest of the game.

"They kind of worked with us and played a lot of man coverage," Meyer said. "If they would have come out and played a bunch of zone, we'd have been in trouble. We didn't have a lot of crossing routes and stuff like that, which you have to do sometimes in zone. Full-field reads, we didn't do a lot of that."

The offense had made its opening statement. Now it was the defense's turn. On first down, the Buckeyes swarmed Gordon for a two-yard gain. Stave rolled out on second down and threw a quick pass to tight end Austin Traylor, who fumbled the ball out of bounds when Darron Lee leveled him. On third-and-4, Gordon got the ball. He danced for a second, looking for a hole. There wasn't one. Bennett submarined Gordon for a one-yard loss, then tugged at his No. 53 jersey in memory of Karageorge.

Ohio State went three-and-out when it got the ball back, but it may have been as significant a possession as the Buckeyes would have. On third-and-14, Jones threw deep into double coverage—over the middle—to Jalin Marshall. The ball fell incomplete. Meyer was furious that Jones had violated his command about avoiding that part of the field.

"I was ready to unload on him," Meyer said.

But Jones was one step ahead of his coach. "As soon as I let the ball go, I said, 'Oh my God. Oh shit,'" Jones said. He ran to the sideline and apologized to Meyer.

"In our leadership training," Meyer said, "we use this great video of Steve Young saying that one of the jobs of a great leader is taking responsibility. He came right over. He said, 'Coach, that's my fault. It won't happen again.'" Meyer was taken aback. He told Jones to tell the offensive linemen he'd made a mistake, and he did. Cardale Jones really was growing up.

Cameron Johnston pinned the Badgers at their 2-yard line with a 73-yard punt, the longest of his career. On Wisconsin's next snap, Dan Voltz reinjured his ankle, causing the Badgers to reshuffle their offensive line. Wisconsin got two first downs on its next possession—a major feat for the Badgers on this night—before having to punt.

Then the avalanche began. After gaining 12 yards to the Ohio State 19, Elliott took the next handoff and saw a huge hole open in front of him. Taylor Decker and Billy Price sealed their men on the left side of the line. Pat Elflein and Darryl Baldwin shoved theirs past Elliott. Jacoby Boren took care of linebacker Derek Landisch, flirting with a clothes-line block before letting go. Elliott broke through the line and ran untouched for an 81-yard touchdown and a 14–0 lead.

On Wisconsin's next possession, safety Vonn Bell read Stave's eyes and stepped in front of intended receiver Kenzel Doe for an interception at the Ohio State 41. The Buckeyes moved the ball to the Wisconsin 1 after passes from Jones to Michael Thomas for 23 yards and to Jalin Marshall for 32. But Elliott dropped a swing pass on third-and-goal, and the Buckeyes settled for a field goal.

Wisconsin had fallen behind in several games in 2014 and rallied. The week before, the Badgers trailed Minnesota 17–3 before taking control. There would be no comeback against the Buckeyes. In fact, Ohio State was just getting started. Daring Stave to throw, the Buckeyes swarmed Gordon almost every time he touched the ball.

"We stacked the line of scrimmage and made the ball go horizontal," cornerback Doran Grant said. "He ran horizontal the whole game. Our defensive line that whole game—oh, my gosh. There was stalemate after stalemate. The defensive line controlled the line of scrimmage, hands down."

A lot of that came from preparation. The motivation from the previous year's loss to Michigan State, Karageorge's death, and all the talk about Wisconsin's dominant run game had caused the Buckeyes, particularly the defensive linemen, to study as if it were the bar exam. They knew Wisconsin's offense cold.

"You see the formation and you kind of know what kind of play they're going to run," Adolphus Washington said. "Me and Mike were literally at the line of scrimmage calling their plays out. One time [Stave] came up there, and we called it out. He made some type of check, and I knew that he was just trading it to the opposite side. I told Mike, 'He's running it to this way now.' [Stave] just looks at me like, 'Wow.'"

The offensive line continued to open holes, and Elliott punished tacklers. Meanwhile, Jones' early confidence never wavered. It helped to have play-making receivers around him, and none were bigger than Devin Smith, who benefited from Jones' arm more than anyone. On second-and-1 from the Wisconsin 44, Smith lined up in the right slot against freshman Derrick Tindal, who would have man coverage. Smith made one move to get behind Tindal, and Jones lofted a pass perfectly over Smith's left shoulder for the touchdown and a 24–0 lead.

"He got waylaid as he was throwing and still hit him right over the outside shoulder," Tom Herman said. "As soon as I watched the film, I was like, 'Wow, that was a grown-man throw right there.'"

The Buckeyes had turned into the Big Scarlet Machine. After another three-and-out forced by Ohio State's defense, the Buckeyes went 69 yards in only six plays, resulting in another touchdown as Elliott ran in untouched from 14 yards out. It was 31–0, and Buckeyes fans had to be thinking things couldn't get better. But they did. The first half ended with an exclamation point. After a

58-yard punt by Johnston and a sack by Rashad Frazier, Wisconsin gave the ball to Gordon hoping just to end its nightmarish first half. But Bennett poked the ball from Gordon, and Joey Bosa scooped it up and ran four yards for the touchdown with 36 seconds left in the half.

Bennett said the forced fumble stemmed from desperation.

"I came off the line, and my angle was wrong," Bennett said. "I was on the back shoulder of the guard while they were going the other way. I saw Melvin with the ball. I kind of went into panic mode because I knew he was going to run in my gap because I was out of it. I pressed the guard off, flew into my gap, saw him right there, and with everything I had because I was a little off balance, I threw my arm at the ball and threw my body into the gap and knocked it loose. Joey was there to clean it up."

Why, with his team ahead 31–0 and Wisconsin 88 yards from the end zone, did Bennett feel such urgency? It came from the culture that had now become ingrained in the program.

"They say that everybody's got a worst fear," Bennett said. "If you've got a close team, your worst fear is letting down your teammates. So if you're like, *Oh, man, I'm not where I'm supposed to be*, you're going to do everything you can do to make up for it and get to where you're supposed to be."

It was a signature play for Bennett, who had four tackles for a loss against Wisconsin. The Karageorge death inspired him, but he had become a different player and leader the second half of the season. "I think it was Coach Fick who said that the No. 1 quality a leader has to have is selflessness," Bennett said. "That's what it means to be a leader—sacrifice and selflessness. Before, I felt a leader meant a guy who works hard and talks the loudest or makes plays. But then I realized it was the guy who cares the most and is willing to do the stuff nobody wants to do and is willing to sacrifice what no one else wants to sacrifice, and I tried to do that in 2014."

With a 38–0 lead at halftime, the Buckeyes knew they couldn't let up in the second half. A College Football Playoff berth that looked like a longshot before the game suddenly looked realistic if a conference championship carried the weight that the guidelines of the CFP said it should. On Ohio State's first possession of the third quarter, the Jones-to–Devin Smith connection clicked again. From the Badgers' 42, Jones threw a deep ball to Smith, who made a circus catch while backpedaling in tight coverage for another touchdown.

* * * *

FOR SMITH, this was the payoff for a trying season on and off the field. His travails began in late June when he was driving back to his home in Massillon and his tire lost traction on a sharp turn. His car slid and hit a utility pole. The car came close to overturning. The driver's side door was the only part of the car not damaged, allowing Smith to escape with only a minor concussion and some scrapes.

"The car was totaled, like crushed," said Doran Grant, Smith's second cousin. "I saw pictures of the car and was like, wow. For him to come out of it with some scratches and a few bruises and a headache? He was getting watched over. I'm thankful for that."

The psychological scars lasted longer than the physical ones. He had trouble sleeping and would sometimes cry himself to sleep, haunted by what would have happened if his car had flipped. His girlfriend, Aliysha Stermer, and his parents helped him cope. "They said, 'You're here now and you've got to get past it,'" Smith said.

When the season started, he had high hopes to be more than just a deep threat. It didn't really happen. In fact, Michael Thomas was listed ahead of him on the depth chart, though Smith did start most of the games as a third receiver. When he caught a total of only four passes in consecutive games against Maryland, Rutgers, and Penn

State, his frustration turned to discouragement. He even fleetingly thought about quitting. "I was never like, 'Forget it, I'm done,'" Smith said. "But it was in the back of my mind: What would happen if I was to quit?"

Again, talks with his parents and girlfriend helped him persevere. His big game against Michigan State—six catches for 129 yards—helped get him out of the rut. Then, two weeks later, came the death of his girlfriend's sister, A'liyia Hancock, in the car accident the morning of the Indiana game. "That was definitely hard," Grant said. "When he's quiet, you know something's wrong. He was quiet. He didn't really talk to anybody. When I found out what happened, I understood and talked to him. Sometimes we cried. It was something we had to deal with. It was hard."

During games, Smith wore Hancock's initials—ARH—on the black sticker under his left eye in memory of her. He wanted to do her proud, and he would in the postseason. For all of his strengths, J.T. Barrett struggled at times with deep passes. That wasn't an issue for Jones, and Smith flourished.

"He's a great kid," Zach Smith said. "One of the funniest kids I've ever been around. Stan Drayton told me that when he first got here. For three months I was calling him a liar. I was like, 'The kid doesn't even talk.' But he has to get comfortable around you before he opens up, and when he does he's hilarious."

Smith is a particularly gifted mimic, with dead-on impersonations of former safeties coach Everett Withers, Mickey Marotti, and Tim Tebow. Yes, he even does Urban Meyer.

*   *   *   *

AFTER SMITH'S third touchdown, the Buckeyes led 45–0. But they were still hungry. In fact, one of them was literally hungry. Pat Elflein had been sick the week of the game and couldn't keep food down. It wasn't until right before the game that he started to feel better. After halftime, his appetite really kicked in. But it wasn't as if he could go to a concession stand. So he asked one of the team's nutritionists to go back to the locker room and get him something to eat. So between series, Elflein munched on some Uncrustables, the prepackaged peanut butter and jelly snack.

"Coach Warinner is drawing up a play and sees me and is like, 'What are you doing?'" Elflein recalled. "I said, 'I'm hungry.' He's just laughing."

Anything can be humorous in the midst of a blowout victory. The Buckeyes padded their lead to 59–0 on a pair of fourth-quarter touchdown runs by backup running back Curtis Samuel. The game had turned into a dream, but to the two Buckeyes coordinators, it was business as usual.

"I'm never at ease," Herman said. "As a play-caller, you're never settled. You don't realize it's going that well because you're always focused on the immediacy of what's next. It's like four minutes left and Coach Meyer said, 'What the hell are you still doing in the press box? Come down and celebrate with us.' So I did, and that was pretty cool because I'd never been down there for that big a moment."

Luke Fickell was just as focused on the task at hand, for a different reason. The Buckeyes were intent on keeping that zero on the scoreboard for Wisconsin. Doran Grant helped the cause with two interceptions in the second half and almost had another on a fourth-down incompletion. On Wisconsin's final possession, with the Buckeyes already celebrating on the sideline, Meyer was congratulating players and coaches. When he approached Fickell, the defensive coordinator shooed him away.

"I think he wanted that shutout so bad," Meyer said.

The Buckeyes got it. Wisconsin didn't cross the Ohio State 25 until the final play of the game when Raekwon McMillan tackled Corey Clement after a 12-yard gain to the 21 as the Buckeye backups finished up. Ohio State had outgained Wisconsin 558–258, including 301–71 on the ground. Elliott had a career-high 220 yards on 20 carries. The Buckeyes' defense held Melvin Gordon to only 76 yards on 26 carries. Devin Smith's three touchdown catches were a career high.

But the man of the hour was Cardale Jones. He needed to throw only 17 times, completing 12 for 257 yards. He was sacked only once and wasn't intercepted. On the championship podium, Jones was announced as the game's MVP. He grabbed the Grange-Griffin trophy and held it above his head, flashing the huge smile that Michelle Nash first saw all those years ago. There was no pain lurking behind it anymore. Nash's reaction came naturally. She cried.

"That was very overwhelming," Nash said. "I was a nervous wreck, and it was like all of a sudden, just all the weight was lifted."

*   *   *   *

DURING THE AWARDS presentation, Big Ten commissioner Jim Delany made a point of calling Ohio State "one of the four best teams in the country." Meyer didn't hesitate when asked his opinion. "I don't think there's any doubt we're one of the top four teams in America," he said.

The locker room was a combination of elation and relief. It was Ohio State's first Big Ten title since 2009. (The one the Buckeyes won in 2010 was vacated because of the NCAA violations.) "You're measured by Big Ten championships, really anywhere, but especially at Ohio State," Meyer said. "I was really happy for our players because none of them had one."

The Buckeyes expected to beat Wisconsin. But 59–0? Nobody could have predicted that. It was as dominating an Ohio State performance against a quality opponent as anyone could remember. It might have been particularly sweet to players on Ohio State's defense. They had heard for years that they had fallen short in upholding the tradition of the Silver Bullets. "I remember the next day when we had our team meeting, Coach Meyer said, 'First, the defense, stand up,'" Doran Grant said. "We all stood up. He said, 'I've been waiting two or three years to say this: I give you the Silver Bullets.' Everyone started clapping. I guess that's when we officially arrived."

It had been a perfect night, but the moment of truth would come the next day. Would Ohio State get one of the four magic tickets to the College Football Playoff? In the concourse of Lucas Oil Stadium after the game, Meyer, walking with Shelley, approached a reporter. Meyer asked him if he thought Ohio State had done enough to get in. Probably, was the response. As for a likely opponent, Meyer was already thinking about that.

"Hope it's not Alabama," he said.

19

SELECTION DAY

THE MOOD IN THE ROOM was uncomfortable at the Gaylord Texan Resort & Convention Center in suburban Dallas as the College Football Playoff selection committee watched Ohio State crush Wisconsin. After all, one of its 12 members is Barry Alvarez, Wisconsin's athletic director and former football coach. Many of those on the committee have or had his job. They knew exactly what he was feeling.

"I think we were respectful and reserved watching that game together because Coach Alvarez's team was in it," said selection committee chairman Jeff Long, the athletic director at Arkansas. "As sitting ADs, we're all so close to our teams. I'm sure it was tough for Coach Alvarez to be there and watch that with us. But he was always very professional and never negative, and he watched it very closely and, as we all did, quietly."

The selection committee was as stunned as the rest of the country by Ohio State's 59–0 victory. "I don't think anyone anticipated Ohio State would control the game the way it did," Long said. "I don't think we anticipated that there would be that kind of margin of victory."

The Big Ten Championship Game ended shortly before midnight. The full selection committee continued discussions for two more hours, Long said. Casual conversation between various members continued for another hour. The committee met for breakfast five hours later and resumed discussions a half-hour after that. None of the contenders for the four coveted spots lost that weekend, so as the committee began to dissect their résumés, they knew it would be a difficult challenge.

* * * *

THERE WAS IRONY in Ohio State needing a playoff to have a chance at the national championship. Jim Delany had long been adamantly opposed to a playoff. So had former OSU president E. Gordon Gee.

"As far as a playoff system is concerned," Gee said in 2007, "there will not be one. They will wrench a playoff system out of my cold, dead hands."

But dissatisfaction with the Bowl Championship Series system, not to mention the money that could be reaped by having a playoff, won over enough converts. Even Barack Obama advocated a playoff. It was eventually decided to have a four-team playoff chosen by a selection committee, similar to how the NCAA basketball tournament field is picked.

Most of the committee members in 2014 were former coaches or athletic directors. But there were some from outside the box. Former Secretary of State Condoleezza Rice, a passionate football fan, is on the committee, as is retired Lieutenant General Mike Gould, and even a former sportswriter, Steve Wieberg. Though the first rankings weren't done until late October, committee members analyzed games from the start of the season. Long recorded as many as nine games at a time on three DVRs. Committee members received downloads of games stripped of commercials that they could watch on iPads. If they wanted, they could even get games in cutup versions, so they could watch a team's offense, defense or special-teams plays separately. Two committee members were assigned to be point persons for a specific conference. Rice and Southern California AD Pat Haden were responsible for the Big Ten. That largely involved communication with the conference office, which would give an overview of its teams in consideration for the top 25.

The Buckeyes had a steep hill to climb. Long watched the Virginia Tech game. He had the same reaction as most people. "Well, they certainly underperformed in that game," he said. "It certainly wasn't the way we expected it to go."

But the committee watched Ohio State's steady improvement. The Buckeyes' standing in the CFP rankings rose accordingly. In the Associated Press poll voted on by 60 media members or the Amway poll voted on by 62 coaches (including Meyer), voters tend not to drop teams unless they lose, particularly late in the season. Long said that one of the committee's guiding principles was that each week, the committee would start from scratch. Because committee members looked at teams with fresh eyes every week, they chose not to speculate about the effect of such things as injuries. Each week's rankings would be viewed as a snapshot in time. So when J.T. Barrett was injured against Michigan, the committee did not hold that against the Buckeyes, who moved up to fifth from sixth after Mississippi State lost to Ole Miss that week. The committee's rationale was that it could judge Ohio State with Cardale Jones at quarterback after the Buckeyes played an entire game with him. Until then, it would judge Ohio State as it had played. Entering the final weekend's games, Long said, Alabama and Oregon were clearly the top two teams. But the next four—No. 3 TCU, No. 4 Florida State, No. 5 Ohio State and No. 6 Baylor—were very close.

"Really, it was 3A, B, C, and D," Long said. "It's a cliché, but it was razor-thin, paper-thin, between Nos. 3, 4, 5, and 6. So the results of that weekend were going to have a big impact on our rankings. One vote different by a committee member could have totally rearranged 3 through 6 going into the final weekend of games. While we had TCU ranked No. 3, we looked at all those teams as 3A, B, C, and D. They were all 3s. That last weekend of games was going to have a tremendous impact on the final rankings."

Not until after the final game—Ohio State's—did the committee begin deliberations, Long said. The process the CFP committee used to analyze and vote on teams is similar to the way the NCAA basketball committee does it. Six teams with similar résumés are evaluated and discussed, with the top three vote-getters put in the field. Three more teams are then added to the mix and that "sifting" process continues until the field is set. Because committee members don't have to explain their vote, there may not be a definitive reason that one team is voted in and another not. It's in the eye of the beholder, and there are 12 beholders on the committee.

Committee members had reams of data, not just about the contenders but about their opponents. Long said the committee was well aware that injuries ravaged Virginia Tech after it beat Ohio State. That somewhat mitigated the damage from that game. "That was discussed and noted, that Virginia Tech was a different team when it beat Ohio State," Long said. "That's the value of a committee. We can see those things. We're evaluating things. We're watching games."

Long said that the conventional wisdom that Alabama and Oregon were clearly the top two teams is correct. But the notion that it would have been impossible to exclude defending champion Florida State, with its undefeated record despite numerous close calls, was incorrect, Long said. "No, it's not impossible they could have been left out," Long said. "That's not true. They could have been left out of the top 4 [despite] being undefeated. That's where a committee that evaluates teams can look at a team and make judgments about how good they are, even though they haven't lost a game."

How close did Florida State come to not qualifying? "It was very close," Long said. "Very close."

But the Seminoles were in at No. 3.

It came down to Ohio State, Baylor, and TCU for the final spot. Before the Wisconsin game, there was much speculation that the Buckeyes were fighting a two-pronged battle in the Big Ten Championship Game. Not only did they have to beat Wisconsin convincingly, but Jones would have to show that he was a championship-caliber quarterback. Long said he wouldn't put it in those terms, though the committee did watch Jones' performance carefully.

"The obvious question was: How would Cardale Jones play in that game?" Long said. "As we saw, he played extremely well. His play in that game showed he was a very talented quarterback, and that Ohio State did not drop off. They were a quality team. There weren't questions about him being able to lead that team."

It didn't hurt that while Ohio State proved definitively that it was the king of the Big Ten, Baylor and TCU were presented to the committee by Big 12 commissioner Bob Bowlsby as co-champs. Despite edging TCU in overtime in October, Baylor had been slightly behind the Horned Frogs in the CFP standings. But that was before beating No. 9 Kansas State in the regular-season finale. When Baylor beat Kansas State, that was enough to push the Bears ahead of TCU—but not Ohio State—in the committee's eyes.

"I think the key that folks need to understand is that some of the criteria for our rankings do not and cannot come into play until the complete bodies of work are done," Long said. "One of those is head-to-head, and head-to-head if teams are indistinguishable [when] you can't tell which one to rank higher than the other. Then head-to-head comes into play. It doesn't really come into play until all of those results are complete."

The more the committee studied Ohio State, the more the Buckeyes' improvement struck a chord. "I think that's a sign of the coaching and the way the team responded to the coaching," Long said.

It has become almost a parlor game to guess the margin of victory Ohio State needed over Wisconsin for the Buckeyes to ascend into the top four. Did it have to be something similar to 59–0? Would 31–14 have sufficed? It was on the minds of the Buckeyes during the game.

"At the beginning of the second half," Doran Grant said, "when we scored another touchdown—Cardale to Devin again [to make it 45–0]—Coach Fickell came over to the defense and said, 'We're playing for style points now. Don't let up.'"

But the committee didn't have a magic number, Long said. "We didn't go in anticipating what Ohio State had to do because there were a number of games that could have affected that final ranking," he said. "They played out in such a way that Ohio State ended up fourth. I don't think the committee looks at, 'Okay, what does Ohio State have to do to get in the top four?' We never think about it that way. We look at the results of the game after they're played."

Long said it wasn't a situation that one or more committee members championed Ohio State's résumé and persuaded others to vote for the Buckeyes. Standing on a table and pleading a case might be the way such situations are portrayed in the movies. It's not what happened that Sunday morning in Texas. It was just a process of continual debate and voting by secret ballot. The vote that put Ohio State in over Baylor and TCU was "extremely close," Long said. Baylor coach Art Briles claimed in January that the vote against his team was 8–4. Unless Long or CFP executive director Bill Hancock divulged it to Briles, which is highly unlikely, Briles was just guessing.

"Individual votes are only known to the chair and the executive director," Long said.

And that's the way, he said, the final vote that put Ohio State into the first College Football Playoff will remain.

*   *   *   *

THE BUCKEYES ARRIVED back in Columbus early Sunday after the championship game. They did not meet as a team to watch the selection show. Meyer and his family watched at their house in Dublin with Gene Smith and his wife, Sheila, and a few others.

"Everyone was nervous," Shelley Meyer said. "We really thought Gene would know. In the BCS, you knew in advance."

Smith didn't know. They'd have to wait like everyone else. Alabama, Oregon, and Florida State were revealed as the first three teams, with the Ducks and Seminoles to meet in the Rose Bowl. The wait for the final team to be unveiled lasted 23 seconds.

"It felt like 20 minutes," Meyer's daughter Nicki said. "Brutal."

Urban Meyer wouldn't look at the TV. He was too nervous. He stared at the ground. Then Ohio State was flashed on the screen. The Buckeyes would play Alabama in the Sugar Bowl in New Orleans on January 1.

"As soon as it popped in there, the whole room erupted," Shelley said. "Screaming, tears, jumping around. It was a really awesome moment. It could have gone either way. It was agonizing. There was so much drama. I even said, 'Oh, my gosh, all this drama over football. I can't take it anymore.' But it was total elation.'"

Nicki said that her dad got up and started walking around when she hugged him. Five years earlier, Nicki returned home for winter break from Georgia Tech after not having seen her father since the summer. He'd lost 30 pounds from the stress of the season. When she greeted him with a hug back in 2009 and felt how gaunt his body had become, it scared her to her core.

This hug was much, much better.

"I hugged him and I just felt his knees buckle, completely buckle," she said. "He was just so happy, so shocked, and so weak for that one minute. We all hugged as a family for like two minutes, which doesn't sound like a long time, but it is a long time to all be holding on to each other. It was really special."

Offensive linemen Pat Elflein, Taylor Decker, and Jacoby Boren went to a Rooster's restaurant on campus to watch the selection show. They ran late and almost missed it. "We hadn't even been seated yet," Decker said. "We ran in and looked at the TV. They announced that we were going to be in it, and people went crazy, high-fiving."

Others watched in the privacy of their dorm or apartment. Doran Grant and Curtis Grant were downstairs in their apartment, while Devin Smith and Chase Farris stayed upstairs when Ohio State's name appeared on the screen. "I pumped my fist in the air," Doran Grant said. "We jumped around, all excited. Then I heard footsteps. It was Devin. He was all excited. Then you hear an earthquake. Chase is literally rolling downstairs."

After everything they'd been through—the departure of key players from the 2013 team, the loss of Braxton Miller, the defeat against Virginia Tech, the death of Kosta Karageorge, the injury to J.T. Barrett—the Buckeyes still had a chance at the national title. It didn't take long, though, for the enormity of their challenge to sink in. "Are we ready for this?" Meyer said. "That's all I kept thinking to myself. I went from real happy to, *Okay, now it's on.*"

20

READY FOR 'BAMA

WITHIN FIVE MINUTES of the College Football Playoff announcement, Urban Meyer was on the phone with Mickey Marotti and
director of football operations Brian Voltolini to start the process
of trying to take down the big, bad Crimson Tide. The CFP would
be uncharted territory for everybody. After the physical and emotional whirlwind of the previous two weeks, Ohio State's players
could finally come up for air. For the coaches and staff, there would
be little respite.

For one thing, the coaching carousel that always starts spinning
after the regular season would affect the Buckeyes. Except for the
departures of Mike Vrabel and Everett Withers after the 2013 season, Meyer had managed to keep his staff intact. Ohio State's con-
tinuing success meant that many of his coaches would be candidates
for head coaching jobs. As he had been three years earlier, Luke
Fickell was approached by the University of Pittsburgh, but Pitt
hired Michigan State defensive coordinator Pat Narduzzi quickly.
Chris Ash interviewed for the job at Colorado State but didn't get
it. The week of the Big Ten Championship Game, Ed Warinner had
preliminary phone conversations with Kansas, where he'd served
so successfully as an offensive coordinator. But Kansas hired Texas
A&M assistant David Beaty the day before Ohio State played Wisconsin. "It just means that it wasn't meant to be, and I wasn't the
guy they were looking for," Warinner said.

Tom Herman's quest to be a head coach would be realized, however. A year earlier, Meyer said, Herman interviewed at Connecticut.

At the end of the 2014 regular season, Herman interviewed for the Southern Methodist job. The Mustangs instead hired Clemson offensive coordinator Chad Morris, a former Texas high school coach. The University of Houston also had an opening, and that seemed like an ideal match. Herman's early coaching years were spent in Texas. The state was part of Herman's recruiting territory at Ohio State, with J.T. Barrett the prized catch. The Cougars have a long, proud history.

"If a guy leaves our staff, I want him to be successful," Meyer said. "Don't go to a place where you can't win. Houston seemed like a good fit."

Herman met with Houston officials in Detroit between flights back from visiting recruits. He met with them again at a private airport in Columbus. In the middle of this, Herman flew to Little Rock, Arkansas, to accept the Broyles Award given to the top assistant coach in the country. That weekend, the Cougars offered Herman the job, which he accepted. Herman decided to stay with the Buckeyes through the playoff. He'd worked so hard and developed such a bond with his players and coaches for three years. There was no way he could be so close to the pinnacle and walk away.

"Had it been a 'lesser bowl,' the decision might have been harder," Herman said. "But it was a no-brainer."

That meant he'd be sleep-deprived for the foreseeable future. He awoke at 5:00, got to the office, and worked on Houston responsibilities until the Buckeyes' staff meeting at 7:00. He did his normal Ohio State work and would squeeze in Houston duties at lunch and late at night. Warinner, who was the co–offensive coordinator in addition to being the offensive line coach, made sure that nothing fell between the cracks.

"Tom did a tremendous job managing both responsibilities," Warinner said.

*   *   *   *

FOR MANY OF the families of Buckeyes players, the elation of making the playoff soon turned to worry and frustration about the cost of going to New Orleans for the Sugar Bowl, let alone a second game in Dallas for the championship if Ohio State won.

Round-trip airfares from Columbus cost about $800. Hotel rooms were also exorbitant. Meyer had become more reluctant over the years to voice his opinion on non-football matters, figuring that it usually just caused him headaches. But this was a cause about which he was passionate. He raised the issue repeatedly, beseeching the CFP to do something to allay costs for families. The CFP is committed to paying each major conference a minimum of $50 million. No money was set aside to defray travel costs for families of players. Ohio State committed to reimburse families $800 per game out of its student-assistance fund. That helped, but it wasn't nearly enough.

"It was wrong," Meyer said. "When you first heard about the playoff, you thought, *How's this going to work?* Then you started living it. I talked to some of our families. Those players and those families shouldn't be stressed because we're winning. I thought it was nonsense. I can't believe that wasn't discussed."

Several parents, most notably Annie Apple, Eli's mother, spoke out about the issue, which became a lightning rod. Some had little sympathy for the parents' plight. Ohio State's football parents association sent a letter to the Big Ten asking for assistance. But the conference, along with the NCAA, said that their hands were tied by the existing rules. The pressure applied by Meyer and lobbying by Gene Smith helped persuade the NCAA and CFP to change its rules. On January 7, the CFP announced that it would reimburse each parent of a player $1,250 for travel costs to the championship game.

For Meyer, the parent-travel issue was important, but it was still a tangential one. One question dominated his thoughts: How do we beat Alabama? The Crimson Tide won BCS titles in 2009, 2011, and 2012 during the Southeastern Conference's seven-year streak of national championships. Their overall history is one of the few in college football that matches or surpasses Ohio State. Alabama has had 11 undefeated seasons. Paul "Bear" Bryant became the coach in 1958 and won six national championships from 1961 to 1979. After Bryant retired in 1982—he died of a heart attack a month later—the Crimson Tide's fortunes slid. Alabama won the 1992 national title under Gene Stallings, but that was an aberration. The program floundered under Mike DuBose, Dennis Franchione, and Mike Shula.

In a state without major pro sports, college football is king in Alabama, and the intrastate rivalry with Auburn makes passion for the sport there perhaps unmatched anywhere in the country. Desperate to return to what it believed its birthright among college football's elite, the Crimson Tide lured Nick Saban away from the Miami Dolphins in 2007. Saban, who coached defensive backs at Ohio State in 1980–1981, had led LSU to the national championship in 2003. If it was possible to exceed the Tide's high standards in Tuscaloosa, Saban did it with those three championships in four years.

By doing so, Saban was probably the only college coach considered above Meyer in the pecking order, and he had a $7 million annual contract as proof of his status. Meyer's Florida teams had an intense rivalry with Alabama. It was after the 2009 SEC title game loss to the Crimson Tide that Meyer had the chest pains that would hasten his departure from Gainesville. Meyer and Saban are similar in personality—extremely competitive, intensely focused and driven, mostly uninterested in small talk. But their personal relationship is warm. At SEC coaches meetings, Meyer said, they would sit together. They talk periodically on the phone. Shelley Meyer and Saban's wife, Terry, both of whom are more outgoing than their husbands, get along well.

"He has a strong belief in what's right and wrong with college football—the NFL and agents and things he's had to deal with,"

Meyer said. "Obviously, we're very competitive in recruiting and on the field. But he has always treated me really well."

As game-planning started for Alabama, Meyer had to decide whether to devote some time and resources to advance scouting for a potential championship-game matchup with Oregon or Florida State. Meyer decided that he needed everybody on his staff focused strictly on Alabama. "It's all hands on deck," Meyer said. "I didn't even know who was in the other game."

*   *   *   *

THE 2014 ALABAMA TEAM wasn't quite the juggernaut that its recent national championship editions were. The Crimson Tide lost at Ole Miss 23–17 on October 4. They had a close call at Arkansas, escaping 14–13. They were extremely fortunate to survive at LSU. Alabama won in overtime 20–13 after the Tigers blew a chance to win in regulation. With the game tied, LSU had the ball at the Alabama 6 with a minute left before settling for a field goal after an unsportsmanlike-conduct penalty. The Tide then drove for a tying field goal to stay alive. In the Iron Bowl against Auburn, the Tide had to rally from being down 36–27 before prevailing 55–44. Alabama's only regular-season league blowout was a 59–0 rout of an imploding Texas A&M team. But Alabama's lack of dominance was mainly chalked up to the overall strength of the SEC West. In the first College Football Playoff rankings, teams from that division had four of the top six spots, with Alabama at No. 6.

Meyer drew on his SEC ties and friendships to learn as much as possible about Alabama. He had a long conversation with one of his protégés, Mississippi State coach Dan Mullen, whose team had lost 25–20 to the Tide. Though Alabama didn't dominate their opponents the way it had in recent years, the Tide revealed few flaws when Ohio State coaches studied them on video. One of Meyer's few disappointments from a player-improvement standpoint in

208 | THE CHASE

2014 was the failure of Ohio State's backup defensive linemen to develop enough to relieve some of the load from the starters. Alabama's depth on the defensive line stood out in stark contrast.

"I thought their interior D-line was phenomenal," Herman said. "You look at, 'Who can't we block? Who can we block?' There was one game we watched on video—a competitive game—and I think they had 10 different D-linemen who played a significant amount. We kind of were looking across at each other like, 'Are you fucking kidding me?' They're like clones of each other, and they're gigantic, and they're talented."

Buckeyes coaches decided to try to use Alabama's depth against the Crimson Tide. Because they weren't used to playing more than three plays at a time before asking for a sub, part of the game plan would be to go up-tempo as much as possible to prevent those substitutions. As for running the ball, well, the Buckeyes weren't so optimistic. Alabama had yielded fewer than 89 rushing yards per game in 2014. "We all thought we would have to throw it to win it, that running the ball was an exercise in futility," Herman said.

Alabama's cornerbacks were considered the Crimson Tide's weak link on defense, not that they were awful. But at least it was a starting point. The problem for Ohio State, according to conventional wisdom, was that exploiting that weakness would be difficult. Give Saban time to prepare, and he'd find ways to confuse and rattle an inexperienced quarterback. Wisconsin had one week to prepare for Cardale Jones, with virtually no significant video to study for tendencies. Alabama had three weeks and a full game to dissect, even if it was a 59–0 blowout.

Jones wasn't too worried about that. "That program, the type of guys they have and the type of man [Saban] is, he's not a guy to reinvent the wheel," he said. "He's not going to change everything up for one player. I could see if it was a receiver. They might double-team him. But because of a new quarterback? He's not going to."

Ohio State's defensive game plan centered on one player—Amari Cooper. The junior won the Biletnikoff Award as the nation's top wide receiver. He'd caught 115 passes for 1,656 yards and 14 touchdowns. Exceptionally polished, with excellent hands and breakaway speed, Cooper would be picked fourth overall by the Oakland Raiders in the 2015 NFL Draft. A year earlier in the Orange Bowl, Ohio State faced another receiver who'd go fourth in the next draft. Clemson's Sammy Watkins torched the Buckeyes with 16 catches for 227 yards. "Everything was designed to stop Amari Cooper," Chris Ash said. "When you watched them, he was their featured player. If you could shut him down, you were going to have a chance to hold the offense down. Everything we talked about defensively, it started from Sammy Watkins the year before. From talking to Coach Meyer and the guys, they did not have a good game plan to try to limit Sammy Watkins, and he had an explosive game."

The Buckeyes would have to be creative because Alabama offensive coordinator Lane Kiffin was inventive in deploying Cooper. This wouldn't be a case where they could stick Doran Grant on Cooper all night. It would have to be a team effort. Though Cooper was the headliner, the Crimson Tide had talent spread throughout their offense. Running back T.J. Yeldon was big and fast, though he was dealing with a nagging hamstring injury. Backup Derrick Henry, a 6'3", 241-pound sophomore, was just as dangerous as Yeldon. He ran for 141 yards as the primary runner in the SEC Championship Game win over Missouri. The offensive line was big and powerful. Fifth-year senior quarterback Blake Sims was the biggest question mark for the Tide entering the season. AJ McCarron had been the starter for three seasons. Throughout his college career, Sims bounced from position to position in a mostly unsuccessful quest for playing time. He was considered a longshot to win the quarterback job in 2014, but he prevailed over Florida State transfer Jake Coker and others. Sims' grip on the job remained a bit tenuous even as he threw for a school-record 3,250 yards. Saban had Coker warm up after Sims threw three interceptions against Auburn but didn't make a switch. Sims rebounded in the SEC championship. He completed 23 of 27 passes for 262 yards and two touchdowns.

With Sims seemingly back on track, Alabama looked poised to keep rolling. Alabama was installed as a nine-point favorite over Ohio State. The Buckeyes had been underdogs against Michigan State and Wisconsin. That didn't faze them. "I'd always wanted to play a big-time SEC team," Taylor Decker said. "For the past however-many years, Alabama has been that measuring mark to see how good you are. If we were going to show we were capable of being national champions, that's how I wanted to do it. I wanted to beat the No. 1 team in the country ranking-wise and leave no doubt that we could play at that level.

"People talk about the SEC bias, and they are an amazing conference from top to bottom. It's deserved. But I don't think there's as big a gap with other conferences as everyone says there is. I think we wanted to show at Ohio State that we could play with the powerhouse in the country, which is Alabama."

Certainly, Jones did. He'd waited three years for the opportunity he now had. Hearing day after day about Alabama and the SEC's dominance stoked his growing fire. "Let's be honest, they were the kings of college football for a lot of years," Jones said. "[We] were hearing what we couldn't do, all these great players they have, [that] this was a scrimmage for them for the national championship game. All that stuff pissed me off. I was like, 'Okay, they're about to see.' I really, really developed a strong hate for them out of nowhere."

But history had not been kind to Ohio State against SEC teams. The Buckeyes were 0–9 against that conference in bowl games until beating Arkansas in the 2011 Sugar Bowl, a victory that was later vacated by NCAA sanctions. Ohio State was 0–3 against Alabama.

With Braxton Miller (top left) and J.T. Barrett (top right) sidelined, Cardale Jones (12, below) got his first career start against Wisconsin. All he did was lead the Buckeyes to a 59–0 demolition of the Badgers, propelling Ohio State into the first College Football Playoff.

(Kyle Robertson [*top*], Jonathan Quilter [*below*])

zekiel Elliott, running for an 81-yard touchdown against Wisconsin, gained more than 200 ards in each of the three postseason games. (Eamon Queeney)

Michael Bennett grabs his jersey after making a tackle against Wisconsin. Bennett, normally No. 63, switched to 53 in honor of walk-on Kosta Karageorge, who died before the Michigan game. No. 53 also adorned Buckeyes helmets. (Kyle Robertson)

Redshirt freshman cornerback Eli Apple (13) overcame a health issue in early 2014 to become a key member of the Buckeyes' secondary. (Adam Cairns)

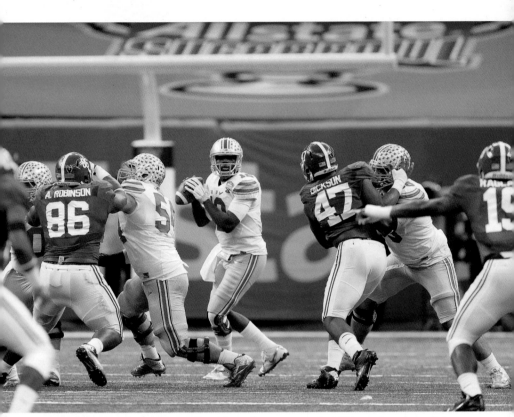

Cardale Jones showed against Alabama that his performance against Wisconsin was no fluke. Of course, it helped that "the Slobs" protected well for him. (Jonathan Quilter)

Steve Miller (88) dreamed about returning an interception for a touchdown against Alabama. His 41-yard pick-six put Ohio State ahead 34–21 late in the third quarter. (Kyle Robertson)

acrobatic catch of Evan Spencer's pass cut Alabama's one-time 15-point lead to only a 21–20 deficit at halftime. (Jonathan Quilter)

Ezekiel Elliott's 54-yard run on Ohio State's first possession against Alabama was the first sign that the Buckeyes could spring the upset. (Eamon Queeney)

Urban Meyer and Buckeyes players hoist the Sugar Bowl Trophy after Ohio State's 42–35 victory over the Crimson Tide, sending them into the College Football Playoff National Championship game. (Kyle Robertson)

Cardale Jones' arm wasn't his only weapon against Oregon. Though the Buckeyes had no bona fide backup for him, Jones was not afraid to use his 250-pound body in the run game. (Jonathan Quilter)

After yielding a touchdown on the game's first possession, Ohio State's defense swarmed Oregon. Here, Adolphus Washington sacks the Ducks' Heisman Trophy–winning quarterback, Marcus Mariota. (Jonathan Quilter)

Ezekiel Elliott's touchdown run caps Ohio State's amazing postseason run. (Jonathan Quilter)

Urban Meyer (bottom), with wife Shelley beside him, celebrates the national championship as Jeff Heuerman looks on with delight. (Adam Cairns) *Heuerman (right) lifts up Jacob Jarvis after the Buckeyes completed their improbable run to capture the first College Football Playoff title.* (Kyle Robertson)

Curtis Grant, holding his son, A.J., sits with (from left to right) Jeff Heuerman, Nick Vannett, and Cardale Jones as teammates celebrate behind them. (Eamon Queeney)

The 2014 national champions. (Kyle Robertson)

Meyer knew that the psychological battle might be as big as the physical one. He told his players that they could compete against the best of the SEC, but he was a few years removed from coaching against those teams. So he enlisted Ash, who had coached at Wisconsin and Arkansas. His message to the players was simple: there's perception and there's reality.

"'The perception is that we're not as good as these other teams,'" Ash said he told them. "'The reality is that we are and we can be better. How do we know that? Because I'm the only one who's been in both seats. I've been in the Big Ten. I was in the SEC just a year ago. I don't care what the media is saying. I don't care what coaches are saying. I have a different perspective than Urban Meyer or Nick Saban or [ESPN analyst] Kirk Herbstreit or whoever it may be. I was just there and now I'm here.'

"I felt confident. I don't know how much confidence there was in some of the players because all they heard was how great Alabama was and how good the SEC is, and nobody else plays good football. I'm sure at some point these guys had doubt. Could we really beat Alabama? My message to them was, yes, we can."

The Buckeyes flew to New Orleans on December 27. Their hotel was around the corner from the French Quarter and Bourbon Street. For college kids, that can be a minefield of temptation. The Buckeyes all but swore it off. Most of them made only token visits. Michael Bennett said the seniors imposed a 10:00 PM curfew on their teammates most nights. "We're not here to enjoy Bourbon Street," he said. "We're here to win a national championship."

Columbus-based Austin Ward was the only one of 43 ESPN analysts to predict that Ohio State would beat Alabama. Bennett believed that the Tide's players arrived in New Orleans thinking the Sugar Bowl, just 300 miles from Tuscaloosa, would serve as almost a victory lap. "I don't think they took us seriously," Bennett said. "I think they watched ESPN a little too much. The week before, they were going out every night on Bourbon Street, hanging out. You're not genuinely preparing for a football game. Not their whole team or anything like that, but maybe a good amount of their players would go out and live it up."

As the game approached, Ohio State's confidence grew. The team was practicing well, particularly Jones. Meyer said the quarterback's practice at the Superdome three days before the game was one of the best he'd ever seen one of his quarterbacks have, other than Alex Smith and Tim Tebow. "It wasn't just how he was throwing the ball," Meyer said. "We had [pumped-in] crowd noise in there. It was management of practice. I remember walking off the field with Tom saying, 'Wow!' The same kid I said was a bona fide nut was leading our team and doing a magical job doing it. It was his team, like really *his* team."

The Buckeyes were ready, and before the game, they got an extra boost of confidence. Ohio State and Alabama played the final game of New Year's Day. The Buckeyes had the whole day to watch their Big Ten brethren in their bowl games. Ten Big Ten teams played in bowl games. All 10 were underdogs. That wasn't too surprising given the conference's dismal bowl record in recent years. Rutgers and Penn State won their second-tier games earlier in the week, but January 1 looked like it might be a bloodbath. The day started as predicted. Missouri beat Minnesota 33–17 in the Citrus Bowl. The two big ones were Michigan State against Baylor in the Cotton Bowl and Wisconsin against Auburn in the Outback Bowl. The Spartans rallied with three touchdowns in the fourth quarter to stun Baylor 42–41, an outcome that took a little air out of the argument that the Bears should have been in the College Football Playoff. Wisconsin was a touchdown underdog against Auburn, in part because the Badgers were in the midst of a coaching change. Gary Andersen abruptly resigned as Badgers coach days after the loss to Ohio State to take the Oregon State job. "I was stunned," Meyer said. "I had no idea. I called him the next day and said, 'What in the heck is that?'"

Wisconsin athletic director and former coach Barry Alvarez reluctantly agreed to fill in for Andersen, who would later cite Wisconsin's strict academic standards as the prime reason for his departure. After the humiliating loss to the Buckeyes, not much was expected from the Badgers in the bowl game under the circumstances. Instead, Wisconsin was up to the challenge. Melvin Gordon, whom the Buckeyes had suffocated, ran for 251 yards and three touchdowns. After the Tigers scored a touchdown to go ahead 31–28 with three minutes left, Wisconsin drove for a tying 29-yard field goal to send the game to overtime. The Badgers kicked a 25-yard field goal in overtime and then stuffed Auburn, forcing a 45-yard field goal that missed, giving Wisconsin a 34–31 victory.

The Badgers had given Meyer the last bit of motivation he needed. Playing on the same themes that Ash had hit, he told his players that they now had proof they could play with an SEC team. The team that they had just crushed 59–0 had beaten an Auburn team that led Alabama by nine points in the second half. "I went crazy," Meyer said of his speech to the team. "I went on the whole perception-versus-reality thing. There's a perception we can't run. There's a perception we're not very good. There's a perception about the Big Ten conference. Then there's the reality. The reality just happened."

The rest of the world may not have thought Ohio State had a chance. The Buckeyes themselves certainly did. They got another lift from Ohio State fans when they left their hotel to board the bus to the Superdome. "We were coming out of the hotel, and there had to be 5,000 people saluting us on our way to the game," Meyer said. "It was overwhelming. I remember that the players were, like, Wow. It was a Super Bowl atmosphere."

The moment they'd worked so hard for and seemed so unlikely had arrived. The Buckeyes were going to find out just how good they really were.

21

SWEET SUGAR

AS SOON AS HE KNEW Ohio State would play Alabama, Urban Meyer projected what it would take to pull off the upset.

"I thought we'd have to play perfect," he said.

If Meyer had known all that would go wrong in the first 22 minutes against the Crimson Tide, he might not have bothered to make the trip. If the previous couple weeks—heck, the whole season—had been a test to see how much the Buckeyes could endure, the start of the Alabama game was a microcosm of that.

Ohio State won the coin toss—thanks to Jacob Jarvis, who told Jeff Heuerman to pick tails, as always—and forced a three-and-out on Alabama's first possession. Doran Grant had tight coverage on a third-down incompletion to Amari Cooper. As he would all night, Alabama punter JK Scott pinned the Buckeyes deep in their own territory with a 53-yard punt.

The Buckeyes would suffer a blow on their very first snap. On a four-yard run, Jeff Heuerman sprained his ankle blocking when got tangled with Alabama defensive end Jarran Reed. It was the latest in a series of injuries that had beset Heuerman all season. First he was slow to come back from the Lisfranc foot injury. Then he'd been kicked in the shin in practice, which, according to the doctors, had hit a nerve in just the wrong spot, causing numbness. Tight ends coach Tim Hinton said that Heuerman had played the second half of the season with a numb foot. But that didn't keep Heuerman out. "Because he's tougher than hell," Hinton said. "He was able to play because he's tough."

Heuerman played some the rest of the way against Alabama, but Nick Vannett took the vast majority of snaps. On Ohio State's second play, Evan Spencer almost made a spectacular catch. In double-coverage, he leaped and made a one-handed grab, but the ball hit the Superdome turf as he landed. It was just a hint of what Spencer would do this night. Jones spun away from a tackle for a 12-yard gain on third-and-6 for a first down, and Jalin Marshall ran for 13 on the next snap.

On second-and-13, Ezekiel Elliott made the first huge play of the game. He took a handoff and went right. Center Jacoby Boren pulled and blocked linebacker Trey DePriest. With his still-sore left wrist, Elliott stiff-armed cornerback Eddie Jackson. All-America safety Landon Collins had the angle on Elliott near the sideline, but he stumbled on the turf and Elliott hurdled him. Suddenly, he had nothing but open space in front of him. Elliott ran for 54 yards before he was pushed out of bounds at the 5. The Buckeyes crowd, outnumbered by the Crimson Tide's but just as vocal, erupted.

But instead of being the first step in taking control of the game, the play set up the first disappointment of many in the first half for Ohio State. Jones was tackled for a loss on first down, threw an incompletion on second, and then wisely threw the ball away under pressure on third down. The Buckeyes had to settle for a field goal.

After Corey Smith pinned Alabama at its 12-yard line with a tackle on the ensuing kickoff, the Buckeyes forced another three-and-out, only to have a chance at favorable field position taken away with another booming punt by Scott, this one 73 yards. Then disaster struck. Elliott ran for what would have been a first down, but Jackson punched the ball out from Elliott's grasp and Collins recovered. On the second play, Derrick Henry broke free on the left side for a 25-yard touchdown run to put Alabama ahead 7–3.

The pattern had been set. Ohio State moved the ball but couldn't take full advantage and would be beset by turnovers, while Alabama cashed in on its chances. On the Buckeyes' next possession,

Jones, who'd started 0-for-5 passing, threw a perfect pass to Devin Smith, who caught the ball going out of bounds at the 1. But again the Buckeyes would be thwarted. Jones bobbled the snap on first down and was tackled for an eight-yard loss. After a short completion to Vannett, Jones' hard third-down pass glanced off Jalin Marshall, forcing another field goal.

Alabama's run game, which started cranking on its short touchdown drive after Elliott's fumble, kept rolling. The Tide gained chunks of yardage on the ground before Sims threw to Cooper for a 15-yard touchdown. After the teams exchanged punts, Ohio State started to move the ball until Jones threw the first interception since taking over the job. He and Devin Smith had a miscommunication. Jones thought Smith was going to break off his route, but Smith kept going. Cornerback Cyrus Jones read the play and made the easy pick, returning it 32 yards to the Ohio State 15. T.J. Yeldon converted a fourth-and-1 at the 6 and then scored on the next play.

Alabama led 21–6. More than eight minutes remained in the second quarter, but the Buckeyes were flirting with disaster. With a couple of famous exceptions against Auburn, Saban's Alabama teams simply didn't squander big leads. Instead, the Tide usually acted like a boa constrictor, methodically and mercilessly squeezing the life out of their opponents. In fact, Ohio State hadn't rallied to win from 15 points or more behind since it came back from 31–0 down against Minnesota in 1989.

But the Buckeyes' belief in themselves did not waver.

"When we were down 21–6, I felt completely comfortable, and I got no vibes from the rest of the team that anybody was worried," Michael Bennett said. "You looked at guys on the sideline, and nobody's head was down, nobody was blaming each other, nobody was getting frustrated. All we did was look at each other and say, 'We've got to stop them, and the offense will get it together.' That kind of maturity from every single person was incredible to me."

*   *   *   *

THE BUCKEYES' COMEBACK began with a moment of immaturity by Alabama. After Reuben Foster tackled Curtis Samuel on the ensuing kickoff return, the Tide's Maurice Smith stood over Samuel, drawing a taunting penalty. The Buckeyes would get to start at their 29 instead of their 14. That might not sound like a big deal, but it would be. Thanks mostly to Scott's punting, the 29 was Ohio State's second-best starting field position of the entire game.

The drive began with a couple of 26-yard, third-down completions from Jones to Marshall. The first came on third-and-10 when, as the pocket began to collapse, Jones threw a dart on a crossing route for a 26-yard gain. The second moved the ball to the Alabama 18.

Elliott broke a tackle on a swing pass to move the ball to the 5. On second-and-goal, Boren, who'd played through ankle and shoulder issues all year, looked like he had suffered an injury that might knock him out for good. While blocking Trey DePriest, Boren got his legs rolled up when Pat Elflein inadvertently pushed Jarran Reed on him. Then DePriest gave Boren a couple of shoves, stretching Boren's legs past what looked like the breaking point. "It looked like he should have torn his ACL," Taylor Decker said.

It turned out that there was a bit of history between DePriest and Boren. DePriest is from Springfield, Ohio, and played against Boren's Pickerington Central team in high school. "I actually ended up getting ejected from one of the games," Boren said. "It was my sophomore year, I think. We were going at it back and forth, and I ended up getting caught [giving] a cheap shot."

Boren said he had forgotten about the incident before the Sugar Bowl. DePriest hadn't. "He tried to break my ankle after he was twisting on it," DePriest said of the high school incident. "I tightened up so he wasn't able to move it."

Now he had a chance to exact some payback. According to DePriest, Boren pushed him after the whistle, though replays don't show that. As Boren lay on the ground and then as he hobbled to the sideline, Boren gave DePriest a piece of his mind. "The entire time he was walking off the field," Decker said, "he was screaming at every one of their players. 'You better watch out when I come back out on the field!' That's just him. That's his attitude when he's out on the field. He had very choice words for [DePriest] and pretty much their entire defense."

With Boren on the sideline, Pat Elflein moved from right guard to center and Chase Farris took his spot. The Buckeyes faced a critical third-and-goal from the 3. Another field goal would have been deflating. They got what they needed. Decker and Billy Price combined for a double-team block on D.J. Pettway, and Vannett blasted linebacker Xzavier Dickson to open a crease for Elliott to score with 2:55 left in the half.

"To me, one of the real untold stories of the game was Nick Vannett," tight ends coach Tim Hinton said. "He plays 85 percent of that game [because of Heuerman's sprained ankle]. The strength of that team is their defensive line, and we don't bat an eye. I thought Nick was phenomenal. The quarterback is the one everyone wants to talk about. I get that. But not only does that happen, but look what happens here with Nick. He played very, very well."

The touchdown made it 21–13. Momentum had switched, and the Buckeyes would maintain it for almost the entire rest of the game. Corey Smith made another huge tackle at the 10 on the ensuing kickoff return. DeAndrew White dropped a third-down pass to force a three-and-out by Alabama. After yet another great punt by Scott, Ohio State took over at its 23 with 1:32 left before halftime. With Boren back in at center, Jones quickly moved the Buckeyes downfield. Michael Thomas broke a tackle and got a first down to start the drive, but he hurt his hip on the play. "I jammed my knee into the ground and it went into my hip," Thomas said. "I had to come out. But after two plays, I was like, 'I can't be on the sideline, I've got to go.'"

Completions to Corey Smith and Vannett moved the ball to the Alabama 40. Jones then scrambled up the middle, shedding a tackle by Ryan Anderson near the line of scrimmage and gaining steam. Collins was waiting for him in the middle of the field. Poor guy. Jones lowered his shoulder and plowed him with his 250-pound body at the end of a 27-yard run. It was a risky play, considering the Buckeyes' lack of depth at quarterback. The only other scholarship quarterback was freshman Stephen Collier, who was redshirting. It would have had to have been an absolute emergency for Meyer to put him in. For the postseason, Marshall, a quarterback in high school, was the Buckeyes' backup.

None of that mattered to Jones. Earlier in the game, he hurdled an Alabama defender. "It wasn't going to stop me from playing the way I play," he said. "That's when you get hurt—when you try to take it easy or tip-toe around. [When people say], 'Stop jumping over people!' Nah, no." With a laugh, he added, "You have to play. You have to be you."

Jones threw the ball away when no one was open on the next play, stopping the clock with 19 seconds left. The Buckeyes then called a play that will be forever remembered. Jones took the snap and handed to Marshall to his left. Marshall went right as if to run a jet sweep but instead pitched to Spencer for what looked to be a double-reverse. Instead, Spencer stopped, planted his feet and threw to the front left corner of the end zone toward Thomas. Cyrus Jones had excellent coverage, but the throw was perfect, just over the cornerback's grasp. Thomas' catch was beyond perfect, if there is such a thing. He leaped to catch the ball and contorted his body so that his left foot barely stayed inbounds. Touchdown.

"I feel I can make the catch nine times out of 10 with someone on me," Thomas said. "If the ball is in the air, I'm going to get it or at least get a PI [pass-interference call]."

The play had originally been installed for the Michigan State game. "When we first put it in, Jalin and I tried it," Spencer said.

"My throw was better than his." So Spencer, though he'd never played quarterback, got the honors. Against Michigan State, though, Spencer didn't like what he saw, tucked the ball and ran. This time, he was going to let it fly.

"Leading up to that game, we ran it a lot," Spencer said. "We wanted to add a couple plays that we could have if we got into a jam. I put the throw on the money a lot in practice. I remember telling my mom and dad and brother when I got down there, 'Hey, we've got this play. Don't be surprised if you see me back there and let one go. If I get the opportunity, I'm throwing it. Trust me.'"

Meyer said the decision to call the play then—a risky call given the time and circumstances—was a collaboration between him and Tom Herman. He said Alabama is tough to throw against in the red zone because of their coverage, particularly with a month to prepare. Ohio State's inability to throw touchdown passes from inside the 10 on its first two possessions bore that out. "So you need something unusual," Meyer said. "It was a great call. It was a great play by two people. [Spencer] did it in practice. He's the guy you want in those situations. And I thought Mike Thomas earned the right, too."

The touchdown made it 21–20, and the Buckeyes went into halftime feeling as good as any trailing team could. The trick play had been the highlight, but the Buckeyes had proven they could go toe-to-toe with Alabama. If not for the two turnovers and failures on the early two possessions to score touchdowns instead of field goals, Ohio State would have been comfortably ahead. The Buckeyes outgained Alabama 348–139, the biggest disparity ever in a first half for a Saban-coached Crimson Tide team. Ohio State's offensive line had taken control of the game.

"We're using two run plays and we're getting six, seven yards a pop," Price said. "Then you start realizing they're not the invincible gods from the SEC. They're blockable. They're guys just like you and me."

From the press box, Herman was amazed. "I did not see the whole thing playing out the way that it did," he said. "You recognize the success you're having and you're, 'Okay, let's go.' I think a lot of that had to do with the tempo and Jacoby Boren, at 5'11" and 285–290 pounds, moving their nose [guard], who's 6'4", 320 pounds. It's like, 'We're on to something here, boys.' We're moving them around and keeping them on the field, and they're getting tired and they're not used to it."

Meyer, too, was skeptical before the game whether Ohio State's linemen could open holes against Alabama. That changed during the game. "One thing about our kids and our coaches is they're honest," Meyer said. "I can ask them, 'Can we block them?' and I can tell by the look in their eyes if they can. They felt we could."

It wasn't just the offense that was playing at a different level. The defense had risen to the challenge as well. It stopped Alabama on five of six third-down chances. Amari Cooper had the touchdown catch but was otherwise quiet. Chris Ash said the strategy was to use tight coverage on Cooper and have safeties help out on deeper throws. "We pressed Amari Cooper," he said. "Nobody else had done that all season. I think everybody else was scared. We pressed our corners on him. Most of the throws to Amari were short, quick throws, probably seven, eight yards or under. We wanted to take those away. We wanted to make the quarterback have to beat us. We didn't think Sims could throw the ball well enough into tight windows to beat us."

That proposition would be tested throughout the second half. Ohio State got the ball to start the third quarter and immediately established that halftime did not stunt its momentum. The Buckeyes got two first downs before facing third-and-8. Ohio State had already completed six third downs when needing at least eight yards, the most Alabama had surrendered in 10 years. Now the Buckeyes went for blood. Jones threw deep to Devin Smith, who was covered man-to-man by Eddie Jackson. That usually is a bad matchup for any defender against Smith deep. Smith got behind Jackson, who then fell. Smith made the easy catch and backpedaled into the end zone for a 47-yard score. The Buckeyes led 27–21, their first lead since it was 3–0.

Alabama started its next drive with an 18-yard keeper by Sims followed by an eight-yard run by Yeldon. Offensive coordinator Lane Kiffin then decided to throw the ball. Bad choice. Linebacker Darron Lee exploded into the backfield to sack Sims on second down. Bennett did the same on third. Scott unloaded a 65-yard punt, which was almost matched by Ohio State's Cameron Johnston. The Australian booted a 60-yarder downed by Devin Smith at the 1 after Ohio State's next drive stalled.

The Crimson Tide faced third-and-7 from their 36 when probably the least-heralded Buckeyes defender made the biggest defensive play of the season. Senior Steve Miller was a career backup from Canton until he was thrust into a starting role following Noah Spence's permanent ban, though he shared time with Rashad Frazier. "You talk about perseverance," defensive line coach Larry Johnson said of Miller. "A great, great worker—probably the guy who worked the hardest every single day. He gave everything he's got. Sometimes, he'd walk off the field exhausted. In games, he showed up and did some stuff that a guy at 255 pounds is not supposed to do against 300-pound tackles, but he did. At times he was overmatched, but his heart was like a lion's."

His work ethic extended to academics, Johnson said. The Buckeyes got back to Columbus after the Penn State game at about 1:00 or 2:00 AM. Instead of going to his apartment, Johnson said, Miller went straight to the defensive line meeting room and studied for an exam. "That's the kind of guy he was," Johnson.

In practice, Miller had told teammates that he would return an interception for a touchdown. "I had a vision about this," he said. "I caught one in practice when we were home, and I was like, 'Man, I've got to get one for the game.'"

Now was his time. Four years earlier when Ohio State played Arkansas in the Sugar Bowl, an unheralded defensive end, Solomon Thomas, dropped back in coverage in a zone blitz and made an interception to seal the Buckeyes' first-ever bowl win over an SEC team, even if it was later vacated. During preparation for this Sugar Bowl, defensive coordinator Luke Fickell remembered that call. Now the Buckeyes would do the same thing with Miller. As Sims dropped back to pass and looked for Cooper, Miller backpedaled into coverage instead of rushing. Sims did not notice him. Miller was right in front of Cooper, caught the ball and followed a caravan of teammates 41 yards for the touchdown. It was, Miller said, the first touchdown he'd ever scored at any level.

"It was pretty special," Johnson said. "We both had tears in our eyes. You were so happy for a guy who gave his heart and soul to the program. It really put an exclamation point to his career."

* * * *

THE BUCKEYES had scored 28 straight points and led 34–21. If it felt too good to be true for Ohio State, Alabama would quickly assert that it wasn't the No. 1–ranked team for nothing. Starting in a hole after Corey Smith—again—and Bri'onte Dunn leveled Alabama kickoff returner Christion Jones at the 16, Alabama quickly moved downfield. After a 15-yard pass to Cooper, Sims sidearmed a middle screen pass to Henry. He shook off an arm tackle by freshman middle linebacker Raekwon McMillan and wasn't pulled down until he gained 52 yards to the Ohio State 17. Four plays later, Sims ran up the middle for a five-yard touchdown to make it 34–28 late in the third quarter.

The Buckeyes failed to get a first down on their next possession. Alabama took over, and after an 11-yard completion to Cooper, Lee sacked Sims for a two-yard loss near the Alabama sideline.

During Christmas break, Lee had gotten sick and lost almost 10 pounds. He barely weighed 220 for the Sugar Bowl. But whatever he was lacking physically, he made up for with extra motivation. Throughout his early youth in Tennessee, Lee couldn't escape the constant talk about Alabama's greatness. Now he had a chance to play against the Tide. That morning, he and Joshua Perry started their day with 10 minutes of silence, just to let their resolve thicken. Finally, Lee spoke. "I said, 'I'm not leaving that field without a W,'" Lee said. "I don't care if I lose my legs, my arms. He's like, 'I'm right there with you.' I just really refused to be denied."

Lee had one extra little bonus goal in mind as well. He and his mom, Candice, were Tennessee Volunteers fans when they lived in Chattanooga. Lane Kiffin became the Vols' coach in 2008 at age 33, the youngest FBS coach at the time. But after only one season, Kiffin left Knoxville abruptly to accept the Southern Cal job. Tennessee fans were outraged, including the Lees. They decided that if the opportunity presented itself, Lee would let Kiffin know how he felt about that. After the sack of Sims, Lee found himself face to face with Kiffin and unburdened himself. "We just had some words," Lee said coyly. "He knows what I said. I'm not going to tell the world. My mom is the only one who knows, and she knows not to tell anybody. It was explicit. I'm not going to lie."

What was Kiffin's response? Lee said Kiffin asked, "Are you crazy?"

While one of Ohio State's brashest players got that off his mind, the player who'd been humbled more than probably any Buckeye was quietly having one of his best games. On third down, middle linebacker Curtis Grant tackled Henry well short of a first down to force a punt. It would be one of a team-high 10 tackles for him. Throughout the year, Grant had split time with McMillan, whom he steadfastly mentored. In the postseason, the Buckeyes would mostly stick with the senior, and he rose to the occasion.

"The greatest thing you can say is that throughout the year, he got better and better," said Fickell, whose position group is the linebackers. "I told Coach [Meyer] at the beginning of the year that everybody loves Raekwon, and I love Raekwon. I said that if Raekwon is the best, he'll play. But I said that I really hope Curtis Grant is our best guy because we'll be a better defense and a better team if Curtis Grant is the middle linebacker. Because I knew what we'd gone through. You want those guys who've failed and failed and failed. They keep failing forward. They've been through the hard times. You know they're that much more invested and have that much more to give, that much of an example to help lead and guide the people around him."

What helped as much as anything was the birth of his son, A.J., in 2012. As A.J. grew, Curtis found his purpose. "Even though I lost my dad," he said, "I was like, 'My son still had a dad, and let's try to make up for things me and my dad won't be able to do." Grant matured so quickly and so much that his fellow linebackers called him "Pops."

"His career didn't go exactly the way he wanted to," Perry said. "He just kept fighting. He put others ahead of himself and wanted to be a great leader. He pushed Raekwon to be better than he is, which is something you'll never see happen. Guys aren't going to push a freshman and try to propel them into their position because it's good for the team. Guys are usually going to be selfish and do what's best for themselves. He's a great example of what it means to be a team leader."

* * * *

AFTER LEE'S SACK and Grant's tackle, Scott again pinned Ohio State deep with a 44-yard punt to the 9. The Buckeyes lost seven yards on their possession, forcing Johnston to punt with little room for error. Johnston has an uncanny knack for getting the ball to bounce perfectly, but this time it didn't. His punt took a huge backward bounce before Heuerman could down it at the Ohio State 23. All of a sudden, Alabama was in position to regain the lead.

But another Buckeye defender peaking late in the season would make a huge play. Safety Vonn Bell's signing out of Tennessee capped Ohio State's stellar 2013 recruiting class. He looked like a five-star player the first time he stepped on the practice field. "To me, he was one of the most talented members of our team," Mickey Marotti said. "The first day, you could see that with him just running around. This is what we're recruiting. Everybody look. This is what we want."

Strongly confident in himself, Bell invented something called the "Vonn Bell Academy." He insists that when his playing career is over, he will open such a place to teach football fundamentals. "My freshman year, we were doing drills, and I remember all the DBs were dropping passes," Bell explained. "I was the only one catching passes, and I said, 'Welcome to the VBA. I'll teach you how to catch.'"

But after a strong first impression, Bell's play slumped. He'd make dazzling plays but wasn't consistent. His practice habits, Meyer said, were "terrible." Ash believed that Bell wasn't properly focused on football, which Bell acknowledged was true. When he didn't start the season-opener against Navy, it got his attention. "It made me look in the mirror and made me think, 'Am I good enough?'" Bell said.

As the 2014 season progressed, so did Bell's performance. But the Alabama game was particularly special to him. Like Lee, Bell grew up in SEC country, and for two years he had to listen while so many people mocked him for choosing to play at a Big Ten school. When he went home to Chattanooga for two days during Ohio State's brief Christmas break, he saw T-shirts at the mall that read, "The Buckeyes Are Done." He soaked it all in.

"I prepared for that game so much it was crazy," Bell said. "It was insane. I practiced for that game like it was my last—getting up with Coach Ash every morning watching extra film, finding the indicators on Amari Cooper. I knew I was going to have to help Eli or Doran."

Early in the game, Bell was beaten on a reception by tight end O.J. Howard, who's one of Bell's closest friends. "I told him I'm getting him back," Bell said.

He would be true to his word. On a play-action pass, Sims rolled right. For a second, it looked like he had Howard open near the goal line. Bell was ready. He swooped over in front of Howard and made the interception.

"Coach Ash and I watched that play over 20 times," Bell said. "I knew when they got close to the red zone, it was one of their favorite plays. I knew they were going to run that play. I almost dared them to throw it. When you look at a formation and see the indicators, Coach Ash always tells you to take a picture of the play and you know it's coming. I took a snapshot in my head. This is where we are, close to the end zone. Get ready to make a play. And that's what I did."

* * * *

IT WAS AS CLOSE AS Alabama would come to regaining the lead. Ohio State had to punt on its possession. When Alabama made contact with Johnston, the ref threw a flag. The Buckeyes thought it would be a roughing-the-punter penalty, which would result in an automatic first down. Instead, it was ruled running into the kicker, which doesn't. A furious Meyer, the former pro baseball player, tossed his headset on the sideline. But Alabama's drive ended when Lee stuffed Sims for a three-yard loss. Ohio State took over at its own 5 with 5:24 left after another excellent punt by Scott.

Jones bulled for a first down on third-and-1 to the 15. That ended a stretch of 19 minutes without a Buckeyes first down and set the stage for the play that proved to be the back-breaker. It was a simple handoff to Elliott, who started left, looking for a seam. He found it, but not in the way the play was designed. Evan Spencer was lined up wide left. He knew he was supposed to block after going in motion, but he didn't see the signal to start moving from Jones.

"We screwed up the play pretty badly," Spencer said. "I don't know if Cardale checked it and I missed something when I read the defense and they changed the play. Cardale checked to something else where I wasn't motioning and I didn't know that. I kept looking. *Cardale, send me in motion, dude.* Then, all of a sudden, he claps his hands and snaps the ball. And I'm like, *Ah, shit, he forgot.* That's what I thought at first. I was panicked. I ran in there and saw Zeke hadn't hit the hole yet. I thought I could still get the guy if we ran the play we were going to run. I'm like, *Screw it, I'm going to go in there and hit him as hard as I can.*"

Spencer did more than that. Not only did he block linebacker Shaun Dion Hamilton, a freshman forced into action because of Tide injuries, but Spencer also took out DePriest with the same block. Price, Decker, and Vannett on the left side of the line blocked their guys out of the play. Elliott was barely touched, if at all, and off he ran for an 85-yard touchdown.

"That play epitomizes that kid because whatever he could physically do to do his job, he was going to do it," wide receivers coach Zach Smith said of Spencer. "So he cracked the linebacker, took out the [other] linebacker, and the rest is history."

Jones laughed about the miscommunication. He said that, when he looked over at Spencer, the receiver was looking at the cornerback lined up against him.

"I didn't want to be like, 'Yeah, come in motion! Come on! Come on!'" Jones said. "I believe he knew what he had to do. It actually worked out because if he would have gone in motion, his corner would have fallen off him a little bit" and been in position to make a tackle.

Jones threw to Michael Thomas for the two-point conversion to make it 42–28 with 3:24 left. The Superdome felt like it would explode from the cheering from Ohio State fans. Victory over mighty Alabama seemed assured. Of course, in a season when little came easily, the final three and a half minutes had more drama than the Buckeyes wanted. Christion Jones returned the kickoff to the 35. After an incompletion, Ohio State surrendered the only thing it shouldn't have—a deep pass. Tyvis Powell bit on a double move, allowing DeAndrew White to race behind him for a 51-yard gain before Bell pulled him down at the Ohio State 14. The Buckeyes forced fourth-and-2. Just before the snap, Fickell and Bell tried to call timeout, but officials didn't see them. Sims threw to Cooper, who beat Eli Apple on a slant for the six-yard touchdown to make it 42–35.

Alabama attempted an onside kick and executed it almost perfectly. Just as it's designed, but seldom done, the ball took one short hop and then a big one, allowing the Crimson Tide to converge. But again, Spencer rose to the occasion, literally. He timed his leap perfectly and grasped the bottom of the ball and fell to the turf before Alabama had a chance to pry it loose.

"Unbelievable play," Meyer said. "That's why he's the MVP."

Meyer may have become a little too enamored with Spencer in the moment, because he made a decision that he feared would come back to haunt him. Just 1:57 remained, and Alabama had only two timeouts left. Alabama packed the line of scrimmage expecting a run play, like everyone else did. Except Meyer saw one-on-one coverage, and his proclivity to go for the kill won out. He called for a deep pass. If Devin Smith were in the game, that might have been less questionable. But he wasn't. The target was Spencer, not known as a deep threat. Spencer couldn't get separation on Cyrus Jones and the ball fell incomplete.

"I thought for sure we'd get pass interference because I didn't think they'd be thinking it, either," Meyer said. "Then the second worst thing [other than a turnover] happens. Incomplete pass and the clock stops. You just have a knot in your stomach the next three minutes. It seems like six hours trying to get the game over with."

It wasn't only fans who wondered about the wisdom of the call.

"Even Shelley asked me about that one. 'Why did you do that? A lot of people are pissed you did that,'" Meyer said. "I said, 'I'd do it again.'"

He paused.

"Maybe."

The Buckeyes did run the ball the next two plays to force Alabama to burn its final timeouts. Johnston's punt was fair-caught at the Crimson Tide 18 with 1:33 left. Sims completed a third-down pass to White for 12 yards and ran for 12 himself to midfield. A pass to Howard moved the ball to the Ohio State 42 with 15 seconds left. Sims then threw a deep pass to White into double-coverage by Apple and Bell that fell incomplete with eight seconds left.

Alabama decided to throw a Hail Mary. Steve Miller applied late pressure but Sims got the ball off. Four Buckeyes surrounded two Alabama receivers—neither of them Cooper—in the end zone, and Powell caught the ball. Then, just to induce one more bit of drama, he brought the ball out of the end zone instead of taking a knee. "They taught us to score," Powell explained with his ever-present laugh. "You don't get that many opportunities to get the ball on defense. So when you get the ball in your hands, you say, 'I've got to make the most of it.'"

His position coach, uh, disagreed. "I wanted to strangle him," Ash said. "We coach it every week. We have a way we're going to handle those situations. Tyvis got caught up in the moment, and all he could think about was ESPN highlights and how he wanted to be on an ESPN highlight. He was celebrating and cheering post-game, and the only thing I was trying to do was find him. I grabbed him and said, 'If you ever do that again, you're going to have a foot up your rear.' I remember standing up in the press box yelling at the glass, hitting the glass, shouting 'Go down! Go down! What are you doing?! Go down!'"

Powell finally was tackled at the Ohio State 29. The improbable had happened. Ohio State had beaten Alabama. This was no fluke. The Buckeyes gained 537 yards, including 281 on the ground. Elliott ran for a Sugar Bowl–record 230 yards on only 20 carries behind a line that had silenced any remaining doubters. For the linemen, it was a matter of pride.

"Top to bottom, they were the best defensive line I'd ever played against," Decker said. "The thing we hung our hat on was being able to run the ball on people, regardless. We were going to try to assert our will and try to run the ball. I felt it was strength versus strength. Those guys were hard to move and played hard. They were 10 guys deep on their defensive line. They were rotating guys through like crazy. I probably played against four or five defensive ends. There wasn't a letup when they subbed."

And still, the Buckeyes moved the ball at will except for that long lull in the second half. Jones barely completed more than half of his passes—18 of 35—but except for the one interception on the miscommunication with Devin Smith, he avoided mistakes. Jones also ran for six first downs, many of them crucial.

It was a triumph of game-planning as well. Alabama ran the ball effectively, but Lane Kiffin didn't stick with it. Running backs T.J. Yeldon and Derrick Henry averaged 6.2 yards per carry, but they combined for only 23 carries. Sims threw 36 times. That imbalance had many Tide fans grumbling afterward. It came as no surprise to Ash. "We knew they weren't going to do it consistently enough," Ash said. "We knew we were going to give up some things in the run game."

For every game, Ash said, coaches identify the one opposing player who's capable of beating the Buckeyes with a big game. Against Wisconsin, it was Melvin Gordon. Against Alabama, it was Cooper, who would finish with nine catches and two touchdowns but only 71 receiving yards. He didn't have a catch longer than 15 yards.

But Cooper was the focal point of the Alabama offense. As a result, Ash said the Buckeyes knew the Tide wouldn't stick with what was working—the run game. "And they didn't, because Amari Cooper was the best wide receiver in college football. They were going to try to get him the ball because he's the best player in college football."

Afterward, the Buckeyes were, as to be expected, jubilant. Elliott, who would be named the Sugar Bowl's outstanding offensive player, jumped on Meyer from behind and gave him a bear hug as the coach walked to shake hands with Saban. Elliott had been overlooked all season. He was only honorable mention by the media for All–Big Ten consideration. The coaches ignored him entirely in their voting. (In fairness, it had been a banner year in the conference for running backs with Melvin Gordon, Indiana's Tevin Coleman, and Nebraska's Ameer Abdullah, among several other worthy players.)

But Elliott hadn't forgotten that slight or the others before the Sugar Bowl. "[Hall of Fame running back] Barry Sanders said before the game, there were two great running backs that were going to play tonight, and they both were for 'Bama," Elliott said after the game. "I felt a little bit left out."

During the awards presentation, Elliott, ever the goofball, did what became known as "salmoning." While the Sugar Bowl president congratulated Meyer, Elliott motioned his hands like a fish swimming upstream. Pat Elflein had started it long before, and other linemen had picked up on it. Elliott made it a thing. Darron Lee, who had seven solo tackles, including two sacks and another tackle for a loss—not to mention the oral takedown of Kiffin—was the game's outstanding defensive player, all 220 pounds of him.

"You don't want to try to rank the best wins you've ever been a part of, but if that wasn't the best, that was one of them," Meyer said. "It was almost validation for everything these guys have done. You've been told for so long that you're not very good. Players start believing it. You start to fight that battle. You almost start to believe it. Are we good enough? And that just validated everything those guys did."

22

SOLVING THE MYSTERY

URBAN MEYER did not know the outcome of the Oregon–Florida State game when the Sugar Bowl's postgame news conference began. Told that Oregon had crushed the defending champion and undefeated Seminoles 59–20 in the Rose Bowl, he reacted with mock horror, pretending to bolt from his chair. "We gotta go," he deadpanned. "We gotta go get ready for that one."

Ohio State had done no preparation for the national championship game in Arlington, Texas. Alabama required every bit of the Buckeyes' attention. They would worry about the title game if they got there. They had gotten there. Now it was time to worry.

Oregon represented the cutting edge of 21st-century college football. Ohio State and Alabama had tradition. The Ducks, who changed their uniform style every game, almost gleefully flaunted that they didn't. They had a mostly undistinguished history until Rich Brooks became coach in 1977. When he arrived, the facilities were primitive. "No meeting rooms, no practice field," Brooks said. "We had five coaches in one room and four in another. My office was like a broom closet. It was, like, six-by-six."

Adjacent to the football building was a cemetery. "The joke was, 'Just look across. That's where all the former coaches are buried,'" Brooks said.

After one early "Civil War" victory over intrastate rival Oregon State, Brooks recalled, the team celebrated in a flooded locker room because the toilets had backed up. "We were standing in eight inches of sewage," he said. "It was unbelievable."

Things have changed in Eugene. Brooks slowly built the program into respectability. In 1989, the Ducks went to their first bowl game in 26 years, beating Tulsa in the Independence Bowl. When Brooks was hired by the St. Louis Rams, Mike Bellotti succeeded him and continued the program's rise. It helped, of course, that the Ducks have had a certain benefactor, Nike co-founder Phil Knight. An Oregon alum, Knight has spared no expense in turning the team's facilities into the Taj Mahal of college athletics. In 2013 the Ducks unveiled a $68 million, 145,000-square-foot football headquarters, which included Italian marble, hand-woven rugs from Nepal, and meeting-room chairs made with the same leather used in Ferraris. The weight room has floors made of Brazilian Ipe wood, which is considered so dense that it can bend nails. Ohio State's 2014 locker room renovation was a keeping-up-with-the-Jones decision. Oregon was Mr. Jones.

Meyer considers Knight one of his close friends. He also is close with Chip Kelly, who was offensive coordinator under Bellotti before succeeding him in 2009. Kelly's ultra-up-tempo offensive style changed the game. The theory was that the best way to beat defenses was to exhaust them. Almost as soon as the ball was spotted, Oregon wanted to snap it.

Kelly took the Ducks to four straight BCS bowls. His 2009 team lost to Ohio State in the Rose Bowl in what might have been Buckeyes quarterback Terrelle Pryor's finest hour before the tattoo-and-memorabilia scandal engulfed him and the Ohio State program. After losing to Auburn in the BCS title game the next season, the Ducks beat Wisconsin in the Rose Bowl and Kansas State in the Fiesta Bowl. Kelly then was hired by the Philadelphia Eagles. Mark Helfrich, who was offensive coordinator under Kelly, took over and continued the same style.

Oregon hoped its 2014 season would be the one that finally put them on top of college football. Quarterback Marcus Mariota was the centerpiece. A gifted passer and runner, Mariota was a Heisman front-runner before the season, and he delivered on that promise, winning the trophy in December. Heading into the title game, he had thrown for 4,121 yards and 40 touchdowns—with only three interceptions—and run for 15 touchdowns. Mariota averaged 10.1 yards per pass attempt, best in the country.

Praised for his humble personality as well as his talent, he easily beat out Melvin Gordon and Amari Cooper for college football's most prestigious individual award. His supporting cast was overshadowed but effective. The offensive line overcame early injuries to become potent. Sophomore Thomas Tyner and freshman Royce Freeman provided an excellent running-back duo in support of Mariota. The receivers were a major question, though. Tight end Pharaoh Brown suffered a season-ending knee injury against Utah. Wide receiver Devon Allen was lost to a knee injury on the opening kickoff against Florida State. Darren Carrington filled that void against the Seminoles by catching seven passes for 165 yards and two touchdowns, only to be suspended for the title game after reportedly failing a drug test. That left Oregon perilously short of depth at receiver beyond Byron Marshall and Dwayne Stanford, a high school teammate of Adolphus Washington at Cincinnati Taft.

Oregon's defense didn't get much attention, but it was formidable. Arik Armstead, who would be a first-round NFL pick, and DeForest Buckner gave the Ducks two mammoth defensive ends in their 3-4 scheme. The back seven was solid if unspectacular, though the loss of All-America cornerback Ifo Ekpre-Olomu to a torn ACL in bowl practice stung.

"The challenge with them was the way they set up their defense with an odd front," Taylor Decker said. "We like to double-team people. With their odd front, it made it difficult to do that, especially with the tackles. It was going to be individual matchups instead of being able to double-team."

The Ducks had only one hiccup on the way to the championship game. On October 2, 24-point underdog Arizona stunned Oregon

31–24 in Eugene. Three offensive linemen didn't play because of injuries, and Mariota was also playing hurt after being sacked seven times the week before. That was the only game all season in which Oregon didn't score at least 38 points. The Ducks ranked second nationally in scoring (47.2 points per game) and third in total offense (552.9 yards). They also were second nationally in turnover differential (1.43 per game).

* * * *

THOSE WEREN'T THE numbers that scared Ohio State, which was pegged a touchdown underdog by Las Vegas. The one that did was 16. That was the number of seconds between snaps that Oregon averaged. The number 16 was posted all around the Woody during preparation.

"It was just a much different feeling going into that game," Meyer said. "Alabama was A to Z. This was going to be one issue: stop the tempo. Their whole system is that they want you to go run around the house three, four times and then go play. The fatigue factor. That's why they go so fast. If we can somehow eliminate that and make them block us and beat us with talent and fundamentals, we think we can beat them. But you had to eliminate 16."

After playing what Meyer described as a "sledgehammer" game against Alabama, the Buckeyes were physically spent. Nobody had ever done what Oregon and Ohio State were facing—winning an intense bowl game and then having to play another with everything at stake.

"It's your 22nd week of football, your 15th game," he said. "You have no depth left because we have some injuries to the backups. I talked to some of the guys I trust, and they said, 'Coach, we're hammered.' So we really backed off as far as the physical-ness of practice. But we had to fight the demon of every 16 seconds a snap."

The Buckeyes' defensive players went on a quick diet to lose a few pounds, which they hoped would help their endurance. "Five pounds makes a huge difference," Michael Bennett said. "When you drop from 295 to 290, you feel like a completely different person."

Facing a fast-paced offense wasn't a foreign concept to Ohio State's defensive players. That element is what Tom Herman had brought to the Buckeyes' offense. "We see that offense every single day," Darron Lee said. "That's what people kept selling short. And that's kind of why the defense was kind of laughing. We knew their plays because we see it every single day."

For all their concern about the task ahead, beating Alabama had removed any last bit of doubt the Buckeyes had about themselves. Chris Ash was on the Wisconsin staff that lost to Oregon in the Rose Bowl two years earlier. He had learned from the experience. "I felt very confident," he said. "I really felt that Alabama was a big hurdle for us to get by. They were a big, strong, physical team from the SEC. If we could get by that game, we could beat anybody. Our players' confidence was sky high. They knew they could play with anybody. Playing Oregon before, I felt confident in our plan.

"Coach Meyer probably doesn't remember this, but we got home from the Sugar Bowl, and a day or two later, we started our preparation for Oregon. I'd been watching Oregon enough. He came in and said, 'How do you feel?' I said, 'Coach, we're going to be just fine.' He said, 'Really?' I said, 'Yeah, coach. We'll be just fine.'"

The defensive game plan was to keep it simple. Coaches figured that if they tried to get complex with their schemes, players would think too much and not react quickly enough. The coaches just wanted the players to get lined up and play. Man for man, they liked the Buckeyes' chances if they could do that and not get sucked into the Ducks' fast-tempo vortex.

"Everybody was talking about their tempo, and speed this and speed that," Doran Grant said. "I was watching their film and I know the athletes we have. I'm pretty sure our whole team thought we were going to win. We were faster than them across the board. We had way more speed than they did. Somebody asked me, 'How was Oregon's speed?' I wasn't trying to be an asshole or anything, but I was like, 'What speed?' They weren't faster than us. It was just a tempo offense."

* * * *

ON THE FIRST DAY of preparation for Oregon, Kerry Coombs gave Ohio State players a cigar box. Each one was painted silver with a helmet stripe and Buckeye leaves. He called them mystery boxes. Coombs is Ohio State's special-teams coordinator as well as cornerbacks coach. Though Coombs took some of the brunt for the Buckeyes' pass deficiencies at the end of 2013, Meyer never lost faith in him. But when Ash was hired to oversee the entire secondary, many perceived that to be a demotion for Coombs. He didn't take it that way. Coombs and Meyer talked before Ash was hired about the change. "Chris was absolutely the right hire, and I understood," Coombs said. "Coach Meyer was clear about what he wanted to see. Our job was to implement it."

The more aggressive style was more in line with how Coombs coached at Colerain and at the University of Cincinnati, anyway. It's his personality. The fact that Coombs is in charge of special teams at all is a testament to Meyer's esteem for him. Meyer's pride and joy is the kicking game. He doesn't delegate that to just anyone.

"He's an incredible motivator," Meyer said. "He motivates me, which is not easy to do. He's one of the best coaches I've ever been around. Being a scheme guy does not make a good coach. To me, that's way down on the list. What makes a good coach is power of the unit, getting your unit to play and being creative and being able to motivate. He's way up there among the guys I've been around."

The Buckeyes' special teams were an often overlooked strength in 2014. With the notable exception of the Alabama game, Ohio State dominated field position. Thanks to the flawless long-snapping of Bryce Haynes, Cameron Johnston's punts, Kyle Clinton's kickoffs, and superb coverage units, Buckeyes opponents had the worst average starting field position in the country in 2014, according to footballoutsiders.com. The Buckeyes used starters in the kicking game more than most teams, but especially as injuries took a toll, backups became the core. Players like Gareon Conley, Craig Fada, Ron Tanner, Camren Williams, and Bri'onte Dunn were essential. Corey Smith, in particular, turned into a demon in kickoff coverage. "He's the best kickoff cover player I've ever seen in my life," wide receivers coach Zach Smith. "If he makes the decision to go hard, he cannot be blocked. I mean it is not possible. He can run—really run—and he's loose."

Special teams can be a thankless, dangerous task. Players race downfield at full-speed looking to launch their bodies as missiles. Other than the adrenaline rush, it's a mystery why anyone would want to do it. Two years earlier, that question came into stark relief. Ohio State was playing Wisconsin, trying to cling to a late seven-point lead after the Buckeyes' offense went into hibernation. Ohio State had to punt. Devin Smith, the gunner, blew past two blockers to tackle Jared Abbrederis, pinning the Badgers deep in their territory. "He went so hard that they didn't even touch him," Meyer said.

As coaches studied the tape, they marveled at Smith's determination to make the play. Here's a wide receiver, a position with a reputation for breeding prima donnas, and he does that. What compelled him to push himself so hard to make that play? Coombs was going to find out. He called it "solving the mystery." The answer boiled down to something Meyer called "selfless strain."

"We got real deep with it," Meyer said. "How do you be a good husband? You put your wife before you. How do you become a good father? You put your children before you. You're selfless. You're there for a greater purpose, which is the team. Why would you run down on kickoff? You're never going to get any notoriety.

"Then *strain*. Going as hard as you possibly can."

Each week in 2014, Coombs would come up with a different motivational theme, which would be represented by a trinket he gave players. For the Navy game, he gave them miniature anchors. For Michigan State, they got dog tags with the date of the game and the mission imprinted on them, in keeping with the military theme for that week. For the Sugar Bowl, Coombs used a World War II theme. New Orleans is the home of the National WWII museum. The amphibious boats, called Higgins boats, which were crucial to the successful landing on D-Day, were built there. Before the invasion at Normandy, with casualties expected to be terribly high, troops wrote postcards home expressing love to their family and explaining the importance of their mission. Coombs decided to have his players, who were the same age as many of those troops, do the same thing. He gave them postcards and asked them to write a note and mail it to someone special to them. Tyvis Powell, for example, wrote one to his high school coach, Sean Williams, who had pushed him so hard with those early-morning workouts in pursuit of an Ohio State scholarship offer. "I let him know that I was going to play for him," Powell said. "Everything in that game was going to be for him."

Coombs also gave the players little clickers that made a sound like crickets. Such clickers were used by D-Day paratroopers who parachuted in behind enemy lines on the eve of the invasion. "They landed at night and didn't know where they were," Coombs said. "Jumping out of a plane, you don't land right next to the guy who jumped out with you. So they're in the wilderness, in the dark. They hear noises and they don't know if it's friend or foe. If it was a friend, they'd double-click back. If they didn't hear a double-click on the other end, they shot, because it had to be the enemy."

The Buckeyes loved the clickers. All week in New Orleans, it sounded as if crickets surrounded the team. Meyer had a clicker as well. After Steve Miller's interception return for a touchdown gave the Buckeyes a 34–21 lead in the third quarter, Meyer pulled the clicker out of his pocket and began furiously double-clicking it.

"They all knew what they meant," Coombs said.

That was the play in which Corey Smith and Bri'onte Dunn almost obliterated Alabama's Christion Jones on a kickoff return.

*　*　*　*

AFTER GIVING PLAYERS their cigar box before the Oregon game, Coombs put the solving-the-mystery question to the players. What is it, he asked, that will cause you to deliver that selfless strain for the team? He told them they needed to fill their box with something meaningful to them. Walk-on linebacker Joe Burger put a letter from his grandfather with some holy water he had given Burger, Coombs said. Curtis Grant put in something that reminded him of his son, A.J.

"I collected the boxes before we left and then I filled them with a series of pictures of special-teams plays from the course of the year," Coombs said. "But in each kid's box, he didn't get any pictures of himself so that they understood that when they solved the mystery they were solving the mystery for their teammates. The idea was, and we talked about it a lot, that you can take this picture of Corey Smith when he's laid out above the ground and his chinstrap is up around his nose and his arm is outstretched and his arms are tackling the returner from Alabama, Christion Jones. There's nothing left. He's absolutely, literally laying everything he has on the line to make this play. Why did he do that? He did it for his team. He did it for his brothers.

"So as you sit there the night before the championship game, and you open your mystery box, you've got those things that are personal to you that you brought, and then you've got this visual representation of your team, your players, your brothers, the brotherhood of trust that you're going to go into battle with and battle for tomorrow night."

Then Coombs issued a challenge.

"I want you to flip through those pictures," he told them, "and I want you to contemplate what it is you will do for those young men. What commitment will you have for those men? What amount of selfless strain will you commit to the team?"

The players brought the cigar boxes to the national championship game and put them in their lockers. It was a final reminder of the bond they had forged. The final leg of The Chase had arrived.

23

COMPLETING THE CHASE

EVERY DAY AT PRACTICE during the 2014 season, Urban Meyer gathered his players on their practice field at the Woody Hayes so that they'd see the "THE CHASE..." banner that hung high above them for two years. At one of the Buckeyes' last practices before leaving Columbus for Dallas, the sign came down. One last mission remained, but not everyone would return with the team from Texas. Tom Herman would go straight from Dallas to Houston after the game to begin his new job. The seniors would soon be off to train for the NFL Combine. So the banner was brought down. Players and coaches were given Sharpies and asked to sign the banner.

"It was a really cool experience to finally have it down, to know we went on a journey two years long and we were coming to the end of it," Joshua Perry said. "It was pretty special for us. To be able to put your name down on it, knowing that as long as Coach Meyer is around it'll be up, it was pretty cool."

The players didn't scribble these autographs. "That's probably one of the best signatures I've signed," Evan Spencer said.

The Buckeyes flew to Dallas on January 9. Their practices had gone well, but every few snaps came a reminder of how precarious their situation was at quarterback. The Buckeyes really had no backup quarterback behind Cardale Jones other than Jalin Marshall, and he'd been an option quarterback in high school. "As we're getting ready for the national championship game," Meyer said, "we had friends at practice. Every third or fourth rep, you have to give it to Jalin. And he, our little 5'10" quarterback, skips one like 10 yards in front of the receiver. The guy looks at me and says, 'Are you ready for the national championship game? How do you like your quarterback?' and we started laughing."

As for Jones, he was as loose and confident as ever. The team stayed at the posh Hilton Anatole in Dallas. With so many fans around, the Buckeyes mostly kept to themselves when not at practice or meetings, especially the prominent players like Jones. "He didn't want to go downstairs because people kept rushing him," Michelle Nash said.

But the day before the game, some young boys wanted to see Jones. So he went to the second-floor balcony and signed Pop Warner footballs that they tossed up to him. Then Jones had them run patterns and threw passes to them. "I said, 'Cardale, please don't tell the little boys to run out there,'" Nash said, "because there was a big water fountain."

For at least a half hour, Jones tossed with them. Sure enough, one boy did in fact fall into the fountain. "They wanted to play catch," he said. "I wanted to play catch, too. There's a time to be serious and a time to be laid back. I'm not going to pass up an opportunity to relax."

Nash knew that a decade earlier, Jones could have been one of those boys, longing for someone like him to take an interest in him. "That just warmed my heart, him with these kids," Nash said.

* * * *

THE FIRST College Football Playoff National Championship was played at a site worthy of the event's magnitude. AT&T Stadium in Arlington, Texas, is nicknamed "Jerry World." It is as extravagant a football palace as would be expected from Jerry Jones, the owner of the Dallas Cowboys. It seats 85,000, with standing room for 20,000 more. The stadium cost $1.15 billion, one of the most expensive stadiums ever built. Its dominant feature is the four-sided, high-definition video board—the larger sideline screens each measuring in at a whopping 72 feet by 160 feet—hanging over the center of the field.

"It was a little bit surreal just being down there knowing what we were playing for," Perry said. "Then when you realized how big that stadium actually is, with the video board, how cool it is and state of the art. They had that little sports bar right down there next to the field. It was one of those deals like, if this isn't the coolest place to play a national championship…"

When they arrived at the stadium, Ohio State players, dressed in suits and ties, came out to survey the scene. After they went back to change, some of the walk-ons and injured players stayed by the bench. At one point, Texas governor and 2012 and 2016 presidential candidate Rick Perry started chatting them up. He even posed for pictures in the O-H I-O pose. The players had no idea who he was.

Jim Tressel was there, too. Three days before the game, Tressel had been voted into the College Football Hall of Fame, his NCAA violations notwithstanding. He is now the president of Youngstown State, where he coached before coming to Ohio State. He chatted amiably with reporters and posed for pictures with OSU band members. They knew who he was.

Tressel joined the other inductees for the pregame coin toss and got a loud ovation when introduced. Unlike in New Orleans, which is SEC country, Buckeyes fans were in the majority in Dallas. About two-thirds of the seats were filled by scarlet-clad fans. After shaking hands with Oregon's captains, Jeff Heuerman walked over and hugged Tressel, who had recruited him. What twisting paths both had taken to reunite at that moment.

Oregon won the toss and wanted the ball first. On the first drive, the Ducks looked every bit the offensive machine they were reputed to be. They went 75 yards for a touchdown, never even needing to convert a third down. Marcus Mariota, who was in complete command during the drive, avoided pass-rushers and found Keanon Lowe for a seven-yard touchdown pass.

"That was a knife through butter," Meyer said.

He was concerned. Chris Ash wasn't. "Not at all," Ash said. "Going through that first drive, Oregon ran enough plays so we had a feel for how they wanted to attack us. We got done with the first drive, gave up the touchdown, calmed the guys down, and said, 'Guys, we're fine. Settle down, play our game.'"

The offense needed time to find its groove as well. Jones powered for a first down on Ohio State's first series but was tackled short of it three plays later. Ohio State caught a break on Oregon's next possession. On third-and-3 from the Oregon 45, Charles Nelson dropped a pass from Mariota. The Buckeyes took over at their 3, and Jones narrowly escaped being sacked for a safety before throwing the ball away on second-and-8. Suddenly, the Buckeyes faced an important third down. If they didn't convert, Oregon would get the ball back with good field position. Another Ducks score, and, well, that was a scenario the Buckeyes didn't want to face.

Jones dropped back into the end zone with maximum protection—seven blockers—to fend off Oregon pass-rushers. No Duck got close to him. Jones found Corey Smith open and hit him near the sideline for a 26-yard gain.

"You talk about opposite ends of the spectrum from Virginia Tech when we counted on him and trusted him and he failed," wide receivers coach Zach Smith said, referring to his end-zone drop against the Hokies. "Now full circle to this. We trusted him to make the play, and he did. All the stuff I went through with that kid, it was almost like knowing that your child is about to have a chance to redeem himself, to succeed. I knew he could and would make the play. I wanted him to make it so bad, not to help win the game but for him to make the play."

Corey Smith's third-down catch ignited the Buckeyes' offense. On the next play, Jalin Marshall made a sensational play when he leaped and grabbed the ball off the back of Oregon cornerback Erick Dargan for another 26-yard gain. "We had been practicing that play in practice all week," Marshall said. "I always had to attempt a crazy catch and I always dropped it. I was determined to catch the ball. When it was up in the air, it was like it was in slow motion. I grabbed it and held onto it on the way to the ground."

Marshall showed his toughness four plays later when he bulled for a first down by the nose of the ball on fourth-and-2. After an incompletion, Jones handed off to Elliott. At first, it looked like a routine play. But Elliott followed the seal block of Nick Vannett to find a crease and then swerved past Dargan for a 33-yard touchdown to tie the score.

Once again, a dropped pass would haunt the Ducks on their next drive. On third-and-12 from the Oregon 28, Mariota avoided a sack, rolled right and spotted Dwayne Stanford wide open near the sideline at the Buckeyes' 40. Mariota's pass was right on target—and bounced right off of Stanford's hands.

Marshall broke several tackles on a 17-yard punt return to give Ohio State possession at the Oregon 46. The Buckeyes needed only four plays—plus a defensive pass-interference call against Troy Hill covering Devin Smith in the end zone—to go ahead. After Elliott ran for 17 yards to the 1, Jones threw to Vannett for the touchdown and a 14–7 lead.

Oregon looked powerless to stop Ohio State. Unfortunately for the Buckeyes, the Ducks wouldn't need to. Ohio State would stop itself with turnovers. The Buckeyes moved inside the Oregon 40 on their next possession when Jones and Elliott botched a handoff. Jones faked it to the running back, pulled the ball back, and then tried to give it back to Elliott after he had already started to block. Oregon recovered.

The Ducks drove inside the Ohio State 3, where they faced fourth-and-goal. Oregon decided to go for it. Mariota handed off to Thomas Tyner. For an instant, a hole opened in the middle of the line. But Curtis Grant came from the right and Tyvis Powell from the left and drilled Thomas just short of the goal line. "I was responsible for the B gap," Powell said, referring to the hole between the guard and tackle. "I'm reading the quarterback. Wherever the quarterback looks, I'm breaking to. When he handed it off, it was like the hole popped open. I said, 'Well, somebody's got to fill it.' I saw Curt running to it, and I'm running to it. I'm like, *Shoot, I've got to at least slow him down because it's wide open.* Then I saw everyone rallying to it, and I'm like, *We're good. We're good.*"

The Buckeyes then blew another scoring chance with another turnover. Jones hit Corey Smith in stride along the sideline. Smith caught the ball and had room to run, picking up another 20 yards down to the Oregon 15 before Troy Hill lowered his helmet and dislodged the ball. Oregon recovered. A 47-yard gain was for naught.

Consecutive turnovers could have deflated the Buckeyes defense, but it seemed to only strengthen its resolve. Ohio State stuffed two run plays. Darron Lee and Adolphus Washington then sacked Mariota to force a three-and-out. The Buckeyes took over and this time cashed in. On third-and-12, Jones bought time in the pocket and saw Devin Smith break free deep. Jones' pass was right on target for a 45-yard gain to the Oregon 6. It would be Smith's only catch of the game, but it would have been hard to have one better timed. After an apparent touchdown run by Jones was reversed on replay review, Jones spun in to the end zone on third down for a 21–7 lead.

Even after Oregon drove for a field goal late in the second quarter to make it 21–10 at halftime, the Buckeyes seemed in control of the game. But the turnover issue persisted. Ohio State got the ball to start the second half. On fourth-and-1, Jones dived for a first down by bouncing outside after initially being stuffed at the line of scrimmage. On the next play, he threw a short pass to Marshall. But the ball deflected off of his hands right to Oregon's Danny Mattingly for a fluke interception.

On the next snap, Oregon hit the Buckeyes with its longest play of the game. Byron Marshall got open deep and Mariota connected for a 70-yard touchdown. It would get worse for the Buckeyes. In Oregon's victory over Florida State, the game's most memorable play was an unforced, blooper-worthy fumble by quarterback Jameis Winston. On Ohio State's next possession, Jones would pull a junior Jameis. Flushed out of the pocket, he tried to throw the ball away, but it slipped out of his hands. Oregon recovered at the Buckeyes' 23 after a play that lost 26 yards.

How'd the ball come free? At least part of the reason is that Jones doesn't always grip the ball with the laces. "I'm comfortable throwing without them," he said. "Just working drills in high school, getting the ball out quick, you don't have time to look at laces. So when I warm up, I don't warm up with the laces. You get in that situation, and it just became really comfortable."

This time, it cost him.

"I was trying to throw the ball away," Jones said. "My hand just came up. I'm like, *Oh, you've got to be shitting me.*"

Here was the moment of truth for the Buckeyes. They had dominated the game, only to repeatedly self-destruct. Trailing only 21–17, Oregon looked poised to regain the lead. The Ducks got a first down and moved to the Buckeyes' 6 where they faced third-and-4. Mariota faded back in the pocket as cornerback Doran Grant rushed. Mariota spotted tight end Evan Baylis in the back of the end zone and threw. But as Baylis leaped and made the catch, Eli Apple shoved him out of bounds before Baylis could get a foot down. Oregon elected to kick the field goal instead of going for it, allowing the Buckeyes to remain ahead 21–20.

Apple said the play was a combination of recognition and fear. He read Mariota's eyes but saw Baylis open. "I panicked big time because the first touchdown they had was similar to that," he said. "I didn't want to give that up again."

The field goal proved to be Oregon's last gasp. Ohio State's defense had been stout, giving up only 10 points following the four turnovers. The Buckeyes had flirted with disaster and were still ahead. If they could stop giving the ball away, it was clear they could put the hammer down. That's exactly what the offense did. Ohio State drove 75 yards, needing to convert only two third downs. On the second, Jones plowed 310-pound nose guard Alex Balducci to get the needed three yards. Two plays later, Elliott scored from nine yards out on the last play of the third quarter to make it 28–20.

The drive was particularly special for one Buckeye who didn't even touch the ball. Dontre Wilson hadn't played since catching that critical touchdown pass against Michigan State with a broken bone in his foot. It had been a slow rehab for Wilson, who would need a second surgery after the season. But he desperately wanted to play in the title game. After all, he was from DeSoto, Texas, near Dallas. Wilson had committed to Oregon before he reopened his recruitment after Chip Kelly left for the Eagles. He wasn't at full strength against Oregon, but he was healthy enough to get a token appearance. So Zach Smith put him in for four plays in the drive. "He deserved to be in there," Smith said. "If he didn't play in that game, he would have been crushed."

Oregon managed only one first down on its next possession. Darron Lee made a diving breakup of a second-down pass, and Armani Reeves had excellent coverage on a third-down incompletion to force a punt. This would be the final game of Reeves' Buckeyes career. Concussion issues caused the junior to have to step away after the season.

After the stop, the Buckeyes offense did what it did the previous drive—manhandled the wilting Oregon defense. The line consistently opened holes for Elliott and provided ample time for Jones to throw on the few times the Buckeyes went to the air. Elliott scored from the 2 to make it 35–20 with less than 10 minutes left. The Buckeyes were now rolling. Oregon's tempo was supposed to tire out Ohio State. Instead, the Buckeyes' powerful offensive line and Elliott's punishing running had done that to the Ducks.

"We were wearing them down," right tackle Darryl Baldwin said. "We just saw the look on their faces. They were just worn down. We knew they weren't ready for the fourth quarter, and they weren't going to be able to come back."

Oregon managed only two first downs in its final three possessions. An offense that torched the Buckeyes on the game's opening possession did not have another sustained touchdown drive after that. "We know who we are," Ash said. "We know our strengths and weaknesses. They hit us on our weaknesses on the first drive. Teams typically aren't patient enough to methodically go down the field play after play and do the same thing over and over. They ran their opening script very well. Their opening script was set up to take advantage of our weaknesses. I don't know this to be true or not, but it felt like when they got off their script and started calling plays, they didn't attack our weaknesses as much as they did on the opening drive. We changed a little up front and started to make a few other calls, but didn't panic with anything. We knew what they were doing, and they just didn't continue to attack us."

Ohio State did not ease off the throttle against the Ducks. The Buckeyes took over at the Oregon 14 with 2:45 left after a fourth-down Ducks incompletion. On fourth-and-1 from the 5 with less than two minutes left, the Buckeyes drew Oregon offside with a hard count. Any fleeting chance the Ducks might have had was gone. Taylor Decker and Billy Price hugged. On the sideline, Meyer threw a triumphant punch in the air with his right hand and then his left. Two plays later, Elliott punched it into the end zone with 28 seconds left.

It was the final carry of an astonishing postseason for Elliott, who had become known for much more than his crop-top uniform look that left his midriff exposed. He gained 246 yards on 36 carries against Oregon, giving him three straight 200-yard games. Two of them had come against two of the country's best defenses. Ohio State's pantheon of running backs matches almost any program's in the country. Nobody in Buckeyes history has ever matched that three-game stretch. In fact, only 1995 Heisman Trophy winner Eddie George, with five, had more than two 200-yard games in his *career*. Elliott finished the season with 1,878 rushing yards, second-most in Ohio State history behind George's 1,927 in his Heisman season.

"Things just started clicking for everyone on the team," Elliott said. "We kind of became unstoppable. Our whole team got better every week. We peaked at the right time. I just had the mentality that no one was going to tackle me. Losing J.T., and Cardale stepping in—I knew Cardale was going to be able to handle himself—but we wanted to keep Cardale comfortable. I wanted to do my best and do whatever I could. Anything that got in my way wasn't going to stop me.

"I think that's how everybody felt. I think we were unbeatable, honestly. I don't think it would have mattered who we would have played—Alabama or the [New England] Patriots. I don't care if we had to play another game after the national championship. We were that tight. We had that kind of brotherhood."

Meyer drew some criticism for not taking a knee after the Oregon penalty. "I never even thought about that," he said. "When you're facing an offense like that, all I thought about was get ahead by as many scores as we can. I look back, and we could have grabbed a knee, but that didn't even cross my mind. Usually, someone like Tom Herman will say something. But on the field, it's just chaos."

Herman had left the press box to get to the sideline. He wasn't going to almost miss the celebration like he almost had against Wisconsin. "I don't live my life worrying about criticism," Meyer said. "But the intent was to get ahead as far as we can because they're an explosive team."

Buckeyes players weren't worried about that. They were just soaking in the moment. Right tackle Darryl Baldwin, a fifth-year senior, was the last link to the Tressel era. He had seen it all. Now he knew after that last touchdown that he'd finish at the summit.

"I came off the field with my teammates and the offensive line, and I looked up and all I could do was start crying," Baldwin said. "I was just so excited about what we were able to accomplish. There was no greater feeling than that moment right there, being able to share everything with my guys. We'd been through so much together for the whole year. All the mat drills, all the 5:00 AM workouts. It was all worth it for that one moment."

The game's final play was a fitting one. Apple intercepted a desperation Mariota pass for the Buckeyes defense's only turnover of the game. Twelve months earlier, Apple couldn't win a sprint against a 340-pound defensive tackle. Now he had made the play to finish off the national championship. "It was very special," he said. "I wanted to hang on to the ball, but I gave it back to the ref. I was in crazy excitement and joy and just wanted to celebrate with my teammates."

*   *   *   *

ONE GROUP OF PEOPLE was being denied the chance to join the celebration, and that situation was on the verge of getting ugly. Players' wives and families were trying to get to the sideline, but security guards wouldn't let them as they assembled in the corner of the field. If hell hath no fury like a woman scorned, imagine the fury unleashed by wives being denied a chance to join their husbands in a championship celebration.

"I'm 50 years old," Shelley Meyer said. "I've not been arrested." This might have been the closest she has come. "They were not letting us get on the field," she said. "Security guards were holding us back, like barricading us. We were demanding to be let on the field, and they wouldn't let us on the field. I missed that last touchdown. I didn't know we got another touchdown until an hour after the game."

The security guards finally relented. "They were horrible," Nicki Meyer said. "Once we finally got through and they let us celebrate, we let that go."

As confetti fell and the awards presentation began, the Buckeyes soaked in the moment. Players held up a commemorative *Columbus Dispatch* page printed for the occasion. Tom Herman found Jones, J.T. Barrett, and Braxton Miller. He hugged and kissed each of them. Michael Bennett, who played through a groin injury suffered in practice after the Alabama game, finally allowed himself to celebrate.

"I was on the sideline when I think we were up 14 with five minutes left," he said. "Everyone starts hugging each other on sideline, and I was like, 'Don't touch me. Don't congratulate me. It's not over.' Then it's 21 points with two or three minutes left, and everyone's coming around congratulating me, and I'm like, 'Don't congratulate me, it's not over.' Then I think it was a minute left, and I was like, 'Okay, it's over, we're national champions.' I just started hugging guys. I went to find Adolphus as soon as I could. That's my homedog. He held down the inside with me."

But even then, the finality of what the Buckeyes had accomplished didn't quite hit him. "I remember almost being confused," Bennett said. "After every game there was a mentality that it's not over, there's another game to play. What do you do when you accomplish the dream?"

For Jones, it was surreal. After all he'd been through, he had led the Buckeyes to a national championship with an almost flawless postseason. In the championship game, he completed 16 of 23 passes for 242 yards and made some crucial runs. The unforced fumbles and bobbled interception were the only blemishes.

When the clock hit 0:00, the enormity of what he'd accomplished hit him. "My heart just dropped," Jones said. "We really just won the national championship. All this confetti is for us. This is really for us."

Exactly 12 months earlier, defensive line coach Larry Johnson left State College, Pennsylvania, for Columbus after 18 years at Penn State. Now he had won the national championship in his first year at Ohio State. It was hard for him to fathom that this had really happened. The same went for Ash, the Buckeyes' other new coach.

"It was probably more relief than anything," Ash said. "And a little bit of shock. Did we really just do this? Did we really just win the national championship, the first-ever College Football Playoff National Championship? I'm watching the confetti come down and the stage going up, and I'm thinking, *Did we really just do this?* As a coach in this profession, that's all you dream about, having a chance to win the national championship. You're finally there, and you always wonder how you'll react and how you'll celebrate. It was like almost more relief. We just won another game. It wasn't just another game. It was surreal. It still is."

Doran Grant and several offensive linemen were among the Buckeyes who did snow angels in the confetti. Evan Spencer played in the championship game with a hamstring injury. He had a quiet game, but that didn't lessen his excitement. "It was unbelievable," Spencer said. "Everything you could imagine, triple it. It was just crazy. The fact that my parents and my girlfriend were there, it was just unreal."

Ed Warinner, who'd reconstructed the offensive line into a force nobody could have expected, took in the moment as validation. He, like all coaches, sacrificed so much to achieve this goal. He hadn't had an off day since July. If coaches weren't preparing for a game, they were recruiting relentlessly. Now all that work had culminated in a national championship. At the end of the game, Warinner and Meyer looked at each other. Meyer winked. The two then hugged. After the game, Warinner sought out his starting linemen and his family. "That's all I cared about at that point—those five guys and my family," he said.

Another family had made the trip to Dallas. Jacob Jarvis, his brother Noah, and their parents also attended the championship game with tickets bought by Meyer. They had not expected to go because of the cost. Eight days before the game, they went to practice because they thought it would be their last chance to see the team before it left for Dallas. Meyer invited Jacob to the huddle after practice.

"Then he came to us privately and said, 'You're going to the game, right?'" Chad Studebaker said. "I said that I didn't think so. It was pretty expensive. He said, 'We really want you to get there and want Jacob and your family to be a part of it. We'll help you get there.' I said, 'Coach, I don't want to impose.' I said that several times. But he was very persistent."

Jacob was understandably thrilled. "I couldn't believe it," he said. "I was shocked. I couldn't wait."

They sat in on team meetings and events and watched the game with seats behind Ohio State's bench and went into the locker room after the game. "He was pretty emotional in the locker room, really excited to be a part of us," said Joshua Perry, fellow Olentangy Shanahan Middle School grad.

That postgame locker room was the scene of some of the more telling and touching moments. A year earlier after the Orange Bowl, Philly Brown had given his younger teammates that impassioned speech about not forgetting the pain of disappointment they felt after the back-to-back losses to end the 2013 season. Now seniors spoke about the overwhelming sense of accomplishment they felt. Bennett's stood out to Perry.

"The captains talked about their experiences and the whole journey," Perry said. "Those guys were emotional. They were in tears. They talked about how hard they worked and how long they worked, and the way we won it with all the adversity we faced. I thought it was pretty cool to see some of the guys we look up to as players really open their chests for us one last time."

After the media was allowed in, Curtis Grant sat in his locker holding his son, A.J. In 2013, after Grant's father died and his Ohio State football career looked destined to be a disappointment, A.J. provided inspiration. Now Grant held him in his arms as a champion. "It was just that feeling of 'Mission complete,'" Grant said. "We can let everything go. We have no worries. We know we finished on top."

Answering questions from reporters, Luke Fickell declined every opportunity to say that he felt vindicated. Nobody had been more of a lightning rod for the Buckeyes' defensive struggles in 2013 than Fickell. Now his defense had held Oregon to only 20 points, and even that was deceiving because of the four turnovers by the Buckeyes' offense. But Fickell would not take the bait. He talked about how proud he was that his players could reclaim the title of Silver Bullets, a moniker coined when he was a player two decades earlier.

Then there was J.T. Barrett. He had to watch in the postseason while the team he'd carried to that point played without him. He'd been confined to a motorized scooter for weeks. But when asked if the championship was bittersweet, he scoffed. No, he said, it was all sweet. He couldn't imagine anything taking away from it, not even his injury.

"I think that is ridiculous," he explained a couple months later. "I think that's just crazy. Not even for myself. For someone who was a scout-team guy, all the things that we do as a team and the things you do individually to put your team in a position to be in the national championship, and to be bitter about that? I think that's just crazy. Do I wish I wasn't hurt? Of course. But you don't think about that at the time. I was already past that. I already had that idea or mindset of, 'It is what it is.'"

Jones, the man of the hour, sent Michelle Nash a note as she rode on a bus back to the hotel. "He texted me and said, 'If it were not for you, I would not be here,'" Nash said.

For Urban Meyer, one thought kept popping into his mind as he soaked in the championship. "The Chase is complete," he said. "We did it. It was a great feeling."

24

POSTSCRIPT

THE CELEBRATION didn't last long for Ohio State's players and coaches. In fact, in Dallas it never really got started. By the time coaches got back to the hotel, the bar was closed.

"I'm still kind of grieving because I haven't had the chance to celebrate with our coaches and my wife. I feel cheated," Mickey Marotti said a month after the championship. "The last ones I've been a part of, we celebrated all night. You get it all out and feel better."

Even if there was no swinging from chandeliers at the team hotel, there was quiet satisfaction and pride. "We were down in the lobby with our family," Taylor Decker said. "Me and Pat [Elflein] were roommates for the game. We went back to the room and were watching highlights and just looked at each other like, 'Man, we're national champions. We actually did it. Against all odds, after all the adversity and people saying we couldn't.' We smiled and said, 'We're national champions.'"

In Columbus and elsewhere, of course, Buckeyes fans reveled. Hundreds of fans broke into Ohio Stadium after 2:00 AM and pulled down a goalpost. The streets around campus were filled with jubilant fans, though Columbus police were criticized for using pepper spray and tear gas to disperse them. That prompted an internal investigation. The Buckeyes flew back to Columbus the day after the game. The next day, the coaches had a staff meeting to discuss recruiting and the off-season. On Thursday, coaches fanned out on the road to meet with recruits. It never stops.

Tom Herman left Dallas the day after the game to his new job in Houston. "I promised myself I'd spend sunrise in Dallas, Texas, and I did," Herman said. "At 10:00 or 11:00 AM, I had to put my wife and three kids on a plane back to Columbus."

Herman and Fernando Lovo, Ohio State's football operations coordinator who would join Herman with the Cougars, drove the four hours to Houston, arriving at about 5:00 PM. "It happened so fast," Herman said of the championship and transition. "It was hard. I don't really know if it really had a chance to sink in."

It was hectic for the players as well, particularly Cardale Jones. It had been an incredible whirlwind. Six weeks earlier, he was a backup, an afterthought who figured he'd transfer in 2015. Now he had put together what might have been the most impressive three-game quarterback debut in the history of football. Suddenly, the NFL looked like an enticing possibility. Jones said in a press conference the day after the game that he wasn't ready to turn pro. But he at least wanted to look into the possibility.

Before that, Jones had a more pressing matter. His uncle, Audie Murphy, was dying of liver cancer. Jones rushed back to Cleveland to see him one last time. Jones took comfort that his uncle had gotten to watch the national championship game, which was noted in Murphy's obituary.

Jones found himself suffering from insomnia coming down from the emotions of the week. "I probably got four hours of sleep total that week, from the national championship game to Saturday," Jones said. That helps to explain the surprising press conference he had in the middle of that. On Thursday, three days after the game, Jones tweeted that he would have a "Life changing announcement at 4:00 PM" at the Ginn Academy run by his high school coach, Ted Ginn Sr. Speculation immediately became rampant that Jones would turn pro. Why else would he have a press conference?

But Jones confounded expectations one more time. He announced that he would return to Ohio State. "It was stressful," Jones said.

"It happened so fast. A month before that, nobody knew who I was. Now you're telling me I could be a late first-round, early second-round draft pick? What? What are you talking about? Go live out your dream, or set your life up for the rest of your life and come back to school."

As enticing as the NFL was, Jones decided it would be wiser to earn his degree—he wants to be a financial planner—before embarking on a pro career. "What really made that decision was understanding it's not about me anymore," Jones said. "Actually, it's not about money. My life is really devoted to making sure my daughter has a better life than I had. I feel like graduating and getting a degree from Ohio State will benefit her more than me going to the NFL right now."

Jones' return ensured that the Ohio State quarterback situation would be the talk of college football for the next eight months. J.T. Barrett's broken ankle healed enough that he was able to participate on a limited basis in spring practice. Braxton Miller's shoulder was more of an unknown, but he had begun light tossing in the spring. Miller had graduated in December, making him eligible to transfer and be able to play without sitting out a year. Persistent rumors popped up about him transferring to various schools, including Alabama and LSU. Miller, as is his wont, stayed silent.

The only clue of his intentions came at a championship celebration 12 days after the title game at Ohio Stadium. All season, Ohio State fans bucked the declining attendance trend in college football to lead the country with an average of 106,296 per home game. After every game at the Horseshoe, Meyer thanked the fans, particularly the students, for their support. Even on a frigid day with no game, about 45,000 filled almost the entire lower deck of the stadium to salute the team. "There's schools around the country that have never had this many people show up to a game," Jeff Heuerman told the crowd.

Meyer described his quarterbacks, who were clowning around together on the stage, as the "Magnificent Three." Whatever competition awaited the three, it was obvious that they were friends and teammates first. Then Miller spoke. "It's a privilege and an honor to be a part of this national championship team," he said. "Guess what? We've got another year to do it."

Ezekiel Elliott reprised his "salmoning" move, which was flashed on the video board. As he spoke, a jersey was superimposed on the board with Elliott's trademark crop-top. The crowd roared as Elliott laughed.

Coaches worked to finish off the 2015 recruiting class, which again was ranked in the top 10 nationally. One of the biggest pieces of drama, and then controversy, came when Detroit blue-chip running back Mike Weber picked Ohio State on signing day over Michigan. The next day, Ohio State running backs coach Stan Drayton left the Buckeyes to take the same job with the Chicago Bears. Drayton and Ohio State were accused of a bait-and-switch on Weber, who tweeted "I'm hurt as hell I ain't gone lie" after the news broke. His Cass Tech coach Thomas Wilcher, who played with newly hired Michigan coach Jim Harbaugh for the Wolverines in the 1980s, initially said he felt deceived, though he was placated after talking with Meyer.

Drayton said he didn't tell Weber about the possibility of leaving for Chicago because he had no expectation that the Bears would offer him the job that day or that he would take it if they did. "There was no offer on the table prior to signing day," Drayton said, breaking his months-long silence about the issue. "I had seen no contract or anything like that prior to signing day."

He said he was in a similar situation in 2013. "We could have been having the same conversation the same year Ezekiel Elliott was recruited," Drayton said. "I had an offer on the table from a National Football League team that I decided not to take. When

I went to Chicago, at that point it became an opportunity I could not refuse."

He said he called Weber from Chicago and told him he would not be coaching him at Ohio State. "With all the speculation that was going on, I wanted him to hear it from the horse's mouth," Drayton said. "At that point, he understood. He did express that he wanted to play for me. I told him these were opportunities that were bigger than just one coach. Mike Weber should not come to Ohio State because of Stan Drayton. That's not why you go to Ohio State. You go to Ohio State to be a part of something very, very special that's bigger than any coach and even you."

Meyer hired Notre Dame's Tony Alford to replace Drayton. He'd already tabbed Nebraska's Tim Beck to replace Herman as quarterbacks coach. Ed Warinner was promoted to offensive coordinator as well as offensive line coach.

Just two months after winning the championship, the Buckeyes were back on the field for spring practice. Barrett and Miller were among many veterans who were held out or limited in practice. Conscious of the toll the long 2014 season took on players' bodies, Meyer allowed those in what he called the 2,000-snap club to back off during the spring. The spring game, as is usually the case, was a forgettable affair—except for its attendance. A crowd of 99,391 showed up for the scrimmage. That broke the national record set in 2009 by Ohio State for a spring game.

Two days later, the Buckeyes flew to the White House to be honored for the championship. Meyer said that President Obama spent 20 minutes before the public ceremony meeting with the team. "I've never seen a president so genuinely involved with our players," said Meyer, who was making his third trip to the White House after a national championship. "Shook every man's hand. Took pictures with them all. Phenomenal. When we were finished, he stayed another 15 minutes afterward taking pictures."

During the ceremony, which he started with three O-H I-O chants, Obama reminded the Buckeyes that he had been an advocate for a college football playoff. The president acknowledged several players by name. He did the "Bosa Shrug" and thanked Elliott for tucking in his shirt and not going with the crop-top look with his suit. About Cardale Jones, he said that anyone with a nickname "12 Gauge" has to be taken seriously. But Obama also turned serious, saying that the adversity the Buckeyes faced revealed their character.

To the Buckeyes, that's what made the championship particularly special. Sure, they had talent. But that's not what enabled them to overcome all the obstacles they faced. Teams at every level and in every sport claim that they are a family. It has become a cliché. The Buckeyes truly believed themselves to be one. How else could they have survived everything without that bond?

"It was just the ultimate team effort over the course of January through January," Warinner said. "For 12 months, a team of players, coaches, and support staff, all bound together and worked as a team and had no agenda and no egos. It's the ultimate reward for having that kind of sacrifice. There was not a selfish player on the team. There wasn't a selfish coach. There wasn't a selfish person around the program. When you have that many people working together toward a common goal and no one cares who gets the credit, it's amazing what can happen. I saw it with my own eyes."

* * * *

THE SENIORS COULDN'T revel long in the championship. They had to prepare for what they hoped was the next step in their football careers. As with their Ohio State careers, many of them faced an uphill climb and more unforeseen adversity. None became a first-round NFL Draft pick, the first time a national championship team hadn't had a first-rounder since the 2002 Buckeyes. Devin Smith was the first Buckeye taken, in the second round by the

New York Jets. Jeff Heuerman went in the third round to Denver. Unfortunately, the injury issues that hampered him his final season continued. He tore his ACL in the Broncos' first minicamp. The Pittsburgh Steelers took Doran Grant in the fourth round. Thought to be a likely second- or at worst third-round pick, Michael Bennett had a perplexing fall all the way to the sixth round before Jacksonville took him, seven spots before Washington took Evan Spencer. Curtis Grant, Darryl Baldwin, and Steve Miller signed free-agent contracts.

Whatever happens in their pro careers, their legacy with the Buckeyes is secure. They were the last players signed by Jim Tressel. Until their senior year, they looked like they'd be one of the rare classes at Ohio State not to win a Big Ten championship. Now they'll never be forgotten in Buckeyes lore.

"We've been through everything," said Spencer, a Buckeye since birth. "We've been through a 6–7 season. We've been through when we had an undefeated season and couldn't reap the rewards at the end of the year. We've been through a season where we were incredibly successful during the regular season and then just didn't get it done in postseason play. We got to last season, and it's like, 'We've done everything else. We've got to get this done,' and we did. Being on this team meant the world to me. It's taught me about myself. It's taught me about how to work. It's taught me about leadership and ultimately friendship and relationships."

Heuerman said months after the championship that the feeling remained surreal. "I get goosebumps even now," he said. "Everybody told us we were absolutely done after we lost to Virginia Tech. You don't believe it, but when so many people say it, it wears on you. There was no one who said we were going to make the playoff. But we actually did it. It's cool to say we're the first-ever undisputed champion."

This was a class that ended up teaching as much as learning. The poster boy for that might have been Curtis Grant. His Buckeyes career had been a bust until he decided to be selfless as a senior, mentoring Raekwon McMillan and the other linebackers.

"One of the proudest things in my coaching career was seeing Curtis Grant standing on the stage at the Big Ten championship, the Sugar Bowl, and at the national championship," Luke Fickell said. "I just stood there and looked and was like, 'Wow.' You have to give him all the credit. To see a guy tear his chest open.... He had it. It was there. But the ability to fight through a lot of things and transform his mind more than anything is something I'm indebted to and will never forget."

* * * *

MEYER HAD A SAYING after the season: what he and the coaches preached was now testimony and no longer just theory. The championship was proof that the culture that they instilled works. It is not an easy path. Players are expected to work hard and mature quickly. If they don't, they risk being left behind because someone else willing to work harder will surpass them.

"You really find out whether you want to be a great player," Decker said. "They're going to expect out of you what it takes to be a great player. [Coach Meyer] talks about it all the time: If you have that greatness in you, how cool would that be to get it out of you? They're going to make it uncomfortable in this program for people who don't want to sacrifice what needs to be sacrificed to be the player they can be. Our program and off-season program and practice is a pressure cooker. You're expected to perform day-in and day-out. Aside from the fact we don't get paid, we're professionals. It's our job. That's the way we're treated and that's why we're able to win a national championship, because we're professionals and we're treated as such."

The demands of the culture Meyer and his staff have built are the reason that a third-string quarterback can lead a team to the national championship. The Cardale Jones who arrived in 2012 had raw tools and little else. Gradually, and sometimes with painful steps backward, Jones bought in to the program. When needed, he was ready. It's telling that Jones volunteered, with pride, that as well as he played in the postseason, his performance did not grade out as a "champion." "All three of those games, people want to talk about how great I did," he said, "but I love our standards around here."

The expectations are at least as great on the assistant coaches, but so can be the rewards. "I always feel like I went to head coaching school for three years," Tom Herman said.

When he arrived at Ohio State, Herman was already a master at the X's and O's. He was already a hard worker. He already had an innate ability to develop a rapport with players. But working under Meyer, Herman said, taught him how essential it is to have everyone on the staff in alignment with a common method and philosophy. With Meyer, there's no gray area, he said. You know where you stand. If you're doing your job properly, he lets you do your job without meddling. "If you're not, he's going to let you know it," Herman said. "Nobody's ever called a stupid son of a bitch. But there's an intensity about the expectation of what's needed to coach for Urban Meyer at Ohio State. If you don't meet that expectation, you're going to know about it, but you're going to be educated about it, too. If you've got confidence in yourself and are honest with yourself, it's not bad. It's a bit refreshing to know you always know where you stand. You're never guessing. It's not like he's saying one thing one day and having the other shoe fall on you the next."

Coaches can accept the demands because they believe they do have a voice. Meyer does not like to be surrounded by yes-men. He wants to be challenged by those around him. "I love that," Meyer said. "I have respect for that. The bobbleheads, I don't have a lot of respect for."

Ash said that Meyer's continuous pursuit of improvement is what most impresses him. "He's constantly pushing the staff to find ways to get better both as a staff and a program," he said. "He's constantly trying to find ways to do business better as a head coach and constantly trying to find ways to improve the plan. 'How can we do better? Why aren't we No. 1 at that? How do we get there? How can we do more for our players?' He's always asking these questions."

*   *   *   *

FOR MEYER, Ohio State's 2014 national championship placed him in the pantheon of college football coaches. Only 50 years old in 2014, he has won three national titles. Bear Bryant, with five, and Frank Leahy and Nick Saban, with four, are the only coaches with more. Saban is the only other coach to have done it at more than one school, and only Leahy was younger than Meyer when he won his third.

Like a parent asked about his children, Meyer has been careful to try not to pick favorites among his championships. His 2006 team will always be special because it was his first and was also unlikely. Florida needed late-season breaks just to get into the title game against Ohio State and was a touchdown underdog against the Buckeyes before overwhelming them. His 2008 team was a dominating one led by Tim Tebow. But the 2014 Buckeyes will always be special to him, not just for what it did but for the kind of coach he became. Meyer wasn't sure he'd ever coach again after he crashed at Florida.

"Without getting overly dramatic, I realize I'm extremely blessed to even be in that situation again," he said. "It was much more of a reflective year. I really appreciated the year. At times in my past, I never did. It was, 'What's next, what's next, what's next?' I just really appreciated our coaches and our players. Imagine being able to do this in your home state. Are you kidding me? I had a lot more reflective moments than I ever had in my coaching career this year because it was like a time warp of, 'Here we are again. I'm in my home state.'"

In April 2015 Meyer signed a contract extension worth at least $6.5 million per year through 2020. If he stays at Ohio State through the length of the contract, it would be the longest he has ever been at one place in his coaching career. He lasted six years at Florida. Meyer believes he's more grounded than he was with the Gators. "I think in 2006 I expected something different," he said. "I remember thinking, *We won the championship. From this point forward, it's all house money.* That's the furthest from the truth."

In Gainesville, Meyer lived near then–Gators men's basketball coach Billy Donovan. They became extremely close. Few reached the heights they did. Between them, they won four national titles in a two-year span. But both endured wrenching difficulties in their personal lives. In 2000 Donovan and his wife had a daughter who was stillborn after her umbilical cord wrapped around her ankle. Both coaches understood that a championship meant only so much.

"Billy Donovan and I had many conversations about this," Meyer said. "It doesn't change who you are. It doesn't change how you've got to go about your business. It doesn't make recruiting easier. It doesn't make classes or issues or people's health any better. It just makes you for the rest of your life be associated with a championship team and the brothers that you did it with."

In Columbus, Meyer has achieved the balance that eluded him earlier in his career. He attends his son Nate's football and baseball games. He flew to watch Gigi play volleyball at Florida Gulf Coast during a bye week. At Florida, when Nicki was in high school, they went to dinner once a week. Too often, he was distracted during those meals. After graduating from Georgia Tech, Nicki moved back to Columbus in June 2014. She works for a company, Accel-WELL, that runs wellness programs for employees. Nicki and her dad resumed their tradition of weekly dinners out. "We didn't miss it even once," Nicki said. "He was very present and full of happiness and life at those dinners."

They became such regulars at one Dublin restaurant that had a live band that the musicians learned how to play one of their favorite songs, Roger Whittaker's "The Last Farewell." Nicki delighted in the time that her dad bantered with a couple of awestruck college kids sitting next to them and bought them beers. Nicki says with pride that her father has upheld the rules specified in the Pink Contract. Nicki got engaged in late December at a surprise 50th birthday party for Shelley. Even though it was right before Ohio State left for the Sugar Bowl, Urban was involved in the pre-proposal planning. "My dad couldn't have been more supportive," Nicki said.

Nicki's fiancé, former Georgia Tech football player Corey Dennis, will be an intern on the Buckeyes' staff in 2015 as he embarks on a coaching career. "I'm marrying into this lifestyle, fully aware of what it means," Nicki said.

She has seen the good and the bad. Living through the bad makes her appreciate last season even more. The championships in Florida were special, but the crash followed. Nicki and Shelley believe that the newfound balance in Urban's life gives him a chance for sustainable success.

"Three national championships are great," Shelley said. "But to know he can do what he wants and be okay, that's even better."

In the spring of 2015, "THE CHASE..." banner was hung back up, but on the opposite side of the Woody Hayes Athletic Center practice field. In its spot was a new banner reading "THE GRIND." The Chase banner now hangs alongside ones containing photos of great Buckeyes teams from the past. Like those teams, the banner now represents glorious history, achieved by a team whose story was so unlikely that it almost felt like fiction.

ACKNOWLEDGMENTS

I HAD NO INTENTION of writing a successor to *Buckeye Rebirth* when Ohio State's 2014 season began. But after the Buckeyes' improbable national championship was completed, I felt compelled to. After writing a book about a team two years ago that couldn't even play in the postseason, how could I not write the story of this miraculous season?

But this season, unlike 2012, didn't happen under the radar. I knew I had to delve deeper into the how and why of how Ohio State overcame so much adversity if this book was to be more than a mere rehash. What really provided the foundation for the season? How did Urban Meyer and his assistant coaches navigate a season that provided more challenges than any coaching textbook can cover? How did the players manage to push through? I wanted to get to the core of the culture that Meyer has built at Ohio State, including its recruiting process and leadership training. I also knew that time, as was the case with *Buckeye Rebirth*, was not my ally. I had four months to interview and write. I needed plenty of help, and I am fortunate to have gotten it.

The first person to thank is Urban Meyer, who was exceedingly generous with his time and insights. His wife, Shelley, and daughter Nicki also provided terrific background into his evolution as a coach and man since his difficult final years at Florida. I spoke, often for multiple hours, with every Ohio State assistant coach. Each one of them was so crucial to this book that it would be a disservice if I didn't mention all of them by name. So, thank you to Luke

Fickell, Tom Herman, Chris Ash, Ed Warinner, Kerry Coombs, Stan Drayton, Larry Johnson, Zach Smith, and Tim Hinton. Thanks also to Mickey Marotti and Mark Pantoni for all of their help.

Having covered the team for the *Columbus Dispatch*, I wasn't surprised by the wisdom and insight provided by Buckeyes players. Friends in the national media told me during the postseason how impressed they were with Ohio State players' maturity and perspective. This really was a special group of players in that regard. The seniors, including Michael Bennett, Jeff Heuerman, Evan Spencer, Darryl Baldwin, Curtis Grant, and Doran Grant, were particularly important in revealing the story of the 2014 season. Especially helpful underclassmen included J.T. Barrett, Cardale Jones, Taylor Decker, Jacoby Boren, Billy Price, Pat Elflein, Ezekiel Elliott, Michael Thomas, Jalin Marshall, Adolphus Washington, Joey Bosa, Joshua Perry, Darron Lee, Eli Apple, Tyvis Powell, and Vonn Bell.

Thanks also to Michelle Nash, Tim Kight, Todd Gongwer, and College Football Playoff selection committee chair Jeff Long for their invaluable insights.

A special thanks goes to Ohio State football sports information director Jerry Emig, who went well beyond the call of duty in facilitating interviews. An SID's job is a difficult one, especially after a championship season in which interview requests can become a deluge. But Jerry handled mine with his characteristic grace and courteousness.

I could not have done this without the support of my employer, the *Columbus Dispatch*. Former editor Ben Marrison was enthusiastic about me pursuing this book and supportive throughout the process, as were sports editor Ray Stein and assistant sports editor Scott Davis. My beat colleague, the incomparable Tim May, also provided support, both with his encouragement and with taking up a lot of the slack in daily duties while I worked on this book. Tim's award as national college football beat writer of the year in 2014 was well-deserved. Thanks also to the *Dispatch*'s photography department, particularly Karl Kuntz and Adam Cairns for picking out the very best out of hundreds of superb shots. Kyle Robertson, ace that he is, took the shots that grace the front cover.

Noah Amstadter of Triumph Books and editor Alex Lubertozzi were crucial in guiding me through the writing process and helping me make this book as good as it could possibly be. A big thank you to Kirk Herbstreit for writing the foreword.

Nobody has been more important than my family. My parents, both Ohio State grads, have always been my biggest supporters. My daughter, Katie, is an inspiration as the gutsiest person I know. My son, Michael, was quite accepting of the sacrifices I had to make and encouraged me with his kindness and humor. And, as I promised my family, a special shoutout to our beloved Lucy. The biggest thanks of all, of course, goes to my wife, Erin. Words can't express how blessed I am to have her as my wife. I could never have done this without her incredible encouragement and patience. She's a hell of an editor, too.